Practical Recording 5

Surround Sound

Christian Birkner

CONTENTS

ABOUT THIS BOOK

Surround Sound is currently the number-one theme in every recording studio. Long the preserve of the cinema for the lack of adequate multichannel equipment for home use, it has become the dynamo of the audio industry in recent years. New media such as DVD now offer a solid technological foundation for high-quality multichannel reproduction, opening up new perspectives and markets.

Practical Recording 5: Surround Sound supplies the essential information concerning speaker configurations, microphone placement, compression formats and editing. The technical fundamentals and formats such as 5.1, EX in its various manifestations and new techniques such as binaural room scanning (BRS) are also covered, as are microphone systems and techniques for multichannel recording. Typical problems such as phase cancellation are discussed and practical solutions suggested, and the difference between time-of-arrival and intensity stereo is explained. Over the course of the book, I'll be examining the most important components of the modern recording studio and how to operate them, explaining the various phases of post-production such as panning, processing, mixing and mastering, ending with a description of the latest coding and transmission formats and storage media.

This practical and easily understood introduction to the basic procedures involved in multichannel audio production is aimed at all who are, or wish to become, involved in surround productions, whether as sound engineers, musicians, sound designers or producers, regardless of whether they work in major studios or operate from home.

FOREWORD

Surround sound was for a long time the preserve of the cinema. The creation of more realistic sonic images in the home through the use of more than two channels was precluded by the lack of a medium with the capacity to store the necessary data. Even with the coming of CD and the inauguration of the digital age, multichannel sound only found its way into the living room in a compromised form.

For some time now, however, surround sound has been the locomotive of the audio industry. New multichannel storage media such as the now provide a sound basis for multichannel reproduction in the home, opening up new perspectives and new markets. Existing productions can be remixed with multichannel audio; new productions can set out from the start with the aim of reproducing realistic sound relationships; films already furnished with multichannel sound can be digitised and the sound reproduced convincingly in the home – and all this far from exhausts the possibilities of the new media. In the light of all this, it's natural that multichannel audio should be one of the most important topics in the audio sector at the moment.

Yet how much influence do these new possibilities have on the production process? Which recording technique should one favour, and with controversial issues such as the respective merits of main and multiple microphone techniques or of SACD and DVD audio, which is the best counsel to follow? At what stage in the production process do we first need to include multiple playback channels in our calculations, and how do the procedures here differ from those employed for dual-channel stereo? How much of the knowledge and experience that we've already gathered is still valid and how much must we reluctantly discard?

This book answers these questions as well as outlining the most important standards, recording techniques and methods of editing audio material and applying sound processing to it.

I would like to say a warm word of thanks to Professor Bernd Steinbrink, firstly for suggesting the theme of this book and secondly for his assistance while I was writing it. Professor Uwe Kulisch deserves a special word of thanks for his ever-present help and counsel.

I would also like to express my gratitude to Jörg Wuttke of Schoeps, Klaus Gehlhaar of TC Electronics, André Inderfurth of SPL and Conny Thiet of *Studio Magazin* for the information with which they kindly provided me as I was doing the research for this book, as well as my appreciation of the stimulating dialogue we enjoyed.

1 AN INTRODUCTION TO SURROUND SOUND

Where We're At

The development of media suitable for multichannel reproduction – such as DVD – and their widespread use offer sound engineers the possibility of providing listeners with more realistic spatial imaging than was the case with previously existing technologies, such as dual-channel stereo. The key enabling factors are the considerably higher data-transfer rates that DVDs can achieve and the greater quantities of data they're capable of storing.

A further advantage of DVD lies in the flexible algorithms and formats established by the specification, which ensure that the medium is capable not only of satisfying current expectations but also of adapting to future tasks, such as the transmission of high-resolution audio content.

Extensive use is naturally being made of the existing possibilities; DVDs have brought a far higher standard of film reproduction to the home, and this is having a very positive influence on the sales and production of DVD players and discs. At the end of 2002, 21% of all German households were equipped with a DVD player, and this figure was expected to rise to 35% by the end of 2003, and while in 2002 VHS cassettes still accounted for around a third of turnover in the home-theatre market, their share was expected to fall below 25% in 2003.[1]

DVD also offers the music industry the long-awaited possibility of producing recordings with a more realistic spatial impression and greater truth of detail. This had been tried before with technologies such as quadraphony and Dolby Surround, but the former was never really able to establish itself and the latter is incapable of satisfying current demands.

Perfectly authentic sound reproduction has long been the objective of sound engineers but one that not even multichannel stereophony is capable of achieving. The latter does, of course, represent a considerable improvement, but it's still impossible to recreate the true experience of hearing something live. It must be said, though, that new technologies such as Binarural Room Scanning (BRS) and Wave Field Synthesis (WFS) do take us quite close to that goal and may, in the foreseeable future, establish a new standard.

At present, however, even surround sound is far from established as the fundamental standard in the home. Dual-channel stereo is still the most commonly encountered playback configuration, and most surround systems in the home – whether realized with four, five or six loudspeakers – are more or less compromise solutions that don't comply with the ITU-R BS 775 recommendation.[2] The playback conditions for multichannel stereo in the home are therefore anything but ideal. Most people who purchase a new DVD player do so primarily for the enhanced picture quality and not because they're interested in the possibilities of multichannel sound reproduction, even though the effects of poor sound are considerably more detrimental to the overall quality of audiovisual impressions than those of a poor picture. If a surround implementation is attempted at all, people often just use their existing hi-fi or television speakers – one encounters all sorts of Heath-Robinson configurations – and even the dedicated surround loudspeaker sets on the market are often hopelessly inadequate to the task for which they were supposedly designed. Even in specialist retail outlets, there's widespread ignorance regarding the official recommendations dealing with surround sound. The resulting uncertainty does nothing to encourage the proliferation of standard multichannel systems, which is what's needed if identical results are to be achieved in all homes.

Another factor to be taken into account is that, in the studio, recording engineers tend to work with the best monitor systems money can buy (with good reason, of course), and these are invariably fine-tuned to the acoustics of the control room in which they're located. (Of course, there might be a second monitoring system in the control room, inferior in quality to the main one, but this, too, will have been fine-tuned in the same way.) Because of this, what recording engineers and producers hear in the studio is superior in quality to even the best that can be achieved in most homes. If you point this out to them, though, they have a tendency get annoyed and say, 'Look, after a hard day's work in the studio, the last thing I want to do is go home and listen to the same stuff all over again in my living room.' And this attitude is understandable, but the comparison would nonetheless be instructive. While on domestic dual-channel stereo systems you can generally expect to find identical speakers for the right and left channels (even if they aren't always correctly positioned), domestic setups catering for multichannel sound can come in all kinds of weird configurations.

Whether this situation is taken into account in the production process or producers prefer to act on the false assumption that reproduction systems generally comply with the official recommendation is obviously something that varies from studio to studio and from production to production. Personally, I feel that it's unwise for producers to ignore the reality altogether and pretend that they live in an ideal world.

Stereophony: A Statement Of Principle

Confident in the knowledge that *mono* means 'single', people have long assumed that *stereo* must mean 'dual', since for many years single-channel and dual-channel hi-fi systems were the only alternatives on offer, but this only bears out Alexander Pope's maxim that a little knowledge is a dangerous thing. The term *stereophony* is in fact not specific as to the number of channels; it's derived from the Greek words *stereo*, meaning 'solid', and *phono*, meaning 'voice' (although the sense of the latter is usually extended to mean 'of or pertaining to sound in general')[3]. The *New Oxford Dictionary Of English* defines stereophony as the use of 'two *or more* channels...so that the reproduced sound seems to *surround* the listener', so it's wrong to think of surround sound as something different from stereo – the various surround formats are, in fact, new forms of stereo – and it's perfectly correct to speak of 'four-channel stereophony', 'six-channel stereophony' or 'multichannel stereophony'.

In the case of the hapless quadraphony, the popular etymology is correct: the term quadraphony *is* specific as to number: it means 'sound transmitted through four channels', although in this case complex encoding and decoding algorithms often had to be used – due to the lack of the requisite number of playback channels – to tease the illusion of four-channels from systems that provided full support for only two. This was the so-called *pseudo-quad*, the inadequacies of which – along with format disputes and the lack of suitable storage media – served to prevent quadraphony from ever becoming established as a viable system.

When the next wave of multichannel solutions for the home entered the market in the early '80s, a new term obviously had to be found that on the one hand wasn't tainted by failure and on the other hand made it clear that more than two channels were involved. Dolby Laboratories, the first company to launch a multichannel system for the consumer market, chose the name 'Dolby Surround', and the term *surround* quickly became the generic term for all such systems.

In terms of content, surround sound can be equated with multichannel stereophony, but currently a tendency can be detected among manufacturers to distance themselves from the term *surround*. There are several reasons for this.

Firstly, there was a desire to make a clear distinction between modern techniques and Dolby Surround, which is an analogue process with matrixed channels. Although Dolby Surround is perfectly respectable for a system launched over 20 years ago, it can't possibly compete with the discrete digital processes of today.

Secondly, today there's a confusing tendency for the term *surround* to be used to distinguish the rear channels of a multichannel system from the front ones – you hear the rear left-hand channel, for example, referred to as the 'left surround' (or 'LS') – so a term which was clear enough when it was first introduced in 1982 has already become clouded by ambiguity.

Thirdly, the term *surround* has been cheapened by elements of the consumer electronics industry that haven't hesitated to apply dubious terms like *Virtual Surround* to processes that often amount to little more than simple phase- or frequency-shifting and which, it was claimed, obviated the need for additional loudspeakers.

The statement of Wolfgang Hoeg and Gerhard Steinke in their 1975 monograph *The Fundamentals of Stereophony* (German title: *Stereophonie-Grundlagen*) that 'truly natural sound reproduction, ie sound reproduction that recreates the relationships that exist naturally in the sound field, is virtually impossible to achieve and seldom even worth striving for'[4] now requires qualification. True, the results will never be perfect, although the latest advances in sound technology have taken us a great deal closer to truly natural sound reproduction than anyone would have thought possible in 1975, but to say that the objective isn't even worth striving for is to say that recording studios all over the world that have invested in expensive reverb devices, the only purpose of which is to apply retroactively to recordings a sense of the very relationships to which Hoeg and Steinke referred, have simply been wasting their money.

If, on the other hand, a natural spatial impression was already present in the recording, there would be less need to apply synthetic reverberation retroactively, even though such reverberation would retain its value as a cosmetic. The need for synthetic reverberation arises because sound engineers have traditionally striven for recordings that were as 'dry' (ie free from natural reverberation) as possible – the advantage being that these are easier to mix – but the logic of going to enormous lengths to exclude room acoustics at the recording stage only to recreate them artificially further on down the line is increasingly being called into question. In the case of a room with good acoustics, the answer might seem obvious, but a word of caution is in order here: an improvement in the spatial impression of a recording often comes at the expense of clear directional imaging (ie the ability to pinpoint individual sound sources within the stereo field) or some other objective dear to the hearts of sound engineers.[5] What further complicates matters is that no two individuals hear (either physically or psychologically) in exactly the same way, which makes the idea of a 'perfect recording' particularly problematic.

But to reject out of hand the possibilities offered by recent technological advances with the defeatist mantra that you're never going to get a recording that sounds 100% natural, and to claim that such an objective is therefore not worth striving for, is feckless in the extreme. It should remain an article of faith that better is *always* worth striving for.

Glossary

This is perhaps the ideal time to provide a brief explanation of some of the terms that have already been touched upon and others that will appear later in the text.

3/2

The loudspeaker configuration recommended by ITU-R BS 775 for multichannel stereo, comprising three front channels (L = left, C = centre, R = right) and two rear channels (LS = left surround, RS = right surround).

5.1

The 3/2 recommendation expanded through the addition of a 'low frequency effects' channel (LFE)[6]; although chiefly of importance in the area of cinema sound, this format is often also encountered in the home (subwoofer).

6.1

5.1 expanded through the addition of a rear centre channel (examples: Dolby Digital EX and DTS ES).

7.1

5.1 expanded though the addition of two side channels; not to be confused with 5.1 systems using two or more loudspeakers for each of the surround channels.

A/D converter
A converter used to convert analogue audio signals to a digital format; usually PCM-based, but an alternative, DSD, now exists.

AC-3
An abbreviation of Audio Coding 3, a lossy compression system used by Dolby Digital and DVD-Video.

ADAT
Digital data format introduced by Alesis that transmits signals (mainly optical) in blocks of eight tracks.

AES/EBU
Digital dual-channel standard (mainly XLR) defined by the Audio Engineering Society (AES) and European Broadcasting Union (EBU). It encompasses a variety of different sampling rates and resolutions, one being the CD standard – 44.1kHz and 16 bits – while another is 48kHz and 24 bits. Channels can be combined for the transmission of higher sampling rates (up to 192kHz).

Ambience
A term enjoying a certain vogue in the music and film sectors where it is used to refer to background sounds (the theatrical equivalent being 'noises off').

Apparent Source Width
During playback, the angular width of the orchestra, choir or other group of sound sources as perceived by the listener, which may or may not be the same as the actual source width.

Arrival-Time Stereophony
Any stereo-miking system in which the stereo effect results solely from the fact that lateral sound reaches one of two (or more) non-coincident capsules before the other(s) – for example, AB. Also known as 'delay-time (or phase) stereophony'.

Bit Rate
Another term for data-transfer rate.

Blue-Laser Optical Disc
Optical storage medium with about six times the capacity of a standard DVD; read by blue rather than red lasers.

Blu-Ray Disc (BD)
Optical storage medium (up to 27GB) developed jointly by ten leading firms; currently the main recording medium in the professional video sector and a possible successor to DVD.

Codec
Abbreviation of *coder/decoder*, an algorithm used to compress and decompress sound and video files.

Coherence
Two recorded signals, L and R, are said to be coherent when they stem from the same sound source. Even if the phase of one is reversed, they will still be coherent.

Coincidence Stereophony
Stereo recording technique using coincident microphones. Since the sound reaches both capsules simultaneously, the directional imaging can only be the result of level or intensity differences (hence the term *intensity stereophony*).

Coincident Microphones
Microphones placed in such a way that their capsules are as close together as possible (usually one is directly above the other).

Correlation
The mutual relationship between the signals of two channels independent of level. If the signal of the two channels are identical, their correlation coefficient is 1. If they are out of phase, it is –1. Ideally, the correlation coefficient should be between 0.3 and 0.78.

Data-Transfer Rate
The speed at which data is read from a storage medium such as a DVD or hard disk, usually expressed in kilobits per second (kbps), megabits per second (Mbps) or gigabits per second (Gbps).

Delay-Time Stereophony
See *Arrival-Time Stereophony*.

Dolby Digital
Multichannel delivery system employing six discrete channels and a fundamental component of the DVD standard, with downmix guaranteed down to monophony. Dolby Digital EX has an additional centre surround channel with a limited bandwidth.

Dolby Surround
Multichannel delivery system employing two discrete (L and R) and two limited-frequency encoded channels (centre and surround).

DSD
Abbreviation of *Direct Stream Digital*, a single-bit encoding process employed by SACD (Super Audio Compact Disc).

DTS
Abbreviation of *Digital Theatre System*, a multichannel process with six (or, in the case of DTS ES, seven) discrete channels. Optional in the DVD standard.

DVD
Abbreviation of *Digital Versatile Disc*, an optical storage medium (5–18GB), DVD-Video being primarily intended for the reproduction of images and DVD-Audio for the reproduction of sound.

Intensity Stereophony
Recording technique using coincident microphones in which the stereo effect relies entirely upon variations in the level with which off-centre sound sources are reproduced by the left and right channels (examples being MS and XY).

ITU-R BS 775
Also ITU 775. The system recommended by the International Telecommunications Union for multichannel reproduction in the studio and home; the *de facto* standard for surround sound.

LFE
Abbreviation of *Low-Frequency Effects*, referring to a bandwidth-limited channel used mainly for cinematographic effects. Optional in the home. The frequency limitation occurs in the subwoofer while the channel itself transmits the full bandwidth.

Lossy Compression
A term used to describe any system of compression incapable of recovering all of the original data when the file is decompressed. In principle, only redundant information is discarded.

MADI
Abbreviation of Multichannel Audio Digital Interface, a digital format for the transmission of up to 56 audio channels (mainly BNC but also optical).

Metadata
Information that describes, and in some cases controls, aspects of the reproduction.

Panning
The assignment of signal components to channels. In the case of dual channel stereo, this is usually done using a 'pan pot', for multichannel stereo, with a matrix.

PCM
Abbreviation of *Pulse-Code Modulation*, a standard process for digitising sound. Various word lengths and sample rates are possible.

Periphony
Another term for *With-Height Surround*.

Planar Surround
Two-dimensional (left-right/front-back) surround with no height (up/down) element.

Quadraphony
Early multichannel system with four discrete channels (front L/R and rear L/R). With 'pseudo quad', the rear channels are encoded in the front ones.

Recording Angle
Confusingly, this term is used by different writers to describe two completely different things:

- The field within which sound sources need to be located for (reasonably) accurate directional imaging to result. The phantom images of sound sources within the recording angle will appear at varying positions between the L and R speakers. The phantom images of all other sources will appear in either the L speaker or the R. The recording angle is bisected by the main axis (0°), while the same recording angle can be expressed either relative to the main axis (±30°) or in absolute terms (60°).
- The angle formed by the axes of two microphones facing in different directions. In XY stereo, for example, where one microphone points diagonally forwards and to the right and the other diagonally forwards and to the left. The angle at the vertex (which in this case would be 90°) is described by some writers as the *recording angle*, but we will prefer the term *stereo angle*, keeping the alternative term for the first case).

S/PDIF
Abbreviation of *Sony/Philips Digital Interface*, a two-channel consumer digital format based on the AES/EBU standard. In general, fixed at 44.1kHz and 16 bits. Transmission is mainly coaxial (phono/RCA) or optical (Toslink).

SACD
Abbreviation of *Super Audio Compact Disc*, a high-resolution music format based on the DVD medium but with special A/D conversion (DSD).

Stereo Angle
The angle formed by the axes of coincident microphones pointing in different directions, expressed either in terms of the main axis, 0°, that bisects it (eg ±45°) or in absolute terms (90°). The stereo angle affects (but is not the same thing as) the recording angle.

Stereophony
The use of two or more channels of transmission and reproduction.

Surround
Multichannel stereo system in which the speakers surround the listener. As an adjective, the term *surround* is often used as a designation for the rear speakers only. Many different implementations of the surround concept exist, such as Dolby Surround, Virtual Surround.

Sweet Spot
The optimal listening position – in the case of domestic multichannel systems, a relatively small area.

WFS
Abbreviation of *Wave Field Synthesis*, a multichannel format in which, unlike most other surround formats, no phantom sound sources are represented, only direct sound sources.

With-Height Surround
See *Periphony*.

From The Edison Cylinder To Multichannel Stereophony
The history of audio technology could fill an entire book itself, so the brief breakdown that follows is simply designed to arrange the fundamental discoveries and inventions in chronological order and show the roots of multichannel stereophony.

The Genesis Of Audio Technology
An essay by Johannes Webers on the history of audio technology begins with the words 'To solve the problems of the future, you need to follow the train of thought of the pioneers.'[9] To do this, you need to go a long way back in time, since sound, and the possibility of recording and playing it back, has fascinated mankind for a very long time. As early as the turn of the 17th century, the celebrated German astronomer Johannes Kepler (1571–1630) was working on acoustics and music theory,[10] so even the title of this section is misleading since the first successful attempts to record and playback speech and sound pre-date Edison.

Léon Scott was in fact the first person to record sound successfully. In 1859, he demonstrated to the Paris Academy of Science a device that he called a 'phon-autograph',[11] which transduced sound waves into a pattern on paper coated with lampblack, but here he was only improving a device that Professor Wilhelm Weber of Göttingen had constructed in 1830.[12] Neither device, of course, was capable of reproducing sound. That was a development that had to wait 20 years until Thomas Alva Edison had invented his 'phonograph'.[13]

The phonograph recorded sound waves on a cylinder wrapped with tin foil that could be scanned, subsequently allowing the music to be played back. While it was recording, Edison's stylus cut a vertical (peaks-and-troughs) pattern in the foil rather than the lateral (right-left) modulation used later by the gramophone record. The idea had in fact been anticipated by the French scientist Charles Cros, who described the same principle in a paper presented before the French academy on 18 April 1877, but Edison is generally given the credit for the invention since Cros didn't produce a model to demonstrate that his machine could actually work.[14] From around 1878 onwards, phonographs were available commercially.

In 1887, however, the phonograph came under fierce competition from Emile Berliner's gramophone.[15] Berliner discovered a system whereby the vibrations were carved into a layer of wax covering a zinc disc, while the disc was continuously rinsed with liquid to prevent the excavated wax (known as the *chip*) accumulating on the disc and clogging the stylus. On this device, the stylus moved from side to side in response to the sound waves rather than cutting more or less deeply into the wax, but the crucial difference between Berliner's invention and Edison's is that Berliner found a way of duplicating his recordings.

First, the wax-covered zinc disc (with the sound pattern carved into the wax) was dipped in acid, which etched a groove in the zinc in the places where the wax had been cut away. Then a negative (male) version of the disc was made in which the pattern, instead of being recessed, projected from the surface of the disc, and this was used to stamp multiple copies of the recording. Initially these were made from hard rubber, but shellac was later substituted. All the same, it wasn't until 1896, when the hand-turned mechanism was replaced by clockwork, that the gramophone became an indispensable item – and would remain so for the next 100 years in the living rooms of even the moderately well-to-do.

Another interesting invention from this era is the auxetophone, which combined the principle of the gramophone with an early amplifier in which the movement of the needle was used to modulate a stream of compressed air. Unfortunately, the auxetophone was so loud that it could only really be used outdoors.[16]

As the gramophone grew in popularity, the first attempts were made to synchronise sound and images, initially by synchronising the movements of gramophones and projectors, but meanwhile in as early as 1898 the German physicist Ernst Ruhmer was working on a sound-to-light process (the 'photographophone') in which variations in the intensity of oscillation of a 'speaking' arc light were recorded upon a moving sensitive film.[17] However, the optical soundtrack only really came of age in 1919, when the German engineers Hans Vogt, Josef Engl and Josef Masserolle demonstrated the Tri-Ergon process.[18] Here the sound was recorded on the same film as the images – thereby guaranteeing synchronicity[19] – in a space outside the sprocket holes known as the *soundtrack*. As with Ruhmer's photographophone, the sound waves were transduced into light by a glow-discharge lamp and recorded on a film in which the variations in sound pressure were represented by variations in the opacity of the film.[20]

A far more important breakthrough, however, was the invention by De Forrest of the triode valve, which ushered in the electronic era. Soon funnels were replaced by microphones, tubes by cables and horns by amplifier-and-speaker combinations. The Tri-Ergon developers even developed a new type of loudspeaker (known as the 'Statophone') for the cinema, which was based on the electrostatic principle, whereby a metal disc was actuated by an electrode.[21] After a somewhat uncertain start (1925 being a particularly black year for the medium), in 1928 'talking pictures' (or 'the Talkies' as they were usually known) achieved their international breakthrough.

In the meantime, radio, too, was making an enormous impact. In 1923, the first German radio broadcast was made from VOX House in Berlin[22] using carbon microphones developed by Eugen Reisz and improved by Georg Neumann.[23] It was Neumann, too, who developed the first condenser microphone, which later became the CM3, or 'Neumann Bottle', one of the most famous microphones ever produced. As well as carbon and condenser mics, ribbon microphones were also popular at this time.[24]

Another milestone was the development of magnetic tape. The idea of using a flexible tape coated with a medium capable of holding a magnetic charge was first advanced by Fritz Pfleumer in 1928.[25] Although tape recordings could be erased and the tape reused, magnetic tape suffered in the early stages from excessive hiss. It was only when Walter Weber[26] developed the technique of AC biasing in 1940 that the tape recorder really took off as a viable technology. With Weber's discovery, it became possible to create recordings with a frequency range of 30–15,000Hz and a dynamic range of 60dB – far superior to the 40dB that was the best that could be achieved with optical sound.[27]

In 1948, the LP (Long Player) record became established.[28] Admittedly, RCA had produced a disc that rotated at only 33⅓rpm (revolutions per minute) in as early as 1931, but at that time there was little demand and production soon ceased.[29] The problem was the poor quality of the sound, as at the time RCA was still using shellac discs. Then, in 1948, when Columbia introduced discs made of vinyl – which crackles much less – the idea was taken up again and this time achieved success.[30] At this time, RCA also produced a smaller gramophone disc that rotated at 45rpm, which became the standard for singles.[31]

From Mono To Dual-Channel Stereophony

Many regard Walt Disney's *Fantasia* – the first film in which stereo was heard by the masses – as the birth of stereophony,[32] but here, too, there is a prehistory. The first attempt at multichannel sound transmission was made by the Hungarian Tivadaor Puskás in Paris in 1881, when he transmitted an opera performance through multiple telephone lines.[33] In 1933 and 1934, the Bell Telephone Company was also experimenting with what it called 'plastic concert recordings', feeding the signals of three different microphones to three independent loudspeakers.[34] Some sources even attribute the invention of the stereo gramophone record to the Bell Telephone Company,[35] although Alan Dower Blumlein – known primarily for the Blumlein Technique of stereo recording using mid and side microphones – had applied for a patent back in 1931 for the technology used by Bell in 1935 in which the signals were cut into both sides of a 45° groove in the record. In fact, the heyday of the stereo gramophone record had to wait until the 1960s, when there by which time there had been dramatic improvements in the quality of LP records.[36]

Whilst a patent existed for the stereo gramophone record, the first high-quality stereo recordings in 1943 and 1944 were in fact stored on magnetic tape. This had the result that tape was increasingly used for the post-synchronisation of film – a technique that by 1950 had gained an ascendancy over optical sound.[37]

Aside from a few rudimentary efforts, the real genesis of stereo radio also came in 1950. Here again the dual-transmitter method was used, in which the left and right signals were assigned to different frequencies and different radio receivers.[38] However, since this was a highly expensive procedure to implement, from the standpoints of both transmission and reception, and since the mono receivers in almost every home were left with the invidious choice of either the left or the right signal, ways were sought to broadcast both channels over the same frequency and in a form that was also mono-compatible.

Between 1950 and 1960, no fewer than 20 different systems were developed,[39] with the American Pilot-Tone eventually triumphing. This multiplex system developed by General Electric and Zenith, in which the mono signal (L + R = M) was transmitted at the normal frequency (40–15,000Hz, known as the *baseband*) and the difference signal (L – R = S) in the inaudible region between 23 and 53kHz,[40] was also adopted in Germany in 1963[41] as well as being recommended by the CCIR[42] in 1966 for stereo broadcasts and subsequently adopted in most countries of the world.[43]

In the '70s, television, too, began to implement dual-channel stereophony. Initially a workaround was used – the stereo signal was simply broadcast separately, using a normal radio frequency[44] – but in 1980 the German channel ZDF began broadcasting a modulated stereo signal.

It had been widely predicted that magnetic tape would spell the end of the gramophone record, but in the event the two technologies survived side by side, with magnetic tape preferred mainly for those applications where the reusability of the medium was of value. In the end it was the CD (Compact Disc), developed by Philips and Sony and introduced in 1981, that finally put paid to the dominance of the gramophone record and the pre-recorded cassette. This was the first digital medium in the audio-equipment market and it offered the consumer a degree of quality hitherto unknown, and so, despite the fact of its incompatibility with all pre-existing playback devices, it quickly became the leading medium for music reproduction.[45] Its advantages lay above all in its frequency range (which, unlike any other medium, spanned the entire audio spectrum), its dynamic range (greater than 90dB), its virtual absence of background noise and its lossless sampling.[46]

The CD therefore inaugurated the digital age in consumer electronics. Analogue-to-digital (A/D) converters were used to measure the amplitude of the signal (a process known as *sampling*) at minute intervals (the size of which was determined by the sample rate), yielding an array of numbers that described – albeit imperfectly – the course of the signal. When the CD was played back, the process was reversed by D/A converters, which recreated a good approximation of the original analogue signal from the numerical data. A sophisticated system of error checking and correction protected the integrity of the data. Factors of crucial importance to the accuracy of the digital image were the word length (which determined the range of possible values that could be used to describe the state of the analogue signal at the moment the 'snapshot' of its value was taken) and the sample rate (ie the number of snapshots per second that were taken of the analogue signal). In the case of the CD, 16-bit resolution and a sampling rate of 44.1kHz became the international standard, the sampling rate being twice the highest audible frequency, as stipulated by the Shannon Theorem.[47]

A further advantage of digital technology lies, of course, in the relatively free choice of transmission channel. The digital information, which consists of nothing more than a series of zeros and ones, can be recorded using a range of different physical processes, such as the disposition of magnetic particles or – as in the case of the CD – the dichotomy between pits (recesses in the disc) and lands (flat areas). Not surprisingly, then, the CD was soon followed by other digital media.

As it happens, neither Sony's MiniDisc nor Philips' DCC (Digital Compact Cassette) – both of which were rewritable media using systems of data reduction based upon psychoacoustic research – were able to make any significant inroads into the dominance of the CD.[48] However, another digital medium, DAT (Digital Audio Tape), was able to satisfy the expectations of manufacturers by establishing itself primarily in the professional recording sector as a high-quality mastering medium. It's also one of the few media available today capable of recording in 24-bit resolution.[49] Whilst the MiniDisc does still occupy a place in the market – somewhere between DAT, CD and cassette – the digital compact cassette has vanished without trace.

Further consolidation of the CD format came in the mid '90s with the recordable CD. CD *burners* – which use a laser to cut the pits in a specially recordable CD (known as a *CD-R*)[50] – are now commonplace components of the home computer, on which they are used for backing up data as well as recording music, and CDs produced in this way can be played back on any domestic CD player. An extension of this technique is provided by the CD-RW,[51] which can be erased and reused in much the same way as magnetic tape.

The latest developments in the realm of digital music media are DVD,[52] SACD from Sony[53] and XRCD.[54] Whilst the last-mentioned technology is based upon the CD but uses a special mastering technique,[55] DVD and the SACD are based on a completely new medium (although the operating principle of each is the same as that of the CD) but offering greatly increased storage capacity – up to 17GB[56] when two sampling layers are present and both sides of the disc are used.

The Development Of Multichannel Stereophony

The improvement that dual-channel stereo represented over mono was enormous, so it took little time to achieve widespread acceptance and standardisation. In no time, the terms *stereophony* and *dual-channel sound reproduction* became synonymous in most people's minds.

But no sooner had standardisation been achieved than the first attempts were made to improve still further the spatial impression by placing speakers behind as well as in front of the listener, and the ill-fated quadraphony was born.[57] The fundamental idea of using four discrete audio signals could at that time only be realized using magnetic tape, but this technology wasn't available in enough homes to make the new system economically viable. It's true that various systems were developed for encoding the signal for the rear channels in the normal dual-channel signal, using matrixing or a process similar to that used by stereo radio, but none of these systems was able to achieve results that were more than mediocre. The final nail in the coffin of the technology was the incompatibility of the various competing systems. It was all rather sad, since the results – in terms of spatial impression – were really quite good. In fact, even today there is talk of transferring old quad recordings to DTS or Dolby Digital and reissuing them.

Unlike in the home, the stereo revolution in film sound featured more than two channels from the start. The size of cinemas, coupled with the desire to draw filmgoers into the action to as great an extent as possible, called for the use of several discrete audio channels. This development was supported by the fact that film sound was independent of the usual consumer media and used its own medium – film – with either optical or magnetic sound. So the first commercially viable multichannel formats for the cinema were developed in as early as the '50s. One particularly lavish system – which involved the use of three image projectors, as well as five front and two surround audio channels – was called Cinerama.[58]

The point of the centre channel was to provide everyone in the cinema with satisfactory localisation of the speaker during passages of dialogue. Due to its complexity, however, Cinerama failed to establish itself as a standard, and it was replaced in 1953 by CinemaScope – 'the poor man's Cinerama', as it was called.[59] The four audio channels, three front and one (surround) effects channel, were stored on the film itself in stripes of magnetic material applied to each release print. In fact, though, the effects track was so narrow that the channel was very hissy and therefore only sporadic use was ever made of it.[60]

The Todd-Ao 70mm format was developed as a compromise between Cinerama and CinemaScope. This was a widescreen format on 70mm film with five front channels and one effects channel,[61] but it was only with the introduction of 70mm film with six discrete magnetic sound tracks in 1970 that the effects channel became a real surround channel. Since the wider tracks brought an improvement in the signal-to-noise ratio, all the tracks could now be used all the time to create a spatial impression.[62] From these six channels and their possible assignments, Dolby developed its 5.1 format and George Lucas his THX concept – the ideal spatial adaptation to existing surround sound. Later even eight-channel THX systems were introduced.[63] In fact, even today, THX has to be considered one of, if not the best sound standard.

Due to the prohibitive expense of 70mm productions, it was also important to improve the sound quality of 35mm productions, and here it was Dolby Stereo – developed by Dolby Laboratories in the mid '70s – that was to become the standard. With this format, instead of magnetic striping, the sound was recorded on two optical tracks, which ensured downwards compatibility, while two additional channels – centre and surround – could be derived from this stereo signal by matrixing.[64] Highly effective steering techniques contributed considerably to the quality and enabled the system to break through, while Dolby Surround and Pro Logic – which found their way into the living room via the video recorder in the '80s – were based on the same technology. That these were able to succeed, where quadraphony (which actually yielded better results) had failed was due mainly to the successful standardisation and the extensive testing of the technology in the cinemas. It was simply a question of adapting already successful technologies to the domestic environment. Nonetheless, the systems involved a degree of compromise, such as the limited frequency range of the surround channel.

In the '90s, digital technology made its entry into the world of multichannel stereo. A particularly significant idea came once again from Dolby engineers, who discovered that they could insert their new six-channel Dolby Digital soundtrack alongside the optical soundtrack in the spaces on the film between the sprocket holes to create a soundtrack that would play back in all surround formats.[65] The six channels now comprised information for three front, two surround and one subwoofer or LFE[66] channel, and this arrangement has become known as 5.1 format.

With the introduction of DVD, Dolby Digital 5.1 became the main standard for multichannel reproduction in the home. Every DVD player can decode Dolby Digital as well as being able to derive either Dolby Surround, dual channel stereo or a mono signal from the six channel source.[67] On this basis, for the first time it's now possible to produce multichannel audio for domestic use while at the same time being certain that it's both downwards compatible and capable of being played back regardless of the loudspeaker configuration in the living room.

But this is far from being the final word in multichannel sound. In 1993, the introduction of the DTS[68] system made a big splash in the cinemas. With DTS (Digital Theatre Sound), audio information from separate CDs or DVDs is played back in sync with the film. DTS-ES even offers an additional channel, placed in the centre rear. Of course, the various channels are compressed to keep data transfer rates within manageable boundaries.[69] DTS is, in fact, the second optional standard for DVD sound reproduction, the first being Dolby Digital.

In 1994, Sony presented a system of its own, SDDS[70] (Sony Dynamic Digital Sound), a high-end surround solution comprising five front and two surround channels plus one LFE channel,[71] and Dolby also introduced a system featuring a central rear channel in 1998, which it called Dolby Digital Surround EX,[72] whereby the centre surround channel – which is analogue and covers a limited frequency spectrum – is matrix-encoded onto the regular left and right surround channels in a procedure reminiscent of Dolby Surround.

It remains to be seen which of these systems will be developed and which will be abandoned in the immediate future. One promising candidate for the multichannel format of the future is the relatively new WFS (Wave Field Synthesis) system. Although at the time of writing very difficult to implement in the home, in the cinema WFS allows the 'holographic' placing of sound sources inside and outside the room through the use of loudspeaker arrays[73]. At the beginning of 2003, in a joint venture between the Fraunhofer Institute and the TU Ilmenau, the first cinema to feature WFS technology opened in Ilmenau. The response among specialists visiting the cinema ranged from positive to enthusiastic.[74]

2 SURROUND-SOUND FUNDAMENTALS

Sound

A Bit Of Physics

As a branch of the natural sciences, acoustics is intimately bound up with physics. Physics not only explains the fundamentals of how sound propagates and decays but also allows us to make complex calculations that assist with the design and manufacture of musical instruments and the equipment we use to record, transmit and reproduce sound. Here, however, we must content ourselves with a few fundamental principles that are important to an understanding of multichannel audio.

To a physicist, sound consists of successive compressions and rarefactions[75] of the air caused by a vibrating source.[76] To be detectable by the human ear, these vibrations must lie within a certain frequency range: from 16Hz to 20kHz (which means from 16 to 20,000 vibrations per second). Since sound is not confined to a single point in space but spreads in all directions from a source, we say that the source imparts its vibrations to an elastic medium (whether gas, liquid or solid) in the form of sound waves. In the case of airborne sound, air is the medium, and the compressions and rarefactions result from the oscillation of air molecules. Like all waves, sound waves can be reflected, bent, absorbed or superimposed. A sound wave is quantified in terms of sound pressure, the speed of sound and the acoustic particle velocity. The sound pressure is the difference between the instantaneous pressure at a point in the presence of the sound wave and the static pressure of the medium; the speed of sound (which in dry air at 20° Celsius is approximately 343 metres per second) describes the speed at which sound waves propagate from the sound source, and the acoustic particle velocity quantifies the speed of movement of particles in the medium about their point of equilibrium in response to the compressions and rarefactions produced by the sound wave. The wavelength, or distance between successive crests of the sound wave (or equivalent points in successive sound waves), is equal to the speed of sound divided by the frequency. The sound-pressure level is referenced to the threshold of hearing, while the sound intensity is a time-averaged directional quantity that indicates the amount of energy per unit of time flowing through a unit area.

We should distinguish between two types of sound waves – plane and spherical – based upon their manner of propagation. The ideal plane wave propagates in one dimension only, with the speed of sound and the particle velocity in phase, which is to say that the angle between the two vectors is zero. The ideal spherical wave, on the other hand, propagates from a single point as an expanding sphere, with the speed of sound and the particle velocity acting in different directions. In neither case is the energy of the wave dissipated either by reflection or by absorption.

Of course, neither plane nor spherical waves are ever encountered in their ideal form. While it's true that most sound waves are to some extent directional, although never one-dimensional, a diffuse sonic image emerges sooner or later as a result of reflections. Even a point source can be used for only very low frequencies as its dimensions need to be very small in relation to the wavelength of the sound. So, for higher frequencies, all sound transducers are automatically directional to some extent. Besides which, to create an ideal spherical wave, a point source would need to be infinitely loud.

Now that we have familiarised ourselves with the fundamental properties of sound and the way it propagates from a source, let's take a look at what happens at the other end, when sound waves reach the human ear.

A Little Biology

THE EAR

As a general rule, human beings pay more attention to what they see than to what they hear; we are 'seeing creatures'[77], and this is also reflected in our language and imagery, which is based primarily upon visual impressions with impressions derived from the other senses playing only a subordinate role.

The human ear is an extremely complex organ and the process of hearing is no less complex. The ear responds to variations in air pressure, which it translates into nerve impulses. Broadly speaking, we can distinguish between the *outer ear*, which captures and concentrates the sound; the *middle ear*, which begins at the eardrum and contains three small bones known as the anvil, the hammer and the stirrup, which transmit the vibrations to a membrane similar to the tympanum; and the *inner ear*, which is made up of fluid-filled tubes that transduce the pressure variations into nerve impulses carrying information concerning the frequency and intensity of sounds to the brain.

It is, of course, the pitch and loudness of the sound, rather than its frequency and intensity, that are the sensations registered in the human brain.

SENSITIVITY TO PITCH

When we consider the sensitivity of human hearing to pitch, we must distinguish between two faculties: the ability to detect the presence of sound and the ability to distinguish differences of pitch between different sounds. The frequency range within which we are capable of detecting the presence of sound varies from individual to individual and diminishes with age but runs approximately from 16Hz to 20kHz. As for differences in pitch, someone with a trained ear is much more adept at detecting such differences than someone with no musical training, and the minimal perceptible difference in pitch between two notes is in any case not constant across the entire frequency spectrum: someone with a trained ear can distinguish changes in pitch of as little as 2% in the range between 1,000 and 4,000Hz, whereas changes in pitch in other frequency ranges – notably the low frequency range – become detectable only when they reach 5%.[78] The interval of time between the sounding of two notes and their duration also strongly influences our ability to detect any difference in pitch between them.

In music theory, the frequency spectrum – which, of course, is a continuum – is divided up into blocks of 12 discrete steps, whereby the frequency of the first note of each block is precisely double that of the first note of the block below, and the frequency of the second note is double that of the second note of the block below, and so on. Where the frequency of one note is double that of another, we say that the first note is an octave higher than the second, and these two notes and the eleven discrete steps that separate them form the chromatic (ie 12-note) scale at the heart of Western music (even though all 12 tones are seldom used with equal frequency over the course of an individual composition). It's important not to confuse the semitone (the distance between two steps of the chromatic scale), which happens to be the smallest interval of which use is made in Western music, with the smallest difference in pitch that the ear is capable of detecting.[79]

SENSITIVITY TO LOUDNESS

The second factor that conditions our ability to perceive sounds is their loudness. Here, too, we must distinguish between two faculties: the ability to detect the presence of sound and the ability to distinguish differences in loudness. In the former case, we can again define a range, which runs from the threshold of hearing (the level of the quietest sounds that can be detected by the human ear) to the threshold of pain. Judgements about which of two sounds is louder rest largely upon perceived differences in the sound pressure level, and we can define the minimum difference in loudness that can be detected in any given frequency range, for here, too, the ear is not equally sensitive at all frequencies; at 1,000Hz, this volume range runs from 0dB (0.0002μbar) to 120dB (≈ 200 μbar). Since the smallest and largest sound pressure levels here are in the ratio

$1:10^{-6}$ we use a logarithmic scale to measure the loudness of sounds. The dB value of a sound is 20 times the common logarithm of the ratio between its sound pressure level and that of the quietest sound that can be detected by the human ear.[80]

The duration that a note needs to have before both its pitch and volume can be assessed by the human ear is defined as the Attack Constant ($te \approx 23$ms). There is also a Decay Constant ($ta \approx 25$ms), which is the interval between a note falling silent and the moment at which precise evaluation is no longer possible.[81]

Sometimes a sound that would otherwise be perfectly audible is rendered inaudible by the presence of a louder sound. This effect – which is known as *intensity masking* and is dependent also upon the difference in frequency between the two sounds – is exploited by many audio compression algorithms, which disregard altogether the signals of masked sounds in order to economise on storage space and eliminate unnecessary data transfer.

TIMBRE

For the sake of completeness, I should mention timbre as a third, if not very objective, criterion of acoustic perception.[82] Each time a sound is perceived by the brain, this perception is accompanied by a subjective impression. These impressions, which are to a certain extent learned, evoke differing responses in different people, especially people of different cultures. The ability to distinguish different instruments by their timbres, like the ability to detect minor differences in pitch, is more developed in certain individuals than in others, as well as being a skill that can be learned, while our liking (or disliking) of particular timbres, while partly explainable by science, is partly, too, a matter of personal taste and culture. The timbre or tone colour of a note is caused by the proportion in which the fundamental tone is combined with the harmonics or overtones.

Equally subjective is our response to the sounding of two or more fundamental tones simultaneously. Sounds that, if heard individually, would be experienced as euphonious can become unpleasant to the ear when heard together; this is true, for example, of notes that are one, two or six semitones apart, a fact exploited by classical harmony to create tensions, the subsequent resolution of which is experienced as satisfying – at least by listeners versed in the tradition. This, too, is a cultural rather than a universal phenomenon. An objective and universally valid assessment of the euphony of sounds, whether heard singly or in combination, is clearly impossible.

Room Acoustics

Imagine a singer treating you to a serenade outdoors – in the snow, perhaps. Now imagine that he or she follows you to a large gothic cathedral and sings exactly the same song again in exactly the same way. Your impression of the two performances would nonetheless be drastically different. Whereas in the open air you would have heard a very dry sound with almost no reflections, in the cathedral there would have been almost more reverberation than voice! The difference lies in the acoustics of the two settings.

Some of the sound from a source travels to your ear in a straight line, and this is called *direct sound*. Sound from the same source, however, moves in other directions at the same time (sound, after all, expands outwards from the source in a spherical pattern), and sooner or later in a cathedral it collides with obstacles, such as walls, pillars or furniture, which – depending upon their nature and form – reflect or absorb it, or, in most cases, partly reflect and partly absorb it. In this way, the room is gradually filled with reflected sound, which takes longer to reach the ear because it arrives by an indirect route. This is known as *diffuse sound* or *reverberation* and is made up of both early and late reflections.

Both types of sound, direct and diffuse, combine to form the sonic image, their exact proportions depending not only on the acoustics of the room but also on the distance between the listener and the sound source. In a reverberant room, the sonic image can become washy and confused – described as lacking definition – for listeners seated too far from the source, and while the human ear under such circumstances is capable of focusing on the direct sound to a certain extent, a microphone can't do this; it records all sound waves that impinge upon the diaphragm. If, therefore, it's desirable to obtain a sonic image that's at the same time realistic and defined, it's necessary to be very careful with microphone placements.

The reverberation time (T) of a room is the interval between a sound source ceasing and the sound-pressure level falling to a thousandth of its previous level. Since the reverberation time is frequency-dependent, the acoustics of a room are usually assessed using a reverberation curve.[83] Often acoustic correction is necessary, especially in recording studios where the acoustics affect the quality of every recording, and tables have therefore been compiled that describe the absorption and reflection characteristics of a wide range of materials. Such tables can be used to optimise the acoustics of a given room.

The shape of the room is also important. For this reason, rectangular rooms are often less suitable than trapezoidal ones. However, as it's sometimes necessary to work in rooms that are less than ideal in their shape, various aids such as bass traps and resonators have been developed available to optimise a room's acoustics for the purpose of recording. Naturally, it's the acoustics not just of the recording studio itself that are important but also of the control room, where the recording engineer monitors and later mixes and processes the recording.

Standards And Recommendations

People will always argue about the sense or senselessness of standards. From a technical point of view, they are undoubtedly important, if not essential, while on the other hand it's often deviations from the standard that breathe new life into old technologies and lead to innovation. And this is true not just in the field of research and development; in the studio, too, where sound engineers are guided to a great extent by subjective impressions, scope must be allowed for experimentation. It's vital that the creativity of developers and recording engineers isn't inhibited through the over-rigorous application of standards, and that the intuitive preferences of consumers isn't disregarded.

Perhaps this is why in recent years there has been a tendency to shy away from talking about 'standards' and to speak instead of 'recommendations'. This doesn't mean, of course, that the need for standardisation in respect of certain media formats – DVD-Audio, for example – should be ignored; there have to be technical standards agreed on a nationwide – indeed, a continent-wide – basis if modern media and technologies are to have any future at all; the mistakes of the past (quadraphony failed because there were too many incompatible formats) mustn't be repeated.

However, in the short (or, even, medium) term, we're never going to achieve any uniformity of multichannel playback conditions either in the cinema or in the home, largely because the technology is still in its infancy and there are a multitude of competing systems out there; if the consumer prefers a non-standard loudspeaker configuration, or if the architecture of the living room precludes the use of a standard one, he's going to improvise. Then there's the fact that only a minority of the loudspeaker sets on the market comply with the recommendations of the market and specific organisations. Of course, these two factors deny recording engineers the assurance that their mix will sound even approximately the same wherever it's heard, and they might even mean that the multichannel mix that is eventually settle upon as standard will only ever sound right in the studio.

This underlines the necessity of creating a separate two-channel mix; it at least will be capable of being reproduced adequately on the systems found in the majority of homes.

Those campaigning for standardisation of multichannel playback configurations have had to be content for the time being with establishing a common practice among recording studios. There is, of course, nothing to stop affluent audiophiles putting together similar configurations in their own homes, but the reality is that such people constitute only a tiny minority of the listening public. It's against this background that the standards and recommendations discussed in the following pages should be considered.

Multichannel Stereophony

The European recommendation ITU-R BS 775 relates to what the International Telecommunications Union describes as 'a multichannel stereophonic sound system with and without accompanying picture'. This is the *de facto* standard for multichannel systems and describes the fundamental conditions and optimum listening configurations for the assessment of mono and multichannel reproduction.[86]

The recommendation is primarily aimed at recording studios and is intended to ensure the creation of optimal listening conditions in reference and control rooms, but most of the advice it contains is also of value in the home. The term 'listening conditions' refers to a sound field created through the use of loudspeakers rather than headphones, the use of which wasn't covered by the recommendation. However, since these listening conditions can't be described objectively, the recommendation is restricted to suggestions relating to the parameters of loudspeakers and the rooms in which listening occurs.

Recommendation ITU 775 is concerned essentially with the production of multichannel audio that will be listened to in the home, so all the parameters assume a relatively small sweet spot, whether for the reproduction of sound and images simultaneously or of sound on its own.

THE LISTENING ENVIRONMENT

The ITU recommendation described above has much to say about ideal monitoring environments and is intended to serve as a guide to architects designing or studios renovating reference rooms and control rooms. Most people are clearly going to have difficulty trying to implement these recommendations in their own homes (those concerning loudspeakers and their arrangement are obviously more helpful in this respect), but it's worth at least noting the recommendations relating to the monitoring environment, if only because they might help you to decide which is the least unsuitable room in your home in terms of surround listening.

According to the ITU, the characteristics of a room considered ideal for the assessment of multichannel recordings are the following:

- **Area:** >40 m² (>25 m² in the home)
- **Room Volume:** >300 m³
- **Reverberation Time:** 0.2–0.4s (between 200Hz and 2.5kHz)
- **Early Reflections:** Around –10dB relative to the direct sound
- **Reverberation:** No flutter echoes, no discolouration of the sound
- **Background Noise:** Around 10dB (or NR 10)[87]

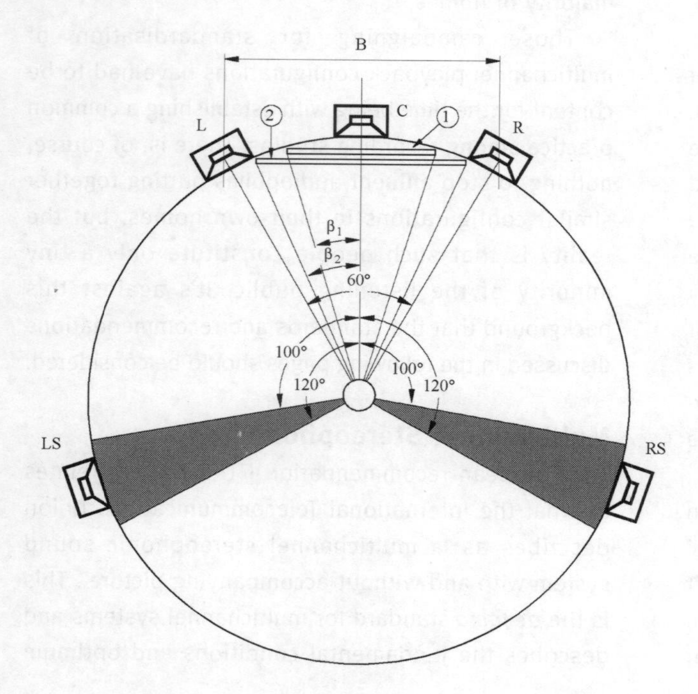

Figure 1: Reference loudspeaker arrangement (L/C/R and LS/RS) in combination with video playback equipment (1 and 2)

LOUDSPEAKERS

The most important section of the ITU 775 recommendation deals with the ideal loudspeaker configuration. Here, too, fundamental parameters have been chosen with studio conditions primarily in mind.

The reference playback configuration is the 3/2 format[88] (L/C/R and LS/RS) with five identical loudspeakers. This represents a compromise between the loudspeaker configurations used in studios for the reproduction of multichannel sound and what can reasonably be expected in the home. An arrangement such as that illustrated in Figure 1 provides a relatively good listening experience.

Naturally, listening conditions in the reference room of a recording studio need to conform to far higher standards than those of the living room, and it would clearly be extravagant to attempt to reproduce them in the home. Nonetheless, an understanding of the recommendations will enable you to create a far better listening environment for multichannel audio in your home than will ever be obtained through the haphazard arrangement of the type of surround loudspeakers sets generally available in the high street.[89] On the other hand, it makes sense for every studio to have at least one non-standard loudspeaker configuration, given that such arrangements are the rule rather than the exception in the home:

- **Height Of Loudspeakers** – 1.2m (0.9–1.4m in the home)
- **Angle (LC + CR)** – 30° (C at 0°, so LR = 60°)
- **Angle (LSC + CRS)** – 100–120°
- **Tilt Of Loudspeakers** – L/C/R = 0°, LS/RS = 15° downwards
- **Distance From Reflecting Surfaces** – 1m (>0.5m in the home)

The ITU 775 recommendation also provides for the simultaneous reproduction of images and sound and the positioning of the video-reproduction device within this configuration. This is especially important since even pure audio media, such as DVD-Audio, allow for the possibility of menu control, so even devices primarily designed for the reproduction of sound must have be able to handle images as well. With a view to the planned (although as yet not widely implemented) switch to HDTV[90], the recommendation takes both normal and high-resolution screen formats into account.

OPTIONAL LFE CHANNEL

The most common extension of the 3/2 standard is the addition of a sub-bass (LFE) channel. Since the bandwidth of this channel (20–80 or 120Hz) is approximately one-tench that of the others, its presence is usually indicated by the suffixes '.1' or '/1'. This channel is generally reproduced by a subwoofer, the position of which is not stipulated, since nothing much turns up on it (the human ear isn't very good at detecting the origins of very low-frequency sounds). In view of the fact that the LFE channel is merely an option, none of the essential audio content should be assigned exclusively to it; in other words, the content of the LFE channel must be shared by other channels. To make sure that the low-frequency signals achieve the necessary penetration, the LFE channel is usually 10dB above that of the other channels. (See the section titled 'Production Parameters', later in this chapter.)

In order to allow a reduction in the size of the five main loudspeakers, there are a large number of solutions on the market in which their low frequency content (ie that below 120Hz) is passed to the subwoofer instead. In this case, the LFE channel is handling not just low-frequency effects but also the normal low frequency content of the audio. There are even solutions involving two subwoofers: one for the low-frequency effects proper and the other to compensate for the fact that there are no proper woofers in the five main loudspeakers. Such configurations are nonetheless considered valid 3/2 or 3/2/1 (5.1) configurations.[91]

EXTENDING THE LISTENING ZONE

To enlarge the listening zone – in large rooms, particularly – it's possible to use several loudspeakers to transduce each channel, with the individual signals sent to a special processor for decorrelation (although

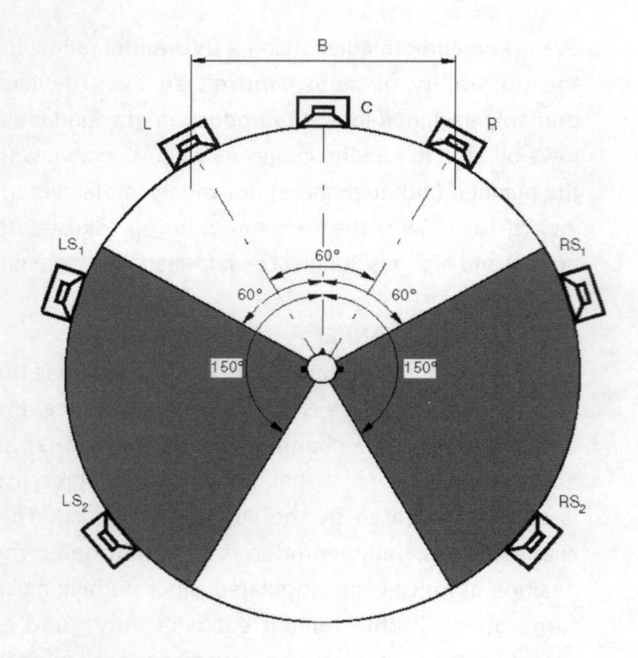

Figure 2: Optional configuration for the 3/2 format with four surround speakers (pseudo-3/4 format)

in practice it's generally only the surround channels that are reinforced in this way[92]). Such extensions are covered by the ITU 775 recommendation, as described in Figure 2. The format that results is, of course, only a pseudo-3/4 format; in essence it is still 3/2.

HIERARCHY OF PLAYBACK FORMATS

In order to guarantee complete reproduction of the audio content by all possible reproduction configurations, and also to make possible the reproduction on standard systems of formats going beyond 3/2, the ITU 775 recommendation stipulates an entire hierarchy with corresponding matrixing suggestions for the summing or distribution of signals to the available loudspeakers. In addition to the 3/2 format, it also takes the 3/1 format[93] into consideration, although no other formats are included. Table 1 on the next page shows the hierarchy.

PRODUCTION PARAMETERS

Certain conventions are necessary to standardise the production process itself so that multichannel projects can be exchanged between different studios and archived. The ITU 775 recommendation therefore contains certain suggestions relating to this part of the production process.

One important parameter is the assignment of channels to the available tracks on a recording medium[94] (Table 2). The recommendation assumes the availability of eight tracks, though in fact most recording devices nowadays offer considerably more.

If Track 4 is not needed for an LFE channel, it can be used for commentary or the monophonic surround signal MS (LS + RS). In the latter case, the summing level must be reduced by 3dB.

If it's not a stereo mix, Tracks 7 and 8 can be used to store the signals of two additional surround channels (3/4) or two additional front channels (LC = half left and RC = half right) for special cinema formats (5/2). The medium should carry a sticker or be accompanied by a sheet indicating the use made of Tracks 4, 7 and 8 and their purpose.

The recommendation also deals with the level ratios between the individual channels as well as the maximum levels permitted. Whilst the degree of attenuation of the individual signals during conversion to other formats is determined by the corresponding matrix, the maximum level varies depending upon the purpose and nature of the recording. The various maximum and alignment signal levels are listed in Table 3.

SYSTEM	SIGNALS/CHANNELS	CODE	LOUDSPEAKER ARRANGEMENT
One-channel mono	M	1/0	front 0°
Two-channel stereo	L/R	2/0	front 0° ± 30°
Two-channel stereo + one surround	L/R//MS	2/1	front 0° ± 30°+ side ± 110° *
Two-channel stereo + two surround	L/R//LS/RS	2/2	front 0° ± 30° + side ± 110°
Three-channel stereo	L/C/R	3/0	front 0° ± 30°
Three-channel stereo + one surround	L/C/R//MS	3/1	front 0° ± 30° + side ± 110° *
Three-channel stereo + two surround	L/C/R//LS/RS	3/2	front 0° ± 30° + side ± 110°
Three-channel stereo + two surround + one LFE	L/C/R//LS/RS + LFE	3/2/1 (5.1)	as indicated
Five-channel stereo + two surround	L/LC/C/RC/R//LS/RS	5/2	as indicated
Five-channel stereo + two surround	L/LC/C/RC/R//LS/RS + LFE + LFE	5/2/1	as indicated

* Channel usually decorrelated and distributed between two loudspeakers

Table 1: Hierarchy of compatible multichannel systems

TRACK	SIGNAL	REMARKS
1	L (left)	
2	R (right)	
3	C (centre/middle)	
4	LFE (low frequency effects)	optional sub-bass or effects signal [alternatively, commentary or monophonic sound signal MS (3dB)]
5	LS (left surround)	alternatively mono surround MS (–3dB)
6	RS (right surround)	alternatively mono surround MS (–3dB)
7	freely assignable	primarily left signal of a 2/0 stereo mix
8	freely assignable	primarily right signal of a 2/0 stereo mix

Table 2: Track assignments for a 3/2 recording on an eight-track medium

---

	ANALOGUE	DIGITAL	
		Exchange TV/Radio	Mastering
Maximum permitted level$_{PMS}$ (permitted maximum signal 1kHz sine)	0dB*	–9dB**	0dB
Alignment signal level$_{AS}$ (alignment signal 1kHz sine)	–9dB*	–18dB**	–18dB**

* Relative to studio normal level + 6dB

** Relative to digital clipping level 0dB

Table 3: Recording levels

When the LFE channel is used, its level needs to be 10dB higher than that of the other channels for an adequate transmission of the signals. The level at the ideal listening position in 3/2 format should be 78dB[95] and the level of the individual channels shouldn't differ by more than 0.25dB[96] (the reference tones, naturally, are stated in each case[97]). The exact recording and control levels are contained in EBU (European Broadcasting Union) Recommendations 64[98] and 68[99] as well as in ITU 645-2[100], and a summary of both these production guidelines can be consulted online at the SSF web site[101].

Surround-Sound Evaluation

An interesting footnote to this round-up of standards is provided by EBU Technical Recommendation R90-2000: 'The subjective evaluation of the quality of sound programme material.' This recommendation seeks to establish a way of quantifying personal judgements relating to a sonic image using certain parameters felt to be appropriate to this endeavour. This is all the more interesting because impressions of sound by their very nature are not susceptible to standardisation in any obvious way, since different individuals hear differently and tend in any case to express themselves in vague or generally unhelpful terms when it comes to the evaluation of sound.

Nonetheless, in EBU 90 an attempt is made to establish a terminology for such evaluations, even though the evaluations themselves necessarily remain subjective. The sonic images created by multichannel stereophony are given special consideration. Table 4 lists the most important terms:

MAIN PARAMETER	SUB-PARAMETERS	COMMON TERMINOLOGY
1 **Quality Of The Front Sonic Image** – In the front sonic image, all the sound sources sound authentic and can be localised well	sound distribution sound stability width of the sonic image localisation/sharpness	wide/narrow precise/imprecise stable/unstable localisable/non-localisable
2 **Side And Rear Sound Quality** – The side and rear sonic image seems balanced	sound distribution sound stability localisation sharpness homogeneity of diffuse sound	stable/unstable localisable/non-localisable
3 **Spatial Impression** – The sound content appears in an appropriate spatial environment	reverberation acoustic balance discernible room size spatial depth	reverberant/dry room direct/indirect large room/small room
4 **Transparency** – Details can be perceived clearly	definition of the sound source time determination	clarity clear/opaque
5 **Distribution** – The individual sound sources appear to be distributed appropriately within the sonic image	front/rear balance direct/indirect balance dynamic range	sound source too loud/ too quiet
6 **Tone Colour** – Accurate reproduction of the characteristic sound of the sources	timbre tone colour (front, side and rear) tone colour of the reverb sound structure	booming/sharp neutral/dull/shrill dark/bright warm/cold
7 **Freedom From Noise And Interference** – Absence of miscellaneous distractions	noise distortion coding errors	bit errors electrical interference acoustic interference environmental noise distortion compression artefacts
8 Overall Impression – Average of the subjective weighting of all parameters		

Table 4: Main and sub-parameters and common terminology[102]

Playback And Delivery Formats

As has already been seen, there are many different multichannel formats in use today, and while all may be informed by the same purpose – to give the sonic image a more realistic spatial impression – each adopts a different approach. Formats also differ in terms of how much they cost to buy and install; some are relatively cheap and easy to install whereas others require a considerable outlay. But, of course, the sound quality of the most expensive systems is generally astounding.

What follows is a brief introduction to the most important systems. They're presented here in no particular order of quality, simply by the number of playback channels they employ and the type of spatial imaging you can expect from them. There's also a distinction made between common systems, more rare systems and new formats from which we can expect to hear more in the future. First, however, we must distinguish between systems for the home and those intended for the cinema.

Reproduction In The Home And Cinema

The roots of multichannel audio are largely found in the cinema, where discrete channels and loudspeakers have been used for some time to create a more realistic cinematic experience. Indeed, the constant struggle for ever more spectacular optical and acoustic effects has been one of the major driving forces behind the development of multichannel sound.

Of course, multichannel reproduction takes a very different form in the cinema from that encountered in the home. Most living rooms are quite small and have a relatively small sweet spot. What's more, they're not used solely for watching TV; they have to serve other purposes that might conflict with the demands of optimal sound reproduction. For the most part, therefore, it's best to stick fairly closely to the ITU 775 recommendation in the living room – in other words, to opt for the basic configuration, in which there are five loudspeakers arranged around the viewers and a sweet spot large enough to accommodate more than one person.

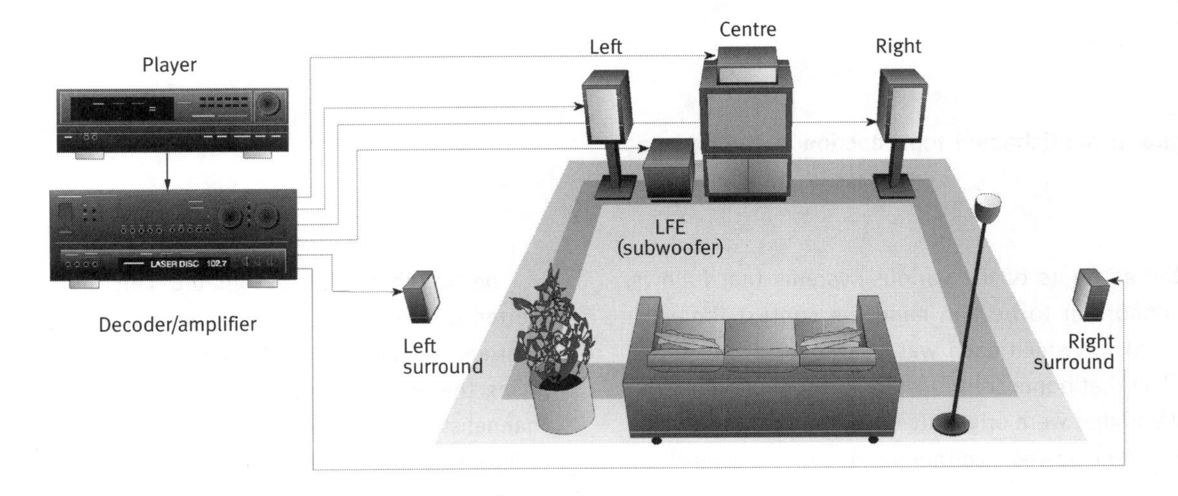

Figure 3: Multichannel reproduction in the home (with non-ITU775-compliant loudspeaker arrangement

In the cinema, the circumstances are completely different: there, we're dealing with what's usually a very large room with a large number of seats, and since everyone who's paid for a ticket has a right to expect decent sound, the sweet spot has to cover the entire seating area. In addition, greater realism is often obtained by concealing the front three or four loudspeakers, as well as placing a subwoofer behind the screen, although this should never be allowed to compromise the quality of the sound reproduction.

Usually, each of the two or more surround channels is assigned to more than one loudspeaker, which means that a processor has to be used to decorrelate the signals of the individual speakers. Furthermore, since cinemas are for the most part used exclusively for the viewing of films, their acoustics can be optimised for that single purpose. Cinema loudspeakers and amplifiers are also far larger and more powerful than any to be found in the home.

For a cinema to obtain a THX certificate, it needs to combine these elements to create something approaching the ideal multichannel listening experience.

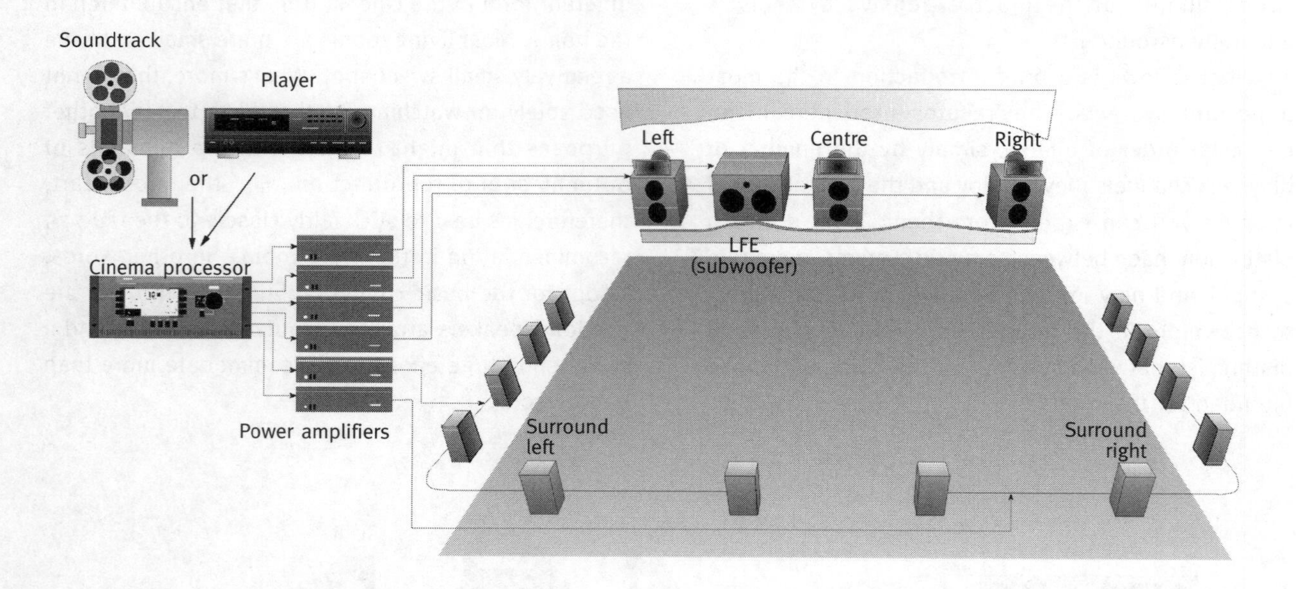

Figure 4: Multichannel reproduction in the cinema

In the accounts of the various systems that follows, it's important to bear in mind the context (home or cinema) for which each was designed, even though the fact that home solutions are now being offered for systems that were originally developed for the cinema inevitably involves a certain blurring of the distinction.

Common Formats

DUAL-CHANNEL STEREOPHONY

As I said, the term *stereophony* is not restricted to two-channel systems, although these remain the most commonly encountered format, even today. At the time they were introduced, dual-channel systems represented such a vast improvement on mono systems that they quickly established a firm hold on the hi-fi market.

The two channels – designated 'Left' and 'Right' – are reproduced through loudspeakers (positioned as illustrated in Figure 5) or headphones, the latter option giving the format the great merit of portability. Dual-channel stereophony is also the best-supported format, in the sense that the classic broadcasting media (radio and television), analogue media (such as gramophone records and music cassettes) and digital media (such as MiniDisc, CD and DVD) all support dual-channel stereophony.

All multichannel techniques, whether for recording or playback, are based on the principles established by dual-channel stereophony. Despite the limited number of channels it provides, the quality of the sonic image is often very high. With many years of experience to draw upon, many sound engineers demonstrate an impressive facility with the medium. If the correct microphones are used in a proper configuration, it's possible to achieve good directional and depth imaging.

Naturally, dual-channel stereophony offers no side or rear sonic image, but this is seldom a major drawback, and however exciting the possibilities of multichannel audio, many noted sound engineers still insist on producing a separate stereo mix in addition to their surround one.

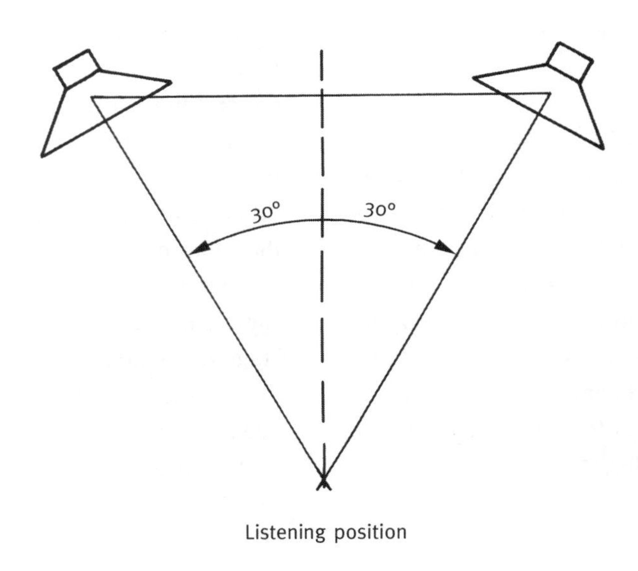

Figure 5: Classic dual-channel stereo configuration

BINAURAL STEREO RECORDING

Binaural stereo recording is an interesting technique involving the use of mics concealed in a dummy head.

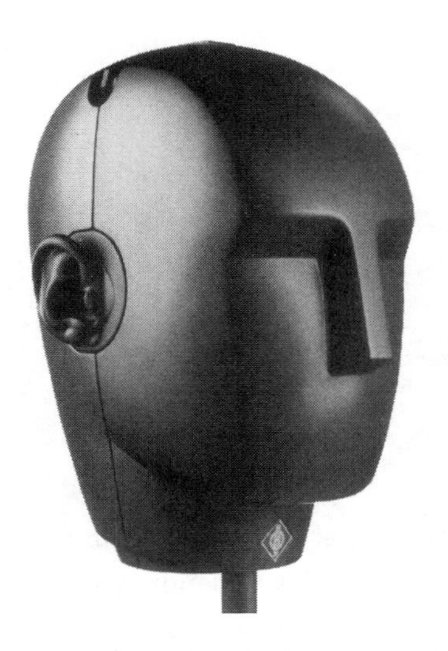

Figure 6: Dummy-head mic (Neumann KU 100) for binaural stereo recording

The head is intended to reproduce as realistically as possible the effect that the geometry and substance of the human head have upon the sound received by the right and left ears. Aware of the important role played by the outer ear in the localisation of sounds, the designers have modelled the outer ear of the dummy on that of a 'typical' human. No two human ears are alike, of course, which means that no two individuals experience the same sound in exactly the same way, but the final design represents a reasonable simulacrum of a 'typical' ear.

A microphone capsule is placed at the end of a 3mm artificial hearing channel within each of the dummy's ears. Because of their relatively linear frequency response and high bass sensitivity, omnidirectional mics are generally preferred.[103]

The signals recorded using the dummy head are astoundingly realistic. The only disadvantage of the format is that it's incompatible with loudspeaker playback; binaural stereo recordings can be appreciated only through headphones. However, as long as these are of sufficient quality, the listening experience is outstanding.

The best binaural stereo recordings combine excellent localisation with spatial depth. One especially notable development of this technique is known as BRS (Binaural Room Scanning), which will be discussed later.

AMBIPHONY AND AMBISONICS

Ambiphony is not, strictly speaking, a multichannel technique; rather, it represents an early attempt to capture room information (ambience) as well as the normal two-channel stereo image. A large number of different ambiphonal microphone techniques were proposed in the '60s, one being L Keibs' system, illustrated in Figure 7. However, there was no ambiphony standard, and the idea wasn't built around any single loudspeaker configuration.[104]

Ambisonic surround sound was developed in the '70s with the aim of satisfying as many of the mechanisms used by the ear and brain as possible in order to localise sounds. It does this by decomposing the directionality of the sound field into spherical harmonic components: W, X, Y and Z. Inside the decoder, these signals are passed through a set of shelf filters with different gains at low and high frequencies to match the various ways in which the ear and brain localise sounds.

One advantage of the system is that it takes account of non-central as well as central listening positions; in other words, the sweet spot in this system is larger than that of a normal quadraphonic system. Another advantage is that the delivery format can cater for a wide range of speaker configurations; only at the final stage of decoding is the actual number and layout of the speakers taken into account. However, due to the need for an additional decoder, ambisonics is not a significant force in the multichannel market.[105]

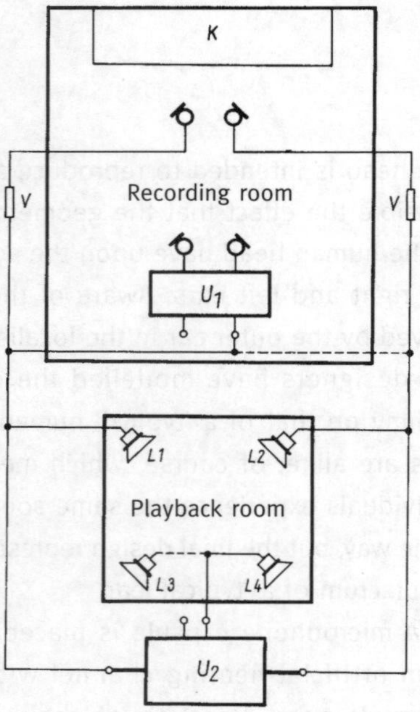

Figure 7: Stereo ambiphony system proposed by L Keibs in 1965

QUADRAPHONY

Quadraphony may be regarded as the most hapless of multichannel systems. In the '70s, it was seen as the next step (after dual-channel stereophony) towards more realistic spatial imaging, and in this respect it was indeed considerably superior to stereo. However, it worked by using four discrete channels for which almost no transmission media existed, at the time.

This, coupled with the fact that no single quadraphonic system ever succeeded in establishing itself as the standard, resulted in quadraphony gradually fading from the scene.

With quadraphonic reproduction, the loudspeakers form the four corners of a square and face inwards towards the listener, with adjacent speakers forming an angle of 90° and non-adjacent speakers facing each other, as shown in Figure 8. A distinction has to be made at the transmission stage between discrete systems – which really do employ four transmission channels – and matrix systems, in which the two rear channels are encoded into the front channels.[106]

Quadraphonic recordings are generally four-channel recordings. One possible recording setup is shown in Figure 8. An interesting feature of quadraphonic miking is that, from a technical standpoint, as a result of the double dual-channel configuration generally employed, it represents the ideal in terms of crosstalk, frequency response and phase response.107 A number of artistic quadraphonic recordings exist, including some by Pink Floyd, in which individual sound sources are distributed within the four-channel spectrum, though they have a rather experimental character. It remains to be seen how many of these historic quadraphonic recordings will be re-released on modern multichannel media; they could, after all, be played back with no problem on ITU 775 systems.

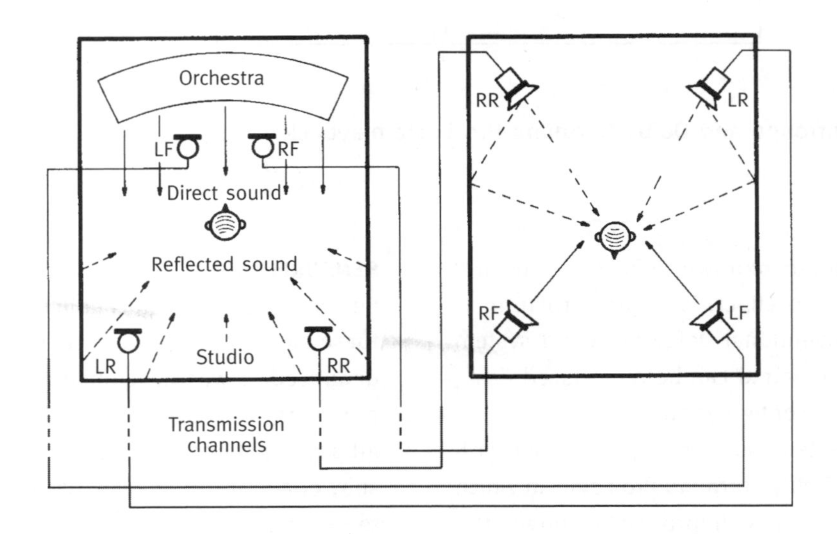

Figure 8: Four-channel quadraphonic recording and transmission

DOLBY SURROUND AND SURROUND PRO LOGIC

Launched in 1982, Dolby Surround was the first surround system for the home. It was designed for playing videos of feature films originally produced with Dolby encoded soundtracks, which remain intact when transferred to a stereo video cassette. Purely musical recordings in Dolby Surround are something of a rarity.

With Dolby Surround, a centre channel and a rear surround channel are encoded in an analogue dual-channel stereo signal.[108] The surround channel – which, as in the cinema, is reproduced by two surround loudspeakers with a slight delay in order to increase the size of the sweet spot, as shown in Figure 9 – has a limited bandwidth (100Hz–7kHz)[109]. The centre channel with Dolby Surround is divided equally between the main L and R channels and forms a phantom sound source when played back.[110]

In many decoders, a Gerzon matrix[111] is used for separate reproduction through a central loudspeaker.

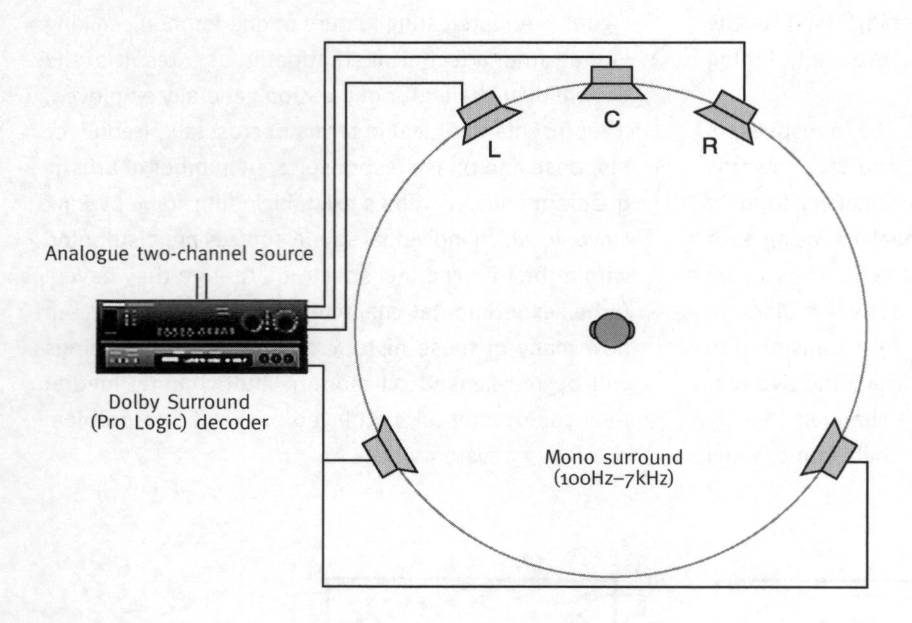

Figure 9: Dolby Surround and Dolby Surround Pro Logic playback

In view of the limited bandwidth of the surround channel, the result, in effect, is a quasi-3.1 format, which, like the conventional Dolby Surround system (without the Gerzon matrix) can be reproduced using an ITU 775 playback configuration.

In 1987, this system was developed further with the introduction of Dolby Surround Pro Logic, in which channel separation was improved through the automatic monitoring of the level ratios. In this kind of system, if one channel is considerably louder than the others, the decoder responds by reducing the levels of the other channels.

Both formats employ two analogue transmission channels. What's important, however, is that the decoders – which are usually integrated into the amplifier – are switched off for dual-channel stereo playback, since otherwise artefact decoding could occur in the surround channel. In such a case, the matrixing of an artificial centre signal could be regarded subjectively as an improvement, but the overall effect on the quality of the dual channel recording is negative.

SENSURROUND

Sensurround is a multichannel system that was used for a short time and passed almost completely unnoticed. It was developed in the '70s as a format purely for the cinema, the idea being to employ infrasound channels (eg sub-16Hz) in addition to the subwoofers in order primarily to give added realism to catastrophe scenes. One of the films that made use of this extra channel was *Earthquake*.[112]

3/2 FORMAT (ITU 775)

The 3/2 format is one of the most important of all the multichannel formats. It forms the basis for the *de facto* standard – ITU 775 – and inhabits the highest level in the suggested hierarchy of multichannel formats outlined in the recommendation. It's generally regarded as the best compromise between what it it's possible to achieve, in terms of spatial imaging, and what it's reasonable to expect people to fork out for in order to install a multichannel sound system in their homes. 3/2 is a five-channel format comprising three front (L/C/R) and two surround (LS/RS) channels, and the

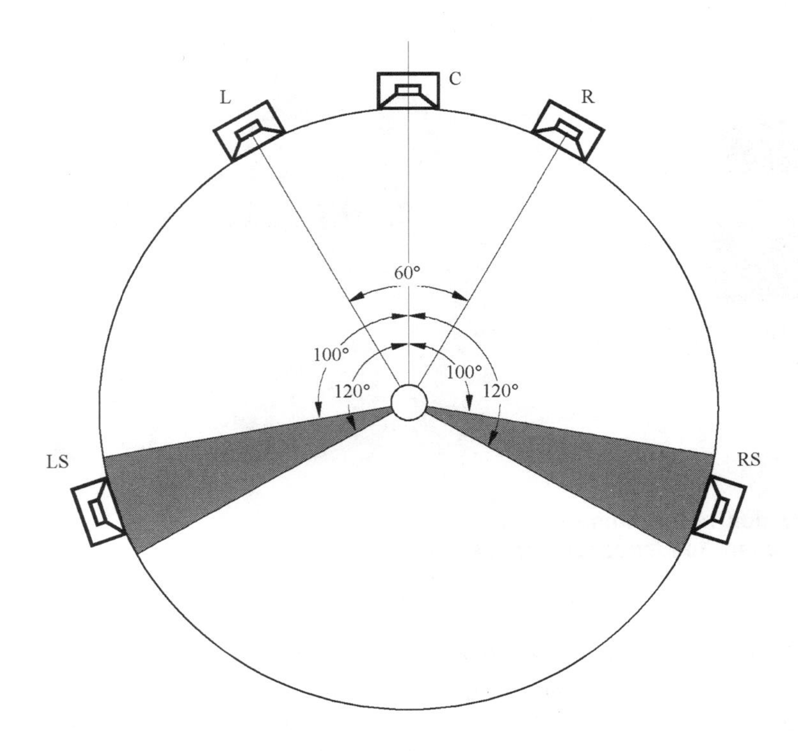

Figure 10: Reference loudspeaker arrangement for 3/2 format (ITU 775)

loudspeaker arrangement recommended by ITU 775 is illustrated by Figure 10.

The sound quality and spatial imaging that can be achieved from the 3/2 format are extraordinarily high quality, although many people feel that the centre channel is unnecessary for the reproduction of films in the home. Centre channels were introduced to the cinema in order to improve intelligibility because of the size of the screen, and it's true that in the home, where the distance between the L and R speakers is far smaller, a central loudspeaker is not really needed.[113] However, for greater compatibility with cinema mixes and improved localisation for purely musical applications, it's still considered advisable to have one.

5.1 FORMAT (DOLBY DIGITAL AC-3 AND DTS-6)

The 5.1 format is a widely encountered variation on the 3/2 theme. The difference lies in the addition of a sub-bass LFE (Low-Frequency Effects) channel to give greater realism to explosions, volcanic eruptions, earthquakes, etc. The bandwidth of this channel is very limited (20–80Hz or 20–120Hz), around one-tenth that of the other channels, hence the decimal point in '5.1'. However, for a discrete 5.1 transmission, six transmission channels (with full bandwidth) are required. There is no matrixing.

Although the 5.1 format is used both in the cinema and in the home, the arrangement of the speakers is different in each case. In the home, an ITU 775 configuration is recommended (you can put the subwoofer wherever you like), whereas in the cinema the loudspeakers are usually arranged as illustrated in Figure 12, with the subwoofer hidden behind the screen. In order to obtain a larger listening area, each of the surround channels is assigned to multiple loudspeakers, for which purpose the signals have to be passed through a decorrelation processor.

The 5.1 format is also the SMPTE[114] standard for multichannel sound for film reproduction.[115] It's most commonly used for the playback of soundtracks delivered in Dolby Digital (AC-3) or DTS-6.

People often confuse the delivery format with the playback format. A delivery format is a system for the encoding and transmission of data; it may be

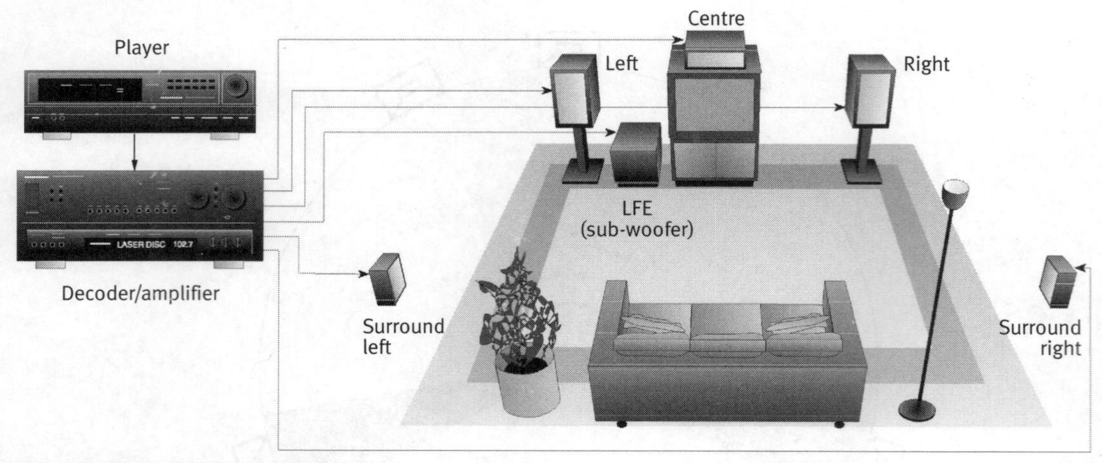

Figure 11: 5.1 reproduction in the home
(with non-ITU775-compliant loudspeaker arrangement)

specifically designed for a particular playback format – as indeed Dolby Digital (AC-3) and DTS-6 are for 5.1 – but it and the playback format for which it is intended (which means here the loudspeaker configuration) are logically distinct. Dolby Digital is one of the delivery formats included in the DVD standard[116] and every DVD player must be capable of decoding it.[117]

In order to make it possible to reduce the size of the five principal loudspeakers, some systems on the market direct the low-frequency content of the five main loudspeakers to the subwoofer. If this means that the subwoofer is obliged to renounce its primary duty (that of reproducing the LFE channel), the end result is not a 5.1 system but a variation on 3/2.

At times, the extension downwards of the 5.1 system's frequency range through the use of the LFE channel can lead to very impressive effects, but whether or not the system gives better results than 3/2 on the whole is purely subjective.

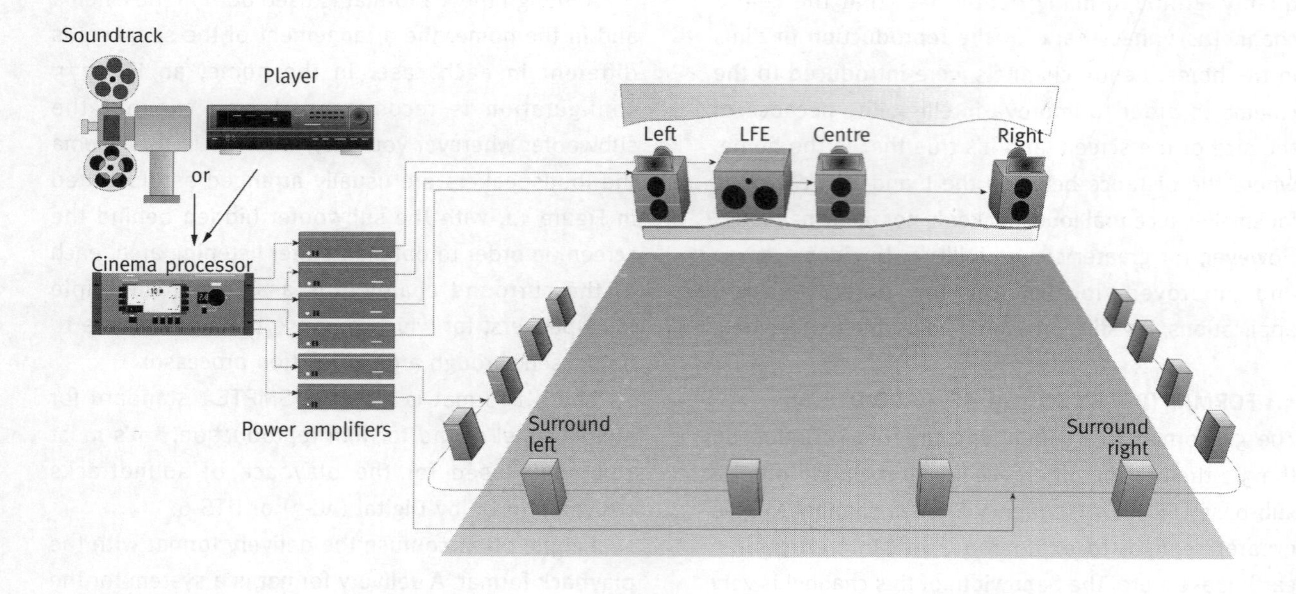

Figure 12: 5.1 reproduction in the cinema

6.1 FORMAT (DTS ES AND DOLBY DIGITAL EX)

The 6.1 format is a further extension of the 5.1 format, the new component being a centre back channel, known as *centre surround* (CS). Like 5.1, the 6.1 format is used both in the home and in the cinema. In each case, the arrangement adopted is essentially the same as for 5.1 but with an additional loudspeaker in the 180° position. Figure 13 shows 6.1 reproduction in the home and cinema.

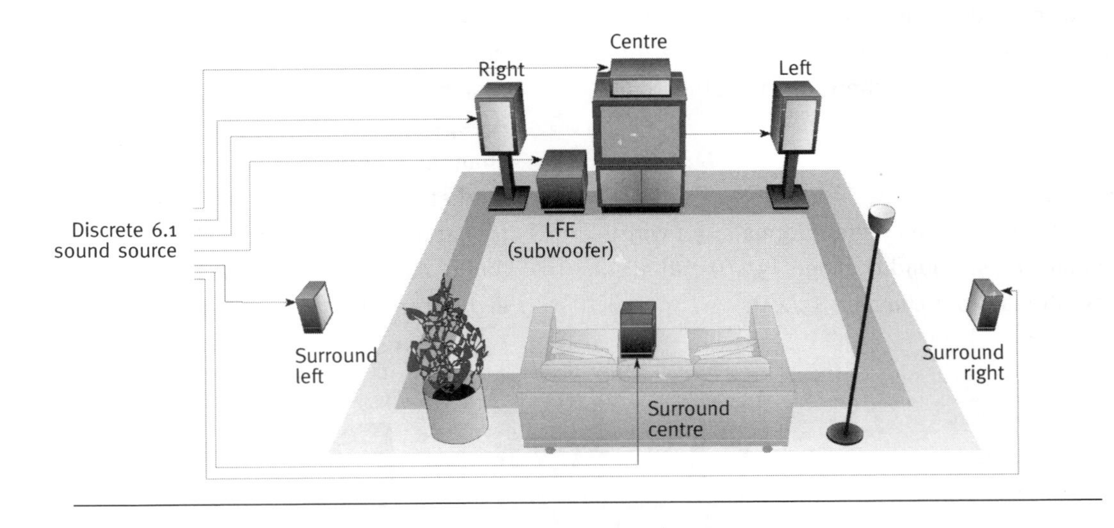

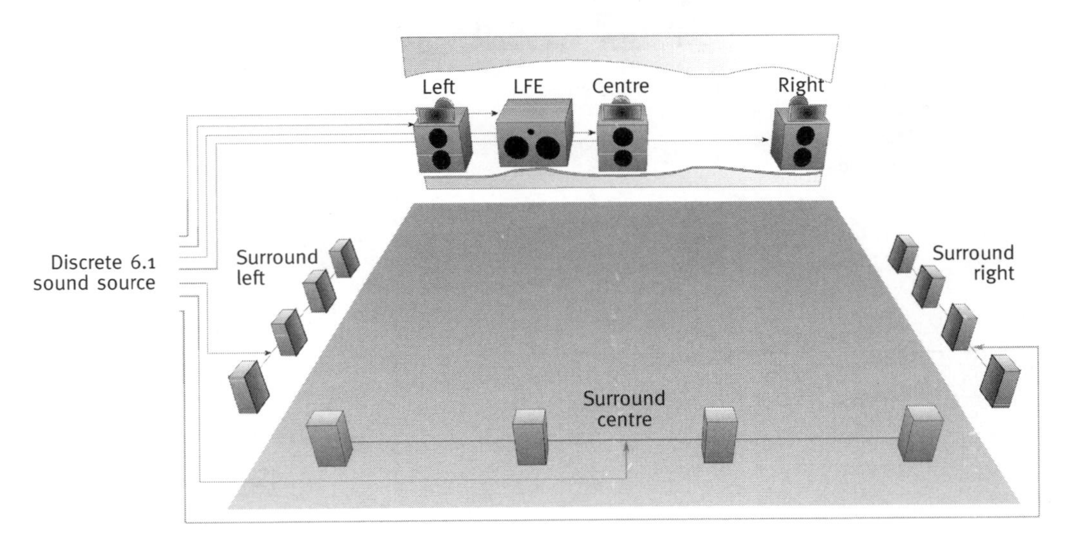

Figure 13: 6.1 reproduction in the home (above) and cinema (below)

The 6.1 playback format is usually associated with the DTS ES and Dolby Digital EX delivery formats, but only DTS ES actually dedicates a discrete channel to the centre surround signal. With Dolby Digital EX, this channel is encoded into the rear surround channels LS and RS using a process similar to that employed by Pro Logic, so it's really only a pseudo-6.1 system, although it does have the advantage of being downwards-compatible with the 5.1 format.[118] The 6.1 format, however, does not correspond to the ITU 775 recommendation.

Thanks to the addition of an extra channel to the

rear sonic image, the 6.1 format's surround localisation is considerably better than that delivered by either the 5.1 or 3/2 formats, but since the capacity of human beings to localise sounds originating behind them is considerably inferior to their ability to localise sounds coming from the front,[119] many sound engineers are inclined to dismiss the gains as insignificant. These are really matters that individuals must decide for themselves based upon their own subjective impressions.

7.1 FORMAT

The 7.1 format is really two different formats: 5.1 with two additional side surround channels (3/4/1) and 5.1 with two additional front channels (5/2/1).

- **3/4/1 format (MPEG-2 Audio and PCM Audio)** – The 3/4/1 format adds two surround channels to the 5.1 format. The side loudspeakers should be positioned (as illustrated in Figure 14) at ± 60°. The rear surround channels are therefore moved to ± 150°. The resulting sonic image facilitates localisation to a considerable extent and the results are especially impressive for special effects. Unfortunately the system is much more expensive than 5.1 to install – especially since there are virtually no eight-channel amplifiers available on the consumer market. The transmission formats for the 3/4/1 format on the DVD include MPEG-2 Audio and PCM Audio, each of which is capable of encoding up to eight channels.

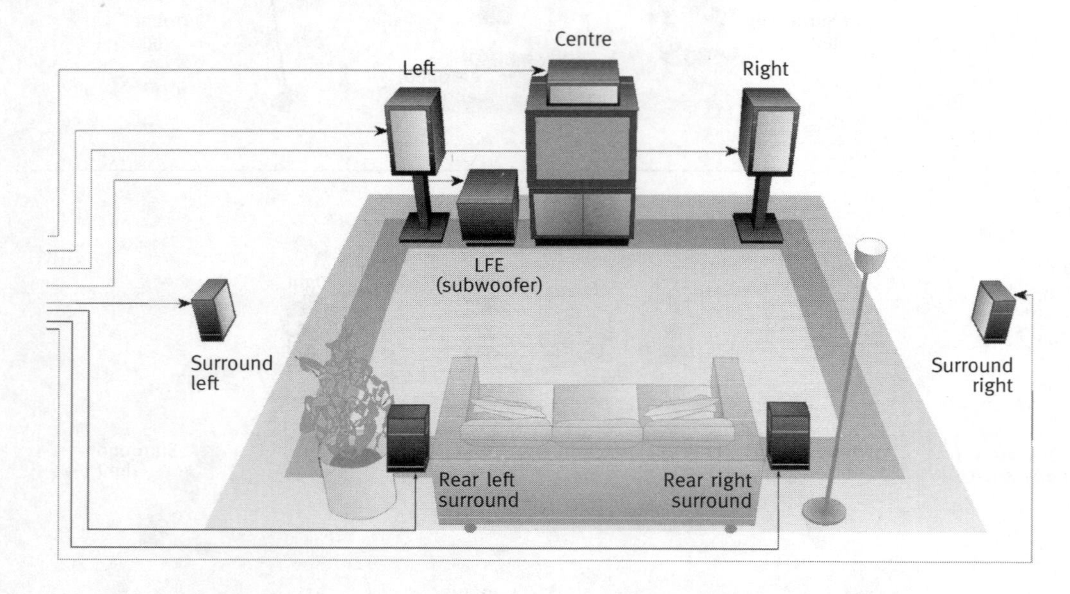

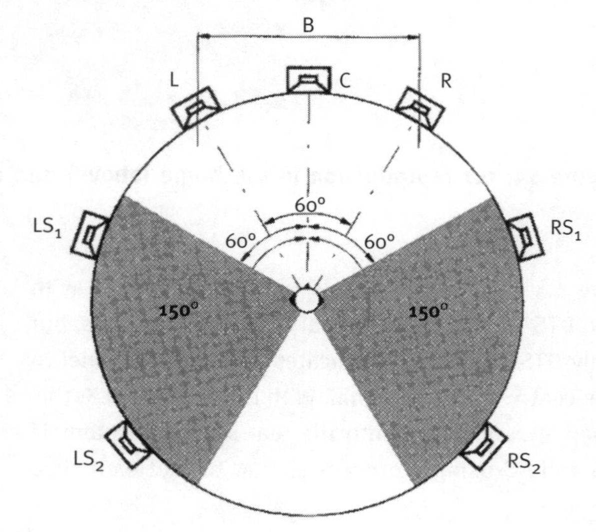

Figure 14: 3/4/1 reproduction (above) and speaker positioning (right) in the home

- **5/2/1 format (SDDS)** – Unlike the format described on the previous page, the 5/2/1 format was designed purely for the cinema, where the two additional front channels are needed to cope with very wide screens. The addition of the LC and RC channels improves the dialogue localisation throughout the seating area. The loudspeakers are generally arranged as illustrated in Figure 15, while the two rear surround channels are usually distributed among multiple loudspeakers. The best-known sound process that employs this format is SDDS.

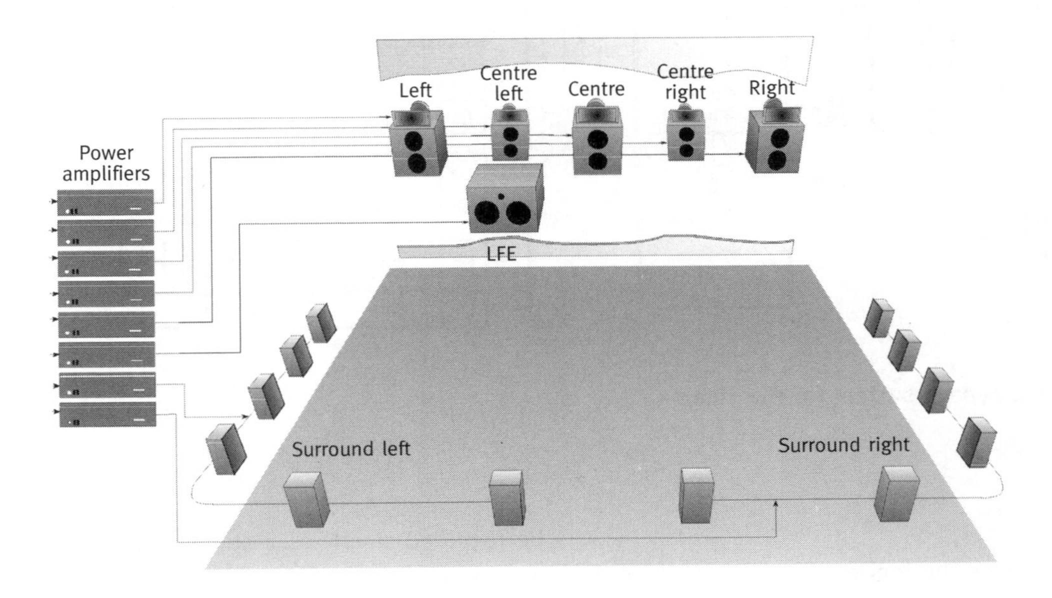

Figure 15: 5/2/1 reproduction in the cinema

THX

Logically, THX (Tomlinson Holman Experiment) belongs in the previous section, since it employs a 5/2/1 format, but I'm devoting a separate section to it because at the moment, according to many experts, it represents the state-of-the-art in cinema sound.

THX is not just a transmission format; it is also a system of certification. To obtain a THX certificate, cinemas must satisfy a large number of conditions relating not only to their sound system but also to their acoustics. Only when a TXH-authorised specialist has visited the cinema to ensure that all these conditions have been satisfied will the cinema be awarded a THX certificate. Figure 16 over the page illustrates the layout of a THX playback system.

Recently, THX solutions for the home have begun to appear. Here, too, the components have to be of a very high standard. THX home solutions usually employ the 3/2/1 format but with a special processor that supervises the quality of the sound.

Unusual Formats

In addition to the commonly encountered multichannel formats, there are naturally a multitude of experimental or more expensive ones that are seldom encountered in practice. For years, sound engineers have been researching ways of expanding and improving existing systems, with a view, for example, to opening up the third dimension. Some of these experimental systems have even made it out of the laboratory, but their implementation is generally so expensive that they will probably never make a significant impact on the market. However, three such formats will be discussed here.

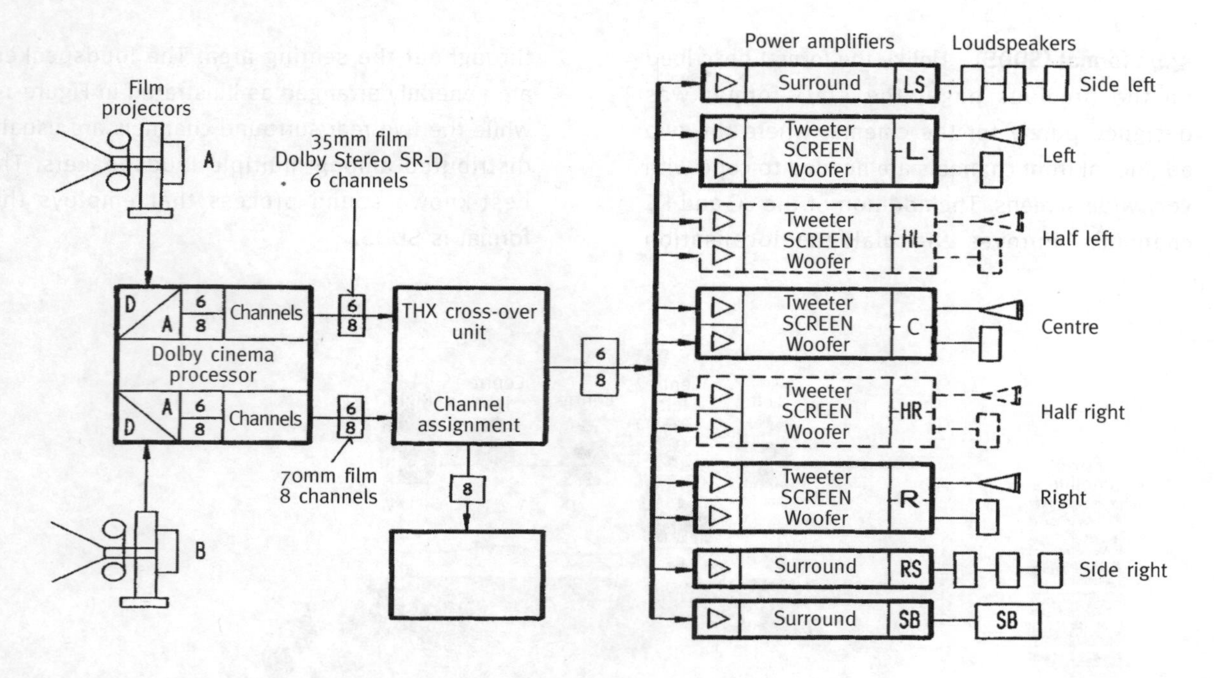

Figure 16: THX playback system for the cinema

9.1 FORMAT

The 9.1 format takes the logical step of combining the two varieties of 7.1. It therefore comprises five front channels (L/LC/C/RC/R), two side surround channels (SSL/SSR) and two rear surround channels (SRL/SRR), as well as an LFE channel. The 9.1 format has the merit of being able to supply the surround loudspeakers with discrete signals instead of decorrelated ones, as is the case with other formats, where the same surround channel is often fed to multiple loudspeakers. Such a system is illustrated in Figure 17. Due to the multitude of channels, the 9.1 format is primarily intended for the cinema. For transmission, eight-channel media can be used with two matrixed channels.

10.1 FORMAT

If the same format is extended through the addition of a rear centre channel, the result is what's known as the 10.1 format. All the same arguments that were advanced for and against the 6.1 format apply also here. Since there is no standard dealing with this format, the configuration illustrated in Figure 18 should be regarded simply as a suggestion. Eight-channel media can be used for transmission, with three matrixed channels.

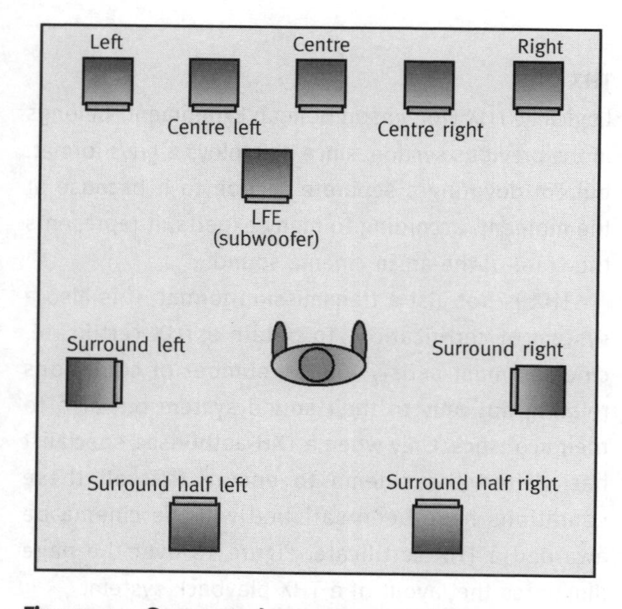

Figure 17: Suggested arrangement for 9.1 playback

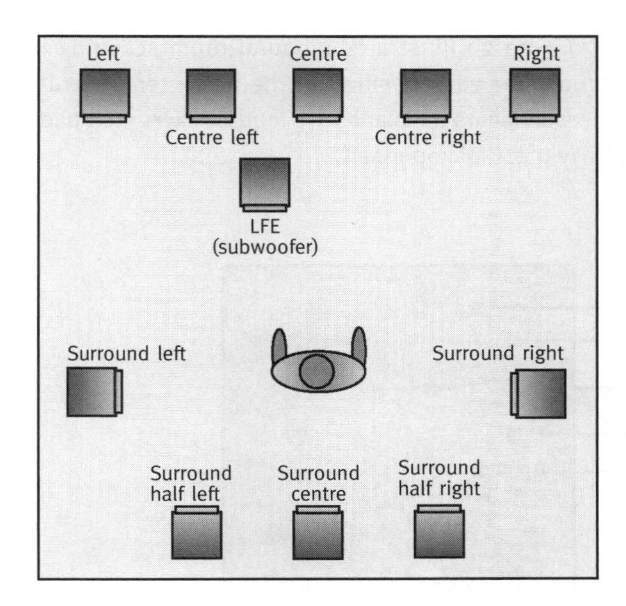

Figure 18: Suggested arrangement for 10.1 playback

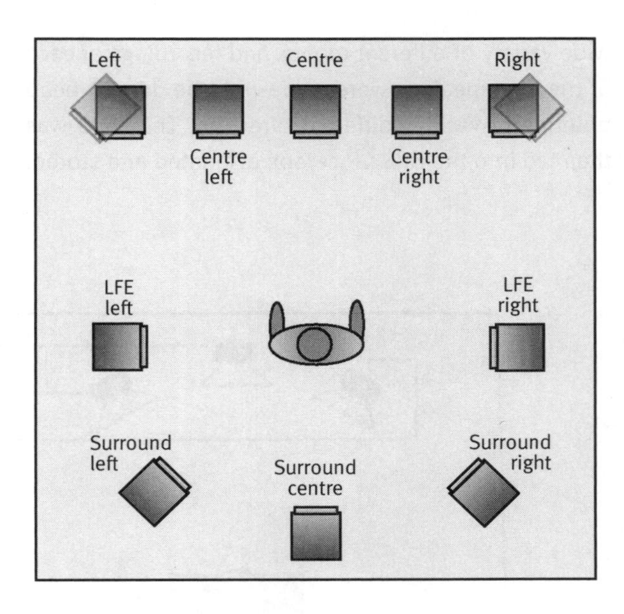

Figure 19: Speaker configuration for 10.2 playback

10.2 FORMAT

The 10.2 format, proposed by THM laboratories, adopts a completely different approach. Building on the 5.2 format, a rear centre channel and two subwoofers are placed ±90° to the right and left of the listening position. The distinctive feature here, however, is the addition of two loudspeakers placed approximately 1m above the main L/R speakers. This introduces a third dimension into the listening experience, a feature known as *with-height surround* or *periphony* (as opposed to *planar surround*, which is limited to two dimensions). The suggested speaker arrangement is illustrated in Figure 19.

When the two upper channels are transmitting discrete sound sources, they should be directed towards the listening position. If they are transmitting primarily diffuse sound, they should be turned ±45° outwards to take advantage of the reflectivity of the wall. In tests, many listeners experienced an improvement in the spatial impression. Unfortunately the format does not increase the size of the listening area, as was originally hoped. 10.2 can be excluded from consideration as a format for the home due to its enormous cost, although for films or presentation purposes, it is certainly worthy of consideration under special circumstances.[120]

New Formats

Over the last few years, new formats based on some very interesting ideas have been proposed for both home and cinema reproduction. These may some day form the basis for new standards. This section considers three such systems, the merits of which are, however, the subject of some controversy.

BINAURAL ROOM SCANNING (BRS)

Developed by Studer, binaural room scanning caused something of a sensation a few years back when it was first demonstrated at conferences and trade fairs. It's informed by the same ideas as binaural stereo (the dummy-head microphone) but with a difference that is of great significance for studio work: like recordings made with the dummy-head microphone, BRS signals can be appreciated only through headphones, but in this case the headphones are no ordinary headphones; they are connected to a *head-tracker*, a device that monitors the movements of the wearer's head. Stored in the BRS processor are the acoustic characteristics of a variety of virtual rooms, based on real rooms that have been subjected to exhaustive acoustic measurements. To gather the necessary data, ITU 775-compliant loudspeaker systems were installed in a wide variety of different rooms, and recordings of each of the loudspeakers were made with the dummy head pointing in various different direction. This data was then fed into the BRS processor, evaluated and stored.

Figure 20 illustrates binaural room scanning in action. For each position of the head, ten separate measurements are made (five loudspeakers multiplied by two ear microphones).[121]

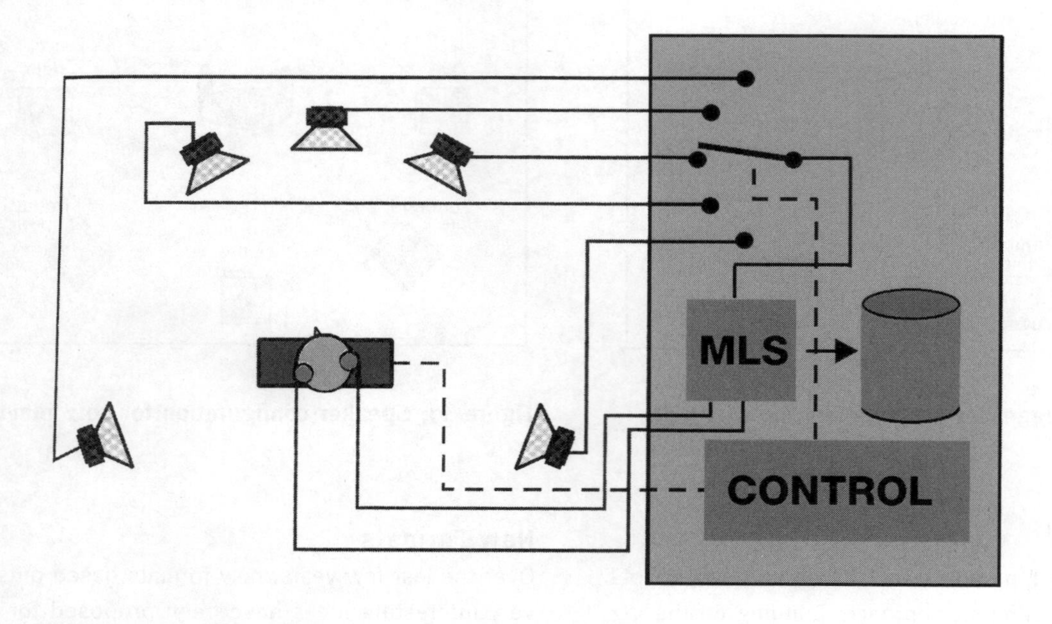

Figure 20: The process of binaural room scanning

When a 3/2 signal is subsequently fed into the processor, you can hear through the BRS headphones how it would sound in any one of the scanned rooms. When you turn your head to face the left front loudspeaker, for example, the sonic image for the new position of your head is calculated and the left front channel will appear to be louder, whilst the acoustics of the original room, too, are accurately simulated.

For studio work, this is naturally an enormous help. In addition to making it possible to produce a 3/2 headphone mix, it allows the sound engineer to hear how the mix would sound in various acoustic environments, such as a domestic living room or the cinema. Furthermore, although the sound engineer may in fact be working in a problematic acoustic environment (such as a cramped studio or outside broadcast van) when performing the mix, it's as though he was working in an acoustically perfect room, as shown in Figure 21. He can even ring the changes in terms of loudspeaker configurations, evaluating the mix in the light of how it would sound through different combinations of speakers in the same room.

Another advantage is that, although several different people may be evaluating the work at the same time, thanks to the headphones, none of them gets in the way of the others; each of them has the benefit of the sweet spot, regardless of where in the room they're sitting. The more affluent audiophile might be interested to learn that the system could be used equally well in the home.

Sound engineers reacted with a certain euphoria to the new technology and frothed with praise at the first prototypes, which made Studer's decision to halt further development and put production on hold all the more baffling. The decision, we were told, came from on high (Studer is part of the Harman Pro Group) and caught even the developers by surprise – at the time the plug was pulled, the BRS processor was virtually ready for series production and there was clearly a demand. There's still hope that we haven't heard the last of binaural room scanning and that the technology will yet find its way to the sound engineers crying out for it, whether it's eventually released by Studer, a different company within the Harman Pro Group or yet another manufacturer producing the system under licence.

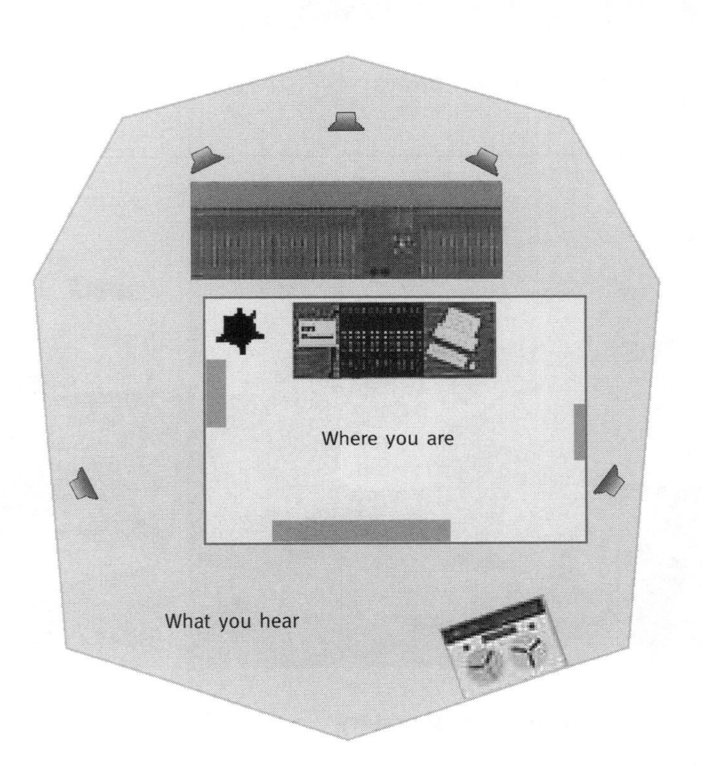

Figure 21: Tube BRS system's virtual listening environment

WAVE FIELD SYNTHESIS[122] (WFS)

Wave Field Synthesis is a lavishly expensive and particularly impressive multichannel system. The starting point here, unlike most other systems, is not the creation of phantom sound sources surrounding the listener but the holophonic recreation of a virtual sound scene in an extended area; it should be possible to localise with precision such a source – whether it be located inside or outside the room – from any point within the room. Both the direct sound emanating from this source and the diffuse sound that would result from it are recreated virtually.

To make this possible, loudspeakers arrays controlled by a special DSP system (as shown in Figure 23) are arranged all around the room (as in Figure 22). When a signal is fed into the DSP system along with information about where it is localised, the system is able to calculate which signals to send to each of the loudspeakers.[123]

One of the underlying ideas behind WFS is the Huygens' long-established principle of wave propagation, in which the wave field of a source can be reproduced by many sources located on the perimeter of the original wave field.

Figure 22: Wave Field Synthesis loudspeaker arrays

Figure 22: Wave Field Synthesis demonstration laboratory

The great advantage of this system is that the localisation of sound sources is now possible from any point in the room since these now radiate in a controlled way from a single loudspeaker or a group of adjacent loudspeakers. There is still such a thing as a sweet spot, from which the ideal volume ratios of the individual loudspeakers can be appreciated, but by this means it has increased considerably in area and it's no longer the only position from which accurate localisation is possible. Furthermore, the WFS format is compatible with every conceivable planar multichannel format, since loudspeakers are located at all angles around the listening position. In other words, the arrangement can be used to implement many different formats – indeed the results of many such systems are actually enhanced by WFS, since each phantom sound source is now reproduced by its own speaker – so all previous media and formats remain valid when an WFS system is installed.

Wave Field Synthesis also allows almost any conceivable acoustic environment to be reproduced, so that the living room of your home can be transformed effortlessly into the finest 20 square metres of Sydney Opera House, within which (assuming discrete recordings) the musicians can be repositioned at will. You could even move your seat into the orchestra if you wished.

The processing power required by WFS is obviously enormous, and several racks full of equipment are needed to implement it. To install such a system in your living would also be relatively difficult, since – quite apart from the processors – in a normal-sized living room you would need to install around eight to ten arrays of 100 loudspeakers and wire them all up!

Nonetheless, wave field synthesis could certainly become a practical option for the home in the foreseeable future, perhaps in an arrangement similar to that illustrated in Figure 24.[124] It has already been tried in the cinema, even if only in a single auditorium in Ilmenau, Germany, which was equipped with a WFS system at the beginning of 2003. The installation was performed in collaboration with the *Fraunhofer Arbeitsgruppe für Elektronische Medientechnologie* (which also developed the IOSONO wave-field synthesis system), and the specialists who were present during the experiment were extremely positive about the results. So, even though there may still be no standard for WFS in the field of movie sound, it appears destined to play an important role in the cinema, especially since the current drawbacks (the space taken up by the processors and the expense of wiring the whole system up) are unlikely to prove an insuperable obstacle to its adoption in the cinema.

Another firm that is very actively involved in the development of WFS is SonicEmotion, which demonstrated the first WFS plugin for Pro Tools at the 155th AES Convention. The plugin, which takes over the function of a pan pot or surround panner, makes it possible for anyone to create WFS mixes from within Pro Tools. Having the right monitoring equipment, of course, is another matter.[125]

The driving force behind SonicEmotion is Renato Pellegrini, who developed Virtual Surround Panning and the BRS system for Studer and was also actively involved in the WFS project CARROUSO. Over the course of the project, in which four universities as well as several well-known companies and institutions participated, the possibility of transmitting WFS data with the help of the AV objects in MPEG-4 was demonstrated. With these objects, it's possible, for example, to describe the spatial-positioning data of audio sources dynamically, and from this data a WFS computer can then derive the necessary information for the placing of the sound source. Since MPEG-4 is certain to play a leading role in future AV transmissions and media due to its open architecture, nothing now stands in the way of the further development of WFS. Hopefully, then, it's not destined to remain forever a 'music of the future'.[126]

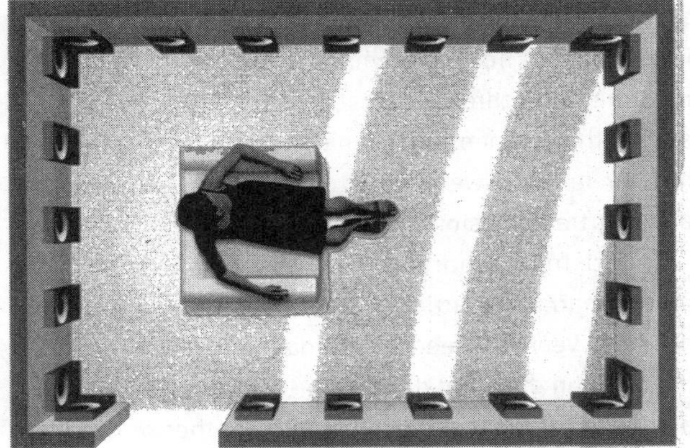

Figure 24: Comparison of 3/2 reproduction and Wave Field Synthesis in the home

2 + 2 + 2 FORMAT

The 2 + 2 + 2 format was proposed by the well-known German sound engineer Werner Dabringhaus – or rather by his label, Dabringhaus and Grimm. Unlike the previous two formats covered in this section, 2 + 2 + 2 is founded on already existing rather than future technology. Dabringhaus took as the basis for his system the six equal channels of the DVD standard and 5.1 format. In light of the objections already raised against using both the centre channel and the LFE channel, he decided to remove them from the equation altogether, by this means liberating two channels to supply a couple of new loudspeakers which he positioned around 1m[127] above the front L and R pair. Depending upon the signal content (direct/diffuse sound), these loudspeakers should either be aimed at the listening position or else positioned at an angle of 90° to one another so as to radiate sound towards the walls. This provides a relatively simple way of implementing a periphonic (ie 3D) audio system. To avoid having to reposition the loudspeakers constantly when switching from 5.1 to 2 + 2 + 2 (for example, when changing from audio to video reproduction), Dabringhaus suggests buying an extra pair of speakers, giving you, in effect, a 7.1 system.

To take advantage of the possibilities, the material must be recorded using a special technique, but according to Dabringhaus this is very simple to implement. Currently the equipment required to do this can be obtained only from Dabringhaus and Grimm or other Japanese sources, although the recording itself poses no problems. Assuming a discrete recording, the three greatest advantages of 2 + 2 + 2 are the three-dimensional sonic image, a larger (though not by much) sweet spot and compatibility with existing transmission formats.

Apart from reports produced by Dabringhaus[128] himself and a few articles in specialist journals, there has been very little feedback to date from users. Clearly the addition of a third dimension – which is also offered by the 10.2 format – is a plus, but whether or not it's worth the extra expense is another matter. What *is* certain is that 2 + 2 + 2 is easier to implement than many of the other extensions to the ITU 775 recommendation and would make it possible for users to reproduce of 3D audio in the home.

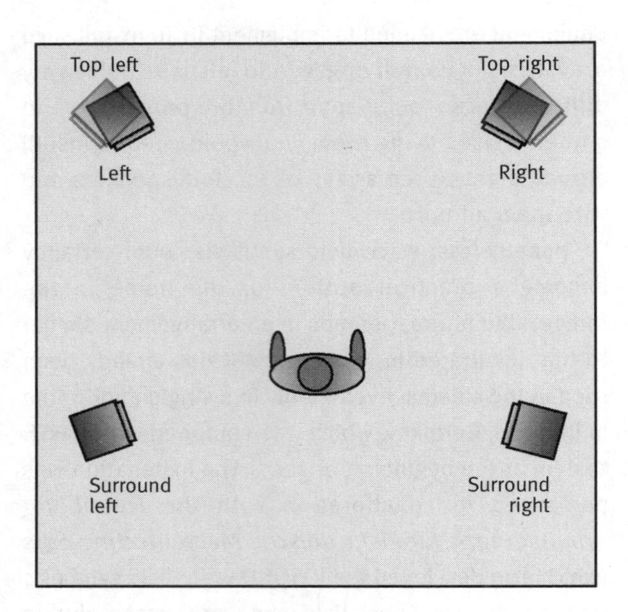

Figure 25: Arrangement for 2 + 2 + 2 playback

Criteria For Multichannel Audio

When you look at the multitude of formats and systems used to play back multichannel audio, one thing you notice at once is that they do not all share the same goals. Quite aside from the dichotomy between home and cinema reproduction, the difference in approach between different formats can often be explained by the fact that they have different objectives – objectives that could never be achieved with conventional dual-channel stereophony.

But these new objectives throw up problems of their own, and suddenly questions that weren't considered important before suddenly need to be answered.

One such matter is the much-discussed issue of the sweet spot. With dual-channel stereo, if you're outside the optimal listening zone, you can still pick up at least 50% of the sonic image, even though you might have sacrificed the spatial effect. With the 3/2 format, you could be left with as little as 20% – and even this is based on the somewhat hypothetical case of the sound being evenly distributed. In reality, the evaluation of a sonic image based on a single surround channel is practically impossible. The importance of being inside the optimal listening zone is therefore far more important in the case of multichannel audio than was ever the case with dual-channel stereo; to make the most of the listening experience, you really do have to be in or near the sweet spot and to stay there.

But how easy is it going to be to drum up support for a technology that can only really satisfy one listener at a time? In the cinema, a solution has been found (for the surround channels, at least) in the form of decorrelation, but here, too, it's important to discover whether it's an acceptable compromise to take discrete signals and blur them artificially solely in order to include more listeners; in the cinema, for instance, this interferes with the localisation of rear sound sources. On the other hand, a low degree of correlation is essential in multichannel audio to avoid a mono-surround effect. The individual channels should carry different signals and the surround channels need to be silent at times.

But what effect does this have upon the spatial imaging? And what are the implications for the diffuse sound field? The answers depend on your objectives. If, for example, you were recording a live concert, it would hardly improve the envelopment if the rear channels suddenly cut out. On the other hand, how much sound emanating from the rear do you really want to hear if the instrument you're trying to listen to – a Spanish guitar on the left-hand side of the stage, for example – is comparatively quiet? In a real concert, any sound coming from behind you in such cases would almost certainly be a source of irritation – someone coughing, for example, or shifting noisily in their seat. Is it worth including such sounds in the name of realism, or would it not be better to create a dry, audience-free recording, even though this would mean losing a certain amount of animation – the applause, for example?

And should you use a main microphone system for such a recording, as the purists would suggest, or should you instead close-mic individual instruments for greater clarity, using panning at a later stage to place them in a virtual room?

Soundtracks provide another extreme where the spatial impression is in constant flux. In order to follow the action, a completely new ambience, consisting of both synthetic and natural sounds, has to be created for each scene, some of which might involve very little in the way of ambient sound. Under such circumstances, which is the best format to adopt? Wouldn't it be a lot easier in the long run to make the switch to 3D sound now, even though, at first, scant use might be made of it?

And what about the people who insist on sticking with their dual-channel stereo systems? Will they still be a significant force in a few years' time, or will the time come when we can safely disregard them and assume that everyone has a multichannel system? Should we then rely on a downmix matrix and accept the fact that dual-channel reproduction will suffer, or is it worth persevering with the idea of providing a separate two-channel mix?

This isn't the place to answers these questions; the important thing is to be aware that they exist. Multichannel stereo is a far more complicated matter than dual-channel stereo, and before embarking on any recording or production using the methods described in the next chapter, it's important to decide in which direction you want to proceed. With dual-channel stereo, you could perhaps get away with having no real plan, but this is a recipe for disaster with multichannel stereo – although that's not to say that you can't experiment. Practice, as we all know, makes perfect.[129]

3 SURROUND RECORDING

Fundamentals Of Recording

As we approach the recording of multichannel audio, it's worth remembering that, however daunting the subject might at first seem, we can take comfort in the fact that the knowledge and techniques involved with working with mono and dual-channel stereophony will stand us in good stead here too, even if they don't take us all the way. The main-microphone technique, for example, is much favoured for the dual-channel recording of choirs and orchestras, whereas a stereo microphone (or a matched pair of mono microphones) strategically positioned to capture a carefully calculated blend of direct and indirect sound will very seldom yield the results you're looking for in a surround recording, and even if you did succeed in getting a halfway decent recording using this method, you could hardly approach the processing and mixing without understanding something more about the nature of the signals you'd recorded. So this chapter begins with the obligatory exploration of the fundamental principles of recording.

Transducer Principles

Microphones are transducers of sound – that is to say, they convert sound energy into electrical energy by converting sound waves into electrical energy variations that can later be amplified. Not all microphones, however, are alike or equally suitable for every application.

Microphones can be divided into two groups – dynamic and condenser – based upon the transducer principle that each employs. In each case, the variations in air pressure indicating the presence of a sound wave are picked up by a very sensitive diaphragm. In the case of a dynamic microphone, the movement of the diaphragm is transmitted to a coil which in consequence moves up and down in a permanent magnetic field[130] (see Figure 26), creating voltage variations that constitute an electrical representation of the sound wave.

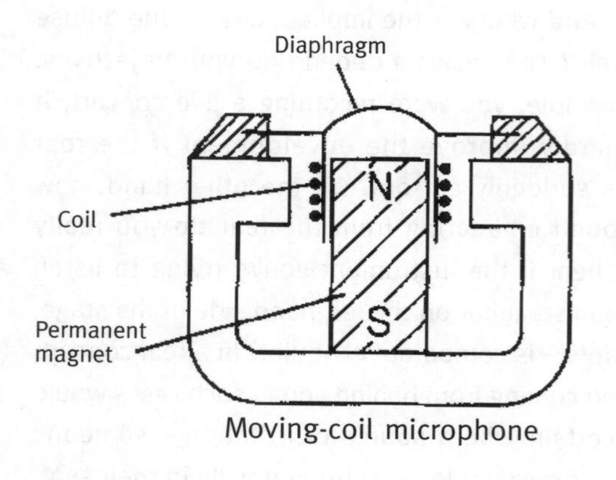

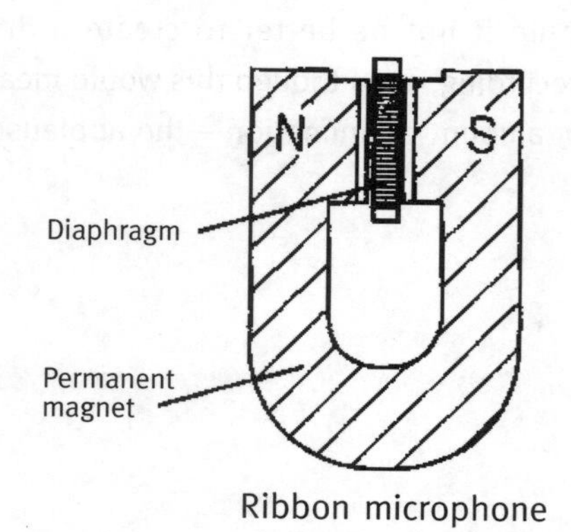

Figure 26: Transducer principles of dynamic microphones

Dynamic microphones have a main resonance frequency – usually in the midrange – which needs to be corrected. Due to their structure, they are also less sensitive than condenser microphones in the lower frequency range, although special designs do exist to improve their response in this area, such as the two-way principle (where two transducer systems work together like the low- and high-frequency drivers of a two-way speaker system), or the variable-distance principle (where special sound holes are provided for low frequencies).

Generally speaking, dynamic microphones can't match the electro-acoustic quality of condenser microphones, but they are considerably more robust and they don't require phantom power for their operation. They are therefore the ideal microphones to withstand the type of rough-handling involved with live work as well as for recording sound sources with very high sound-pressure levels, such as drums. Good dynamic microphones, such as the Shure SM 58, are relatively affordable and are standard items of equipment for any studio or stage.

In condenser microphones, the diaphragm is constructed as one plate of a parallel-plate capacitor. Either that or, if not itself an electrode, it's sandwiched between two acoustically transparent electrodes, as shown in Figure 27. As the diaphragm vibrates in response to a sound wave, the distance between the plates (and therefore the voltage across them) fluctuates, creating a signal that's an electrical representation of the sound wave.

Since the output impedance of the capsule is extremely high, each condenser microphone requires a preamplifier, which is generally built in,[131] and this in turn requires its own 48V power supply, which is known as *phantom power*.

Valve mics (tube mics in the US) are a variety of condenser mic currently enjoying a renaissance of popularity. Judging purely by their technical specifications – ie by measurements of their performance – it's hard to understand this development, but many people judge them to provide a considerably warmer sonic image.

From an acoustic standpoint, condenser microphones are superior to dynamic microphones and are therefore traditionally preferred for recording. One reason for this is the fact that they have a considerably higher signal-to-noise ratio, they have a higher output voltage (in most cases) and they create less distortion. In the realm of multichannel recording, for example, they enjoy an almost complete monopoly.

Although they can handle extremely high sound-pressure levels (as high as 130dB), condenser mics are extremely sensitive to solid-borne sound (footfalls, impact vibrations, handling noise and so on) and require a supply voltage. High-quality condenser microphones

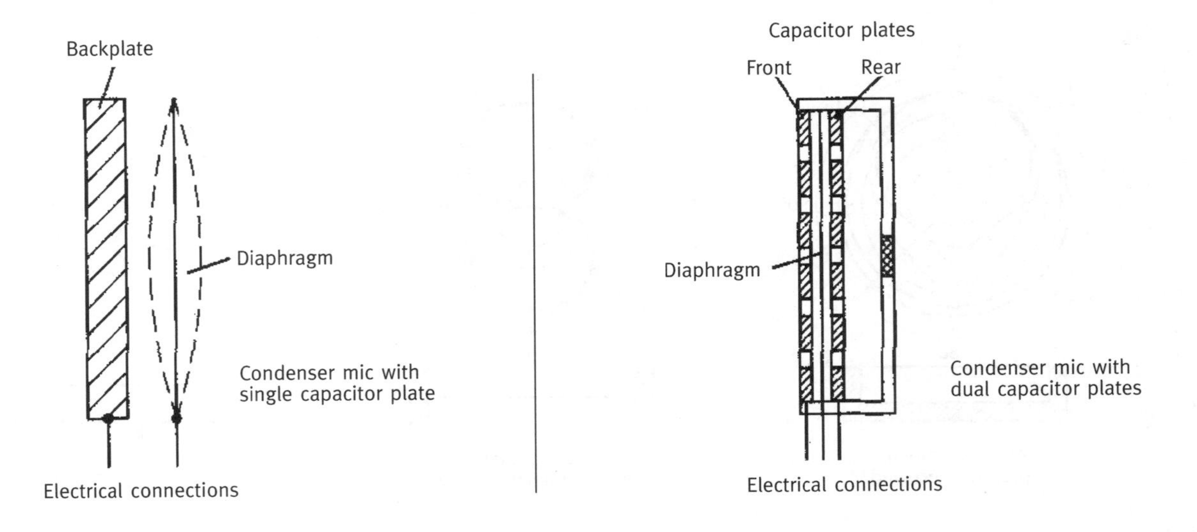

Figure 27: Transducer principles of condenser microphones

– such as the Neumann U 87 – are expensive, too, and to get the best out of them you also need a high-quality (and therefore inevitably very expensive), preamplifier. In spite of all this, such microphones have become the standard transducers in studios all over the world simply because of their peerless sound.

Acoustic Operating Principles And Polar Patterns

The extent to which a microphone is sensitive to sound coming from different directions is known as its *directional characteristic* or *polar pattern* (the term *pickup pattern* is also used), and an important determining factor here is the acoustic operating principle it employs.

Here it's important to distinguish between three types of microphone: pressure receivers, pressure-gradient receivers and sound-velocity receivers. Pressure receivers are for the most part equally sensitive to sound arriving from all directions – in other words, their response is omnidirectional, and generally linear throughout the entire frequency range. Their sonic image is very powerful.

Pressure-gradient and velocity receivers, on the other hand, are invariably directional, and their sensitivity tends to drop off in the low-frequency range. Of course, various techniques can be employed to counteract this tendency, but pressure-gradient receivers still seldom match the fullness of sound you obtain from a pressure-receiver mic.

Pressure receivers are invariably omnidirectional,[132] which is to say that the direction from which a sound emanates has no impact upon their response, except at high frequencies, where a certain degree of directionality creeps in, as shown in Figure 28a. Although they are also pressure receivers, the response of boundary microphones (which are placed on large reflecting surfaces to exploit the special acoustic conditions that prevail there) is, for obvious reasons, hemispherical rather than spherical. Boundary microphones are often used in the theatre.

A microphone is said to be 'bi-directional' or to have a 'figure-of-eight directional characteristic' when it's most sensitive to sound coming from the front (0°) and rear (180°) and least sensitive to sound coming from the sides (90° and 270°), where – as shown in Figure 28 (B), its response is down 20–25dB on the on-axis response. Besides being useful for applications such as interviews, where you're looking to capture the voices of both speakers while rejecting sound from the side, microphones with a figure-of-eight characteristic are key components of MS stereophony, where their signals are combined with cardioid or omnidirectional mics, or a second figure-of-eight

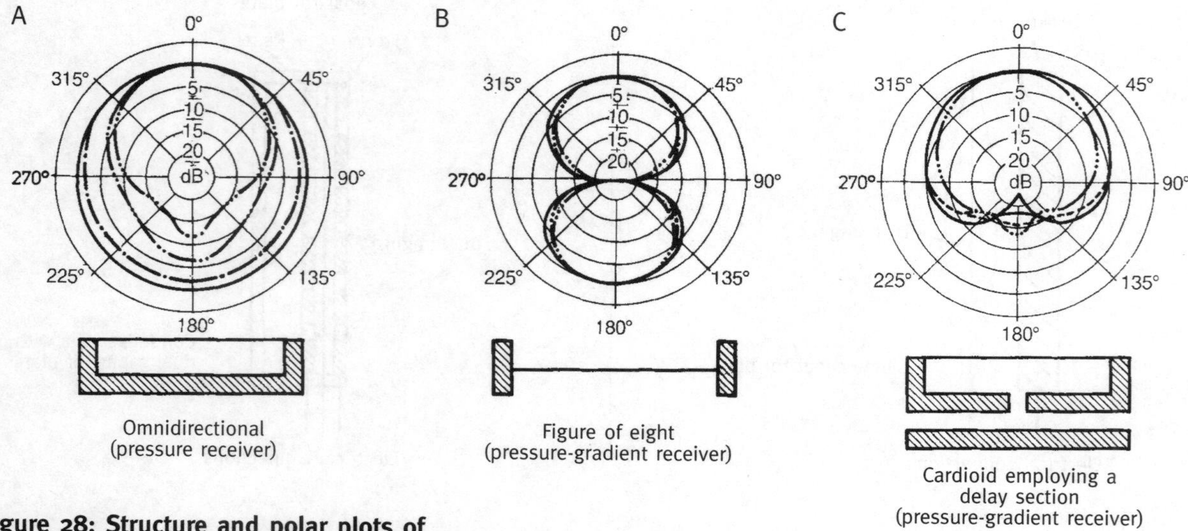

Figure 28: Structure and polar plots of omnidirectional, figure-of-eight and cardioid mics

microphone, and matrixed to achieve excellent directional imaging.[133]

Cardioid Mics

The third group of microphones comprises *cardioid microphones*. A cardioid mic is most sensitive to sound coming from the front (0°), less sensitive (usually –6dB) to sound coming from the side (90° and 270°) and least sensitive to sound coming from the rear (180°), where the response may be as much as 20dB down on the on-axis response, as shown in Figure 28 (C). In other words, the directionality of these mics is fairly marked, making them less susceptible to feedback, which is largely why cardioids (usually dynamic models) are the most common type of microphone.

Cardioid microphones can be divided into four sub-groups, as shown in Figure 29. Of the four, the wide-angle cardioid is the most sensitive to sound coming from the side (–4dB) and rear (–10dB) and therefore is the least directional.

A supercardioid has a narrower but more pronounced on-axis response, which means in effect that, provided the microphone is pointed directly at the sound source, it's possible to place it further away. A supercardioid is less sensitive than a wide-angle cardioid to sound coming from the side but more sensitive (than a wide-angle cardioid) to sound coming from the rear, as is indicated by the small lobe at the bottom of the diagram.

It's the same story with the hypercardioid, only more so: the off-axis sensitivity is less than that of a supercardioid and far less than that of a wide-angle cardioid, but the sensitivity to sound arriving 180° off axis is greater than either, so that the polar pattern comes to resemble that of a bi-directional microphone.

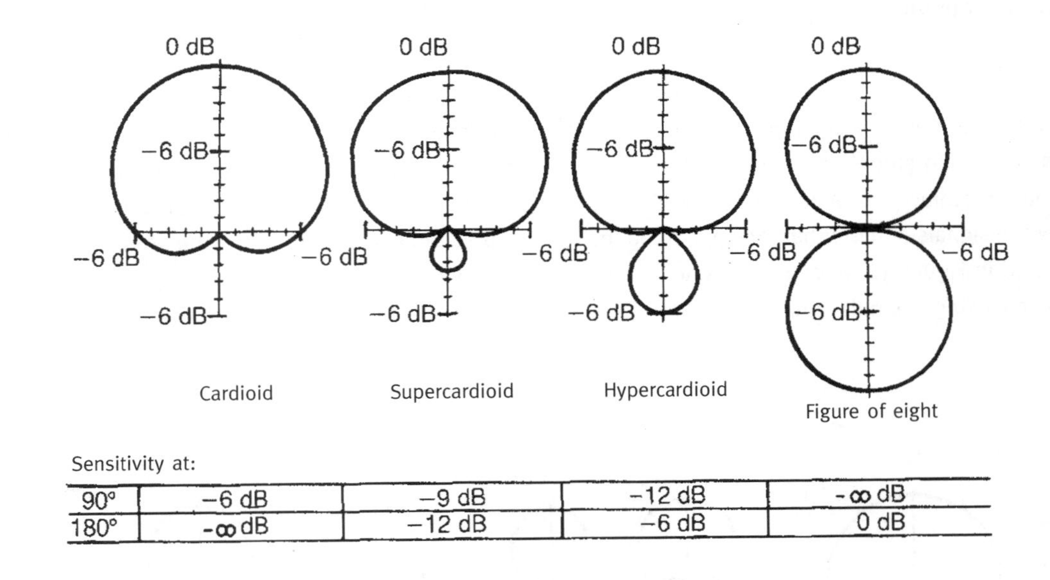

	Cardioid	Supercardioid	Hypercardioid	Figure of eight
90°	−6 dB	−9 dB	−12 dB	-∞ dB
180°	-∞ dB	−12 dB	−6 dB	0 dB

Figure 29: Cardioid, supercardioid, hypercardioid and figure-of-eight polar patterns compared[134]

It is, in fact, possible to achieve still higher directivity – the pattern known variously as *club-shaped*, *lobe-shaped*, *line cardioid* or *ultra-directional*, as shown in Figure 30 – through the use of an interference tube. Microphones of this type are popularly known as *shotgun microphones*. Here the effect of the interference tube is to eliminate almost completely sound coming from the side. The sensitivity to sound arriving from the rear (180° off axis) is similar to that of a hypercardioid.

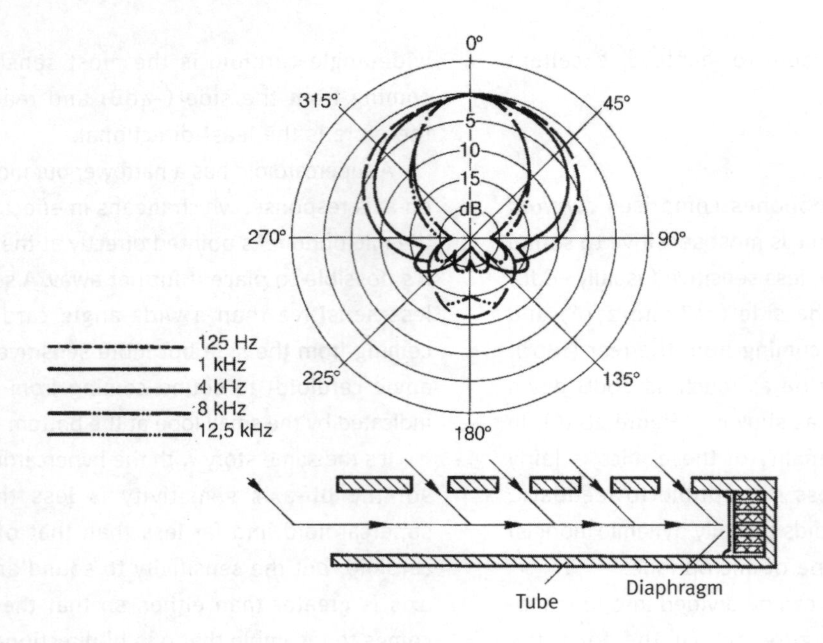

Figure 30: Polar pattern and operational principle of a shotgun microphone

While it is possible to design a separate microphone to achieve each of the aforementioned polar patterns, in most cases you can achieve the same effect by combining and matrixing the signals of more than one microphone, as demonstrated in Figure 31. Indeed, the same variety can be achieved using a single microphone with two diaphragms and the requisite circuitry. Dual-diaphragm microphones – some of which are remote-switchable models – offer the most practical solution; many of the top studio microphones offer the possibility of switching between omni, figure-of-eight and cardioid polar patterns, combining high-quality sound with great versatility.

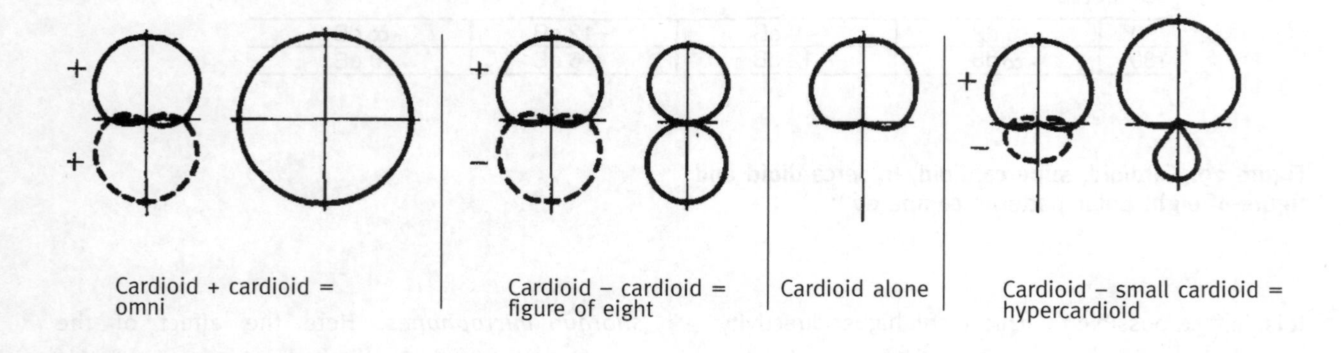

Figure 31: How a variety of polar patterns can be obtained by matrixing the signals of a double diaphragm microphone

Mics In Practice

When creating multichannel recordings, the availability of a variety of polar patterns allows you to implement a wide variety of miking techniques – some highly complex and others remarkably simple.

First you have to be clear in your own mind about what sounds you want each channel to carry, the best microphone placement to obtain them and what type of microphone is best suited to the purpose. An adequate monitoring solution for each channel is also essential.[135] Regardless of whether you employ an established microphone technique or instead you decide to experiment, you'll need to think seriously about the ideal polar patterns to use and the ratio of direct to indirect sound you wish to achieve. Figure 32 illustrates the different miking distances required to obtain the same balance of direct and indirect sound using mics with each of the various polar patterns.

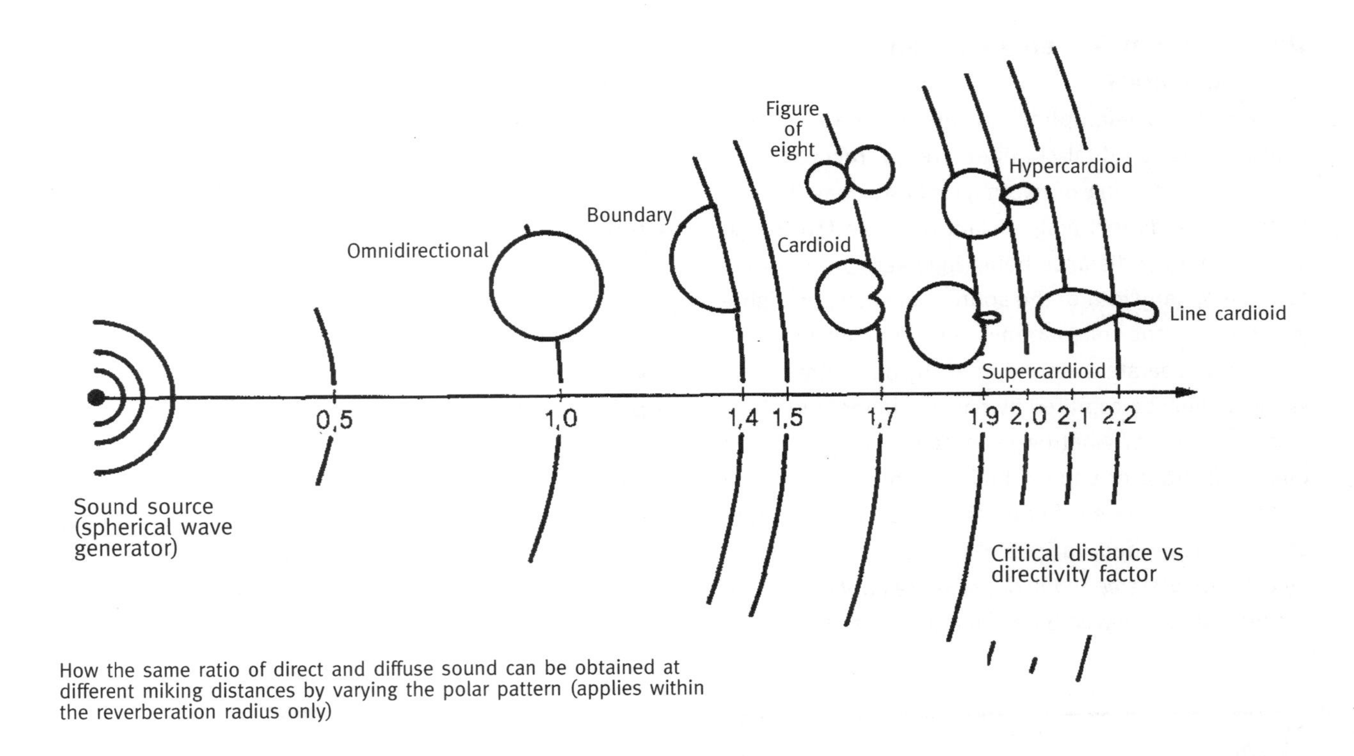

Figure 32: Miking distances (in metres) within the reverberation radius to obtain the same ratio of direct to indirect sound

Another factor to take into account here is the frequency response of the microphones at your disposal. There's no standardisation here, and the microphone with the most linear response isn't necessarily the most suitable for the purpose you have in mind. The best advice here is to experiment and use your ears.

Microphone Techniques

Armed with this knowledge about the various types of microphones and their directionality, we can turn to the business of recording. Surround recording poses a particularly interesting challenge, since as well as the need to obtain a clean recording of the frontal sound sources,[136] you will also be attempting to capture the 'room element', by which we mean the diffuse sound that results from the reflection of direct sound from the walls, floor and ceiling. As well as experimenting with different types of microphone, it's useful to try out different microphone configurations and techniques.

Since the microphone techniques used for multichannel recording are largely based on those developed for dual-channel stereophony, I'll begin with a short account of the latter. The sequence in which they are presented should not be taken to imply any preference.

Dual-Channel Stereo Techniques

AB STEREOPHONY

The AB stereo microphone technique is one of the foundations of dual-channel stereo recording. It involves the placing of two microphones parallel and facing forwards (0°) a significant distance (40–80cm) apart, the ideal distance being inversely proportional to the angular width of the source, as shown in Figure 33. Because the microphones are non-coincident (ie physically separated), sound from any off-centre source will inevitably be captured by one just before the other, just as sound originating from anywhere other than directly in front of you or directly behind you will be picked up by one ear before the other. The resulting effect is described variously as *delay stereophony*, *time-of-arrival stereophony* or *phase stereophony*. When the recording is played back, time-of-arrival differences greater than 1–1.5ms lead to the formation of phantom sound sources between the speakers.[137]

AB recordings often convey an especially convincing spatial impression, although the localisation of individual sound sources is blurry. The technique is therefore especially well suited to applications where you're more interested in conveying a sense of the space in which a performance is taking place, also capturing the natural reverberation of the room, but you're less interested in communicating the exact position of the various sound sources. If you are recording an organ in a concert hall, for example, the position of each individual set of pipes is hardly essential, whereas the acoustics of the room doubtless contribute significantly to the overall impression. If, on the other hand, you wish to draw the attention of listeners to soloists within an ensemble, the AB technique is less useful.

A voluminous and very powerful sonic image can be achieved through the use of omnidirectional mics, particularly at low frequencies, while the incipient directionality at higher frequencies serves to give a balanced spatial impression.[138] If, in addition to single or stereo miking, you wish to capture the room component, the AB technique is the best technique because of the non-correlated recording signals. Depending upon the desired correlation frequency, the microphones should be placed 1.5–3m from each other and around 10–15m from the main microphone.[139]

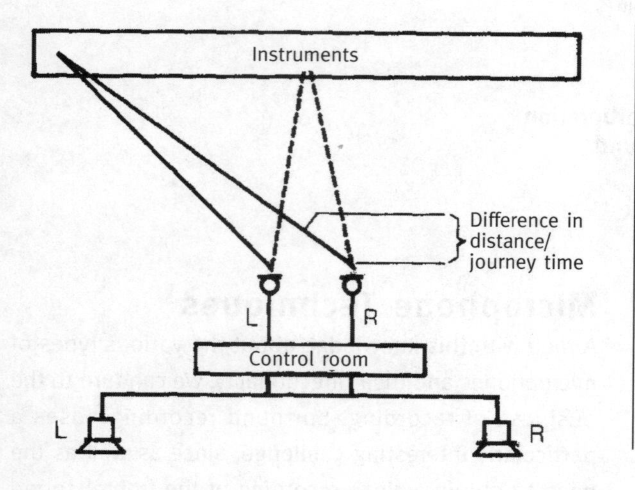

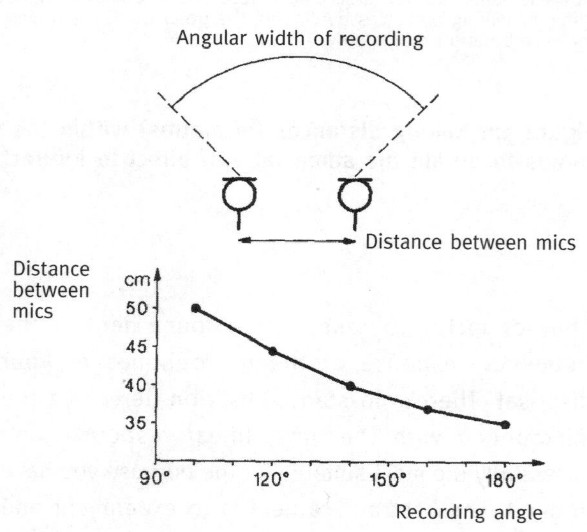

Figure 33: Interaction between the placement and spacing of the mics and the angular width of an AB recording

AB recordings are not mono compatible, as phase differences of the coherent signals would lead to cancellation and reinforcement. One solution to this problem is to play back either the left or the right channel, but not both. In most cases – and especially if omnidirectional microphones are used – all the sound sources are likely to be well represented by each of the two channels.

XY STEREOPHONY

The XY and AB techniques represent the two extremes of dual-channel stereo recording. The XY is a coincident microphone technique, meaning that the two mics (or mic capsules) are placed as close together as possible, but instead of the two mics being parallel and facing forwards, as was the case with AB recording, the X and Y microphones are angled outwards. The stereo effect is the result of level and intensity differences between the two capsules, which is why this technique is also described as *intensity stereophony*.

With the XY technique, one capsule is placed directly above the other, with one pointing diagonally forwards and to the right and the other pointing diagonally forwards and to the left, as shown in Figure 34. The angle formed by the axes of the two microphones is known as the *stereo angle* (also known as the *opening angle* and the *angular offset* of the microphones).

However, it's a mistake to point one mic at the rightmost sound source and the other at the leftmost and expect to create a convincing stereo image; the apparent source width would be too narrow and the result would be a quasi-mono sonic image. The stereo angle in fact needs to be wider than that of the source.

It's also essential that both microphones have the same directional characteristic. Omnidirectional microphones are clearly unsuitable for the XY technique, the choice in most cases being between cardioid or supercardioid microphones.

What makes directional imaging possible when listening to XY recordings is the fact that, since directional microphones are more sensitive to on-axis sound (sound originating from the direction in which they are pointing) than that arriving from the side, all sound sources other than those lying along a line bisecting the angle between the two mics will be captured more strongly by one mic than the other. Therefore, when the recording is played back, phantom sound sources will appear in the space between the two loudspeakers. The localisation of individual sound sources in XY recordings is in fact very good, even though the sonic image has a tendency to be 'middle heavy', which is to say that the sources appear to be bunched near the centre of the stage. The weakness of XY recordings is their poor spatial imaging and the fact that the sound tends to be very bright, with the bass unnaturally lacking in emphasis.

Very different results can be obtained by using microphones with a figure-of-eight characteristic in an XY configuration. With these mics, because of their superior rejection of sound arriving from the side, a narrower stereo angle can be used. Of course, the recording now covers two distinct areas, one in front and the other behind the microphones. Here, too, since pressure-gradient receivers are being used, there's a tendency for the lower frequency range to be somewhat attenuated.

All these factors make this configuration ideal for the live recording of speech, since the attenuated bass reduces handling noise and footfall while the microphones also capture audience reaction, if positioned out of phase. The XY technique is also particularly well suited to recordings in which precise localisation of the sound sources is desired – for example, to allow the pinpointing of soloists or to emphasise the movement of sound sources.[140]

MS STEREOPHONY

Like the XY technique, the MS technique employs coincident microphones, and the stereo effect therefore depends upon differences of intensity rather than phase. The basic setup for both techniques is very similar, though the XY offers sound engineers the freedom to vary the width of the stereo image at the post-production stage, which in this case means when they come to edit and process the signals.

The MS configuration consists essentially of one microphone pointing directly forwards (0°) to capture the mono signal (the polar pattern of this microphone is not material) and a microphone with a figure-of-

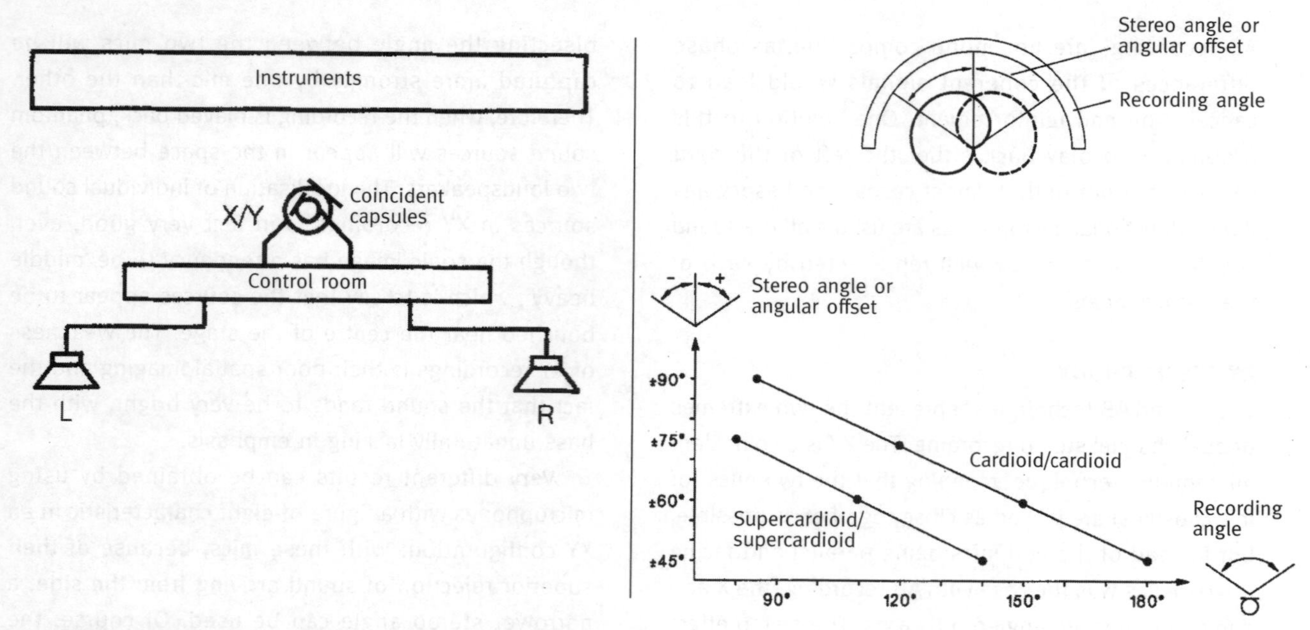

Figure 34: XY recording with two cardioids (left) and the relationship between the placement and angular offset of the microphones and the recording angle (right)

eight characteristic placed as close to the first microphone as possible but at an angle of 90°. (Being bi-directional, this microphone is simultaneously pointing to the right and to the left.) The first microphone provides the mid (M) signal and the second provides the side (S) signal, in which all the directional information is contained. The S microphone is naturally more sensitive to sound waves coming from the sides of the stage (right and left) and less sensitive to sound originating in the centre. By matrixing the M and S signals in the following ratio...

$$L = (M + S) \times \frac{1}{\sqrt{2}}$$

$$R = (M - S) \times \frac{1}{\sqrt{2}}$$

...you obtain L and R signals equivalent to the X and Y signals obtained by XY stereophony.

It's possible to alter the apparent source width simply by altering the ratio of the M and S components.[141] By changing the polar pattern of the M microphone, for instance, you can adapt the angular width of the recording area to match the width of the source or else to include certain sources and reject others. The options are illustrated in Figure 35.

Like XY recordings, recordings created using the MS technique offer very good localisation of individual sound sources, as well as the ability to vary the level ratios between middle and side sources. The spatial depth of the recording, however, is far from being as impressive as that obtained from the AB technique. The ability to use various types of microphone for the M signal makes it possible to create a significantly more powerful and less shrill sonic image than is possible under the same circumstances using the XY technique. The need to use a microphone with a figure-of-eight directional characteristic for the M signal necessarily means that the lower frequency content of the side signals will be somewhat attenuated.

The MS technique is especially good at allowing precise localisation of individual sound sources within an ensemble and is very useful for the recording of moving sound sources. The localisation of phantom sound sources often seems more precise than with XY recordings, especially those for which a narrow recording width has been selected. With MS recordings, also, the pure M signal is invariably mono compatible.

All these factors give the MS technique a theoretical superiority over the other popular coincident microphone technique, XY, and its results can be processed far more flexibly. Nonetheless, arguments exist for both techniques; very good recordings can be made using the XY technique, which, if nothing else, offers direct access to the L and R signals.

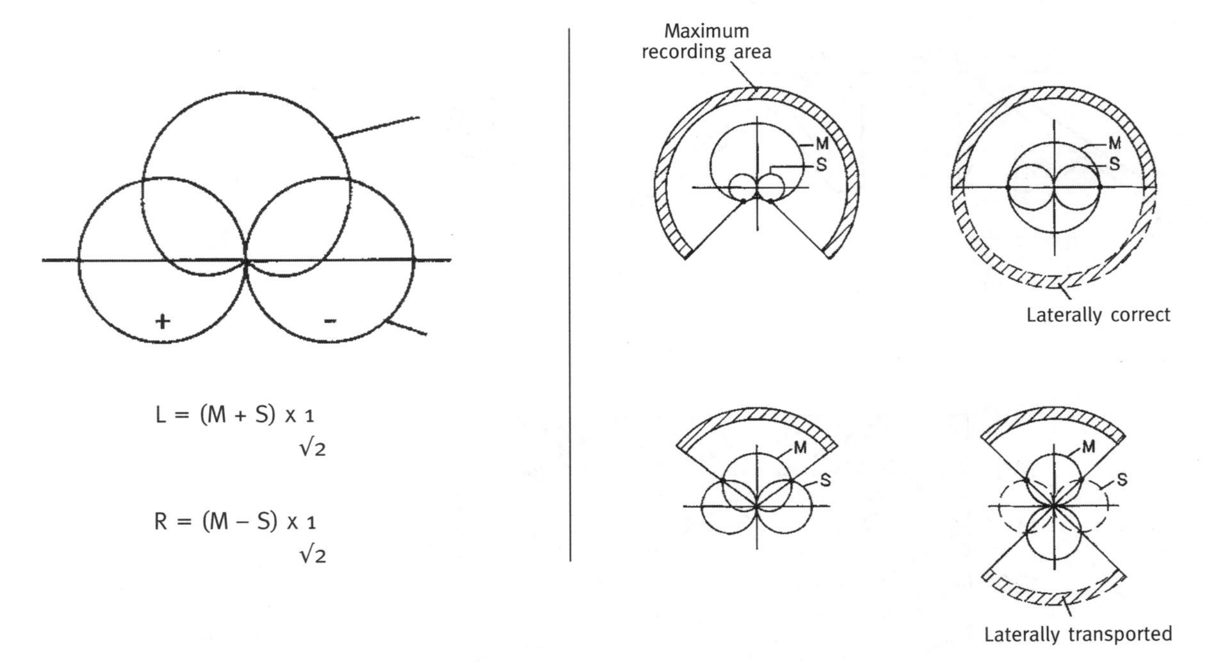

Figure 35: Changing the area covered by an MS recording by varying the polar pattern of the M mic

ORTF[142]

If the AB technique offers a very good spatial impression but poor localisation of the individual sound sources, and the XY technique offers very precise localisation but a confused spatial impression, the question obviously arises, is it possible to combine the two techniques in such a way as to retain only the advantages of each and eliminate their weaknesses? Hybrid recording techniques – of which the ORTF technique is the most famous – represent an attempt to answer this question.

The ORTF technique involves placing two cardioid microphones 17.5cm apart with a stereo angle of ±55°. As a practical aid to simplify the task of positioning the microphones, it's possible to buy ready-made ORTF configurations that can be mounted on a normal microphone stand, as shown in Figure 36; clearly, there isn't much that can go wrong with such systems, and the results they give are nearly always highly satisfactory.

The ORTF technique is a special case of microphone configurations inspired by the curves. In Figure 36, the cross-hatched areas represent unsuitable configurations. Using this diagram, hybrid recording techniques can be adapted to the recording area. The ORTF technique covers a recording area with an angular width of 95°, which is adequate for most purposes.

The stereophonic effect is the result of differences in both phase and intensity, and these combine to create very precise inter-speaker imaging. The ORTF technique is appreciated for its combination of good localisation of sound sources with a balanced spatial impression. Through the use of bass-corrected cardioid microphones, it's also possible to achieve a very powerful (if at times unduly bright) sonic image.

Because of the wide stereo angle used, recordings made via the ORTF system are always mono compatible as there is very little correlation between the L and R signals.[143]

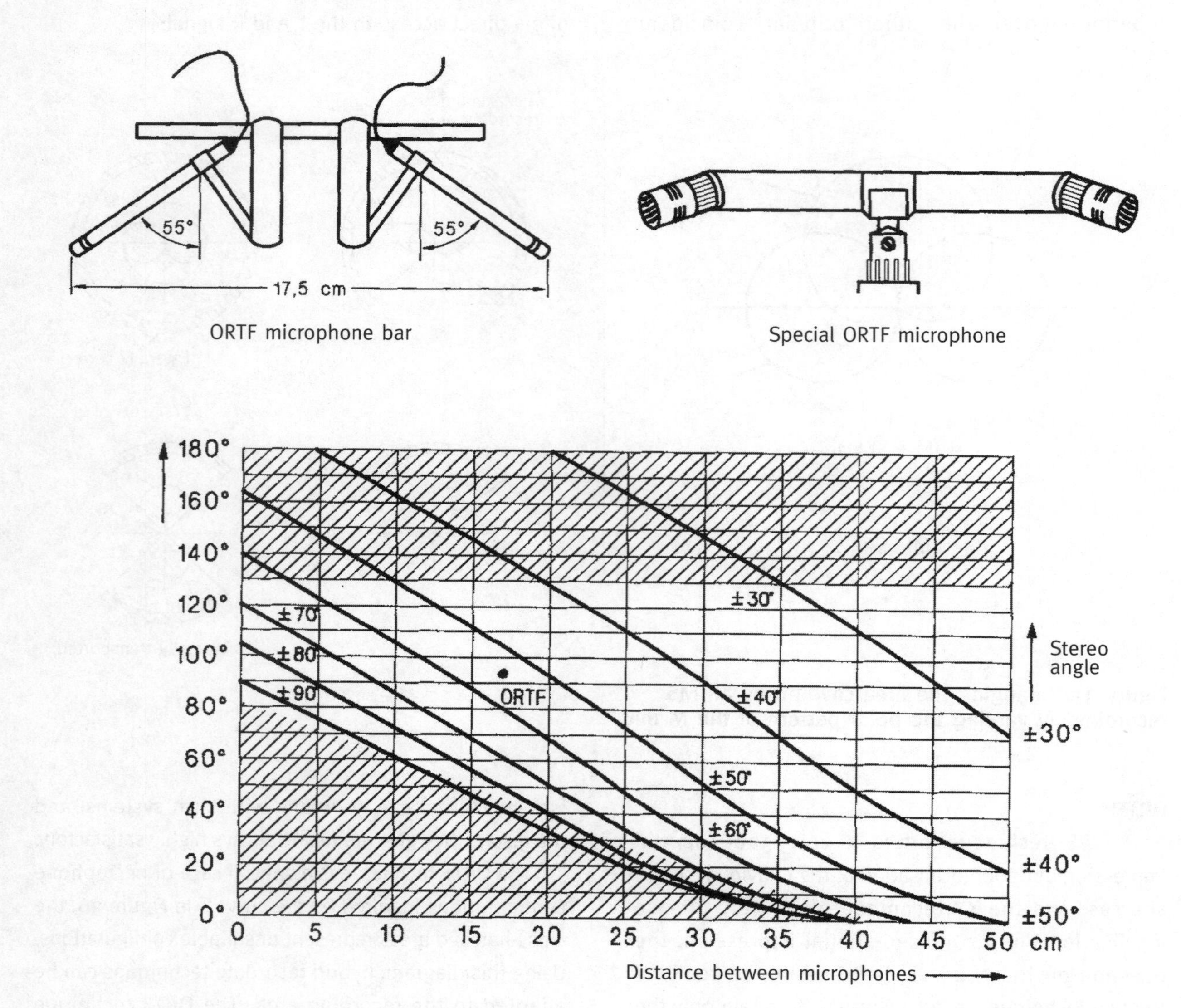

Figure 36: The ORTF technique (above) and Williams curves for hybrid recording (below)

ACOUSTIC-PARTITION STEREOPHONY

Unlike the techniques that have just been discussed, acoustic-partition stereophony attempts to simulate natural hearing in the same way as binaural stereo (using the dummy-head microphone). With this technique, two microphone capsules – usually omnis, on account of their more linear frequency response – are pointed in opposite directions (±90°) with the capsules the same distance apart as human ears. An acoustic partition is placed between the two microphone capsules to simulate the diffraction of sound waves by the human head. Versatile, high-quality main microphones can be constructed in this way. Although it's possible to imagine any number of ways of implementing this principle, two methods in particular are already well established: the spherical surface microphone and the OSS configuration using the Jecklin disc.

The spherical surface microphone, which was first produced around 12 years ago, comprises two omnis at an angle of 180° recessed into a sphere with a diameter of 20cm, as shown in Figure 37. The time-of-arrival and intensity differences produced by off-axis sound sources are very similar to those experienced naturally. Tone discolouration is eliminated by flush-mounting the capsules (with the body of the microphones recessed within the sphere).

However, the sphere needs to be carefully placed. If the recording angle is too wide, lateral sound sources will be received too strongly by the nearer microphone and too faintly by the microphone in the sphere's shadow. For this reason, the spherical surface microphone should be reserved for sources with an angular width of 90° or less.

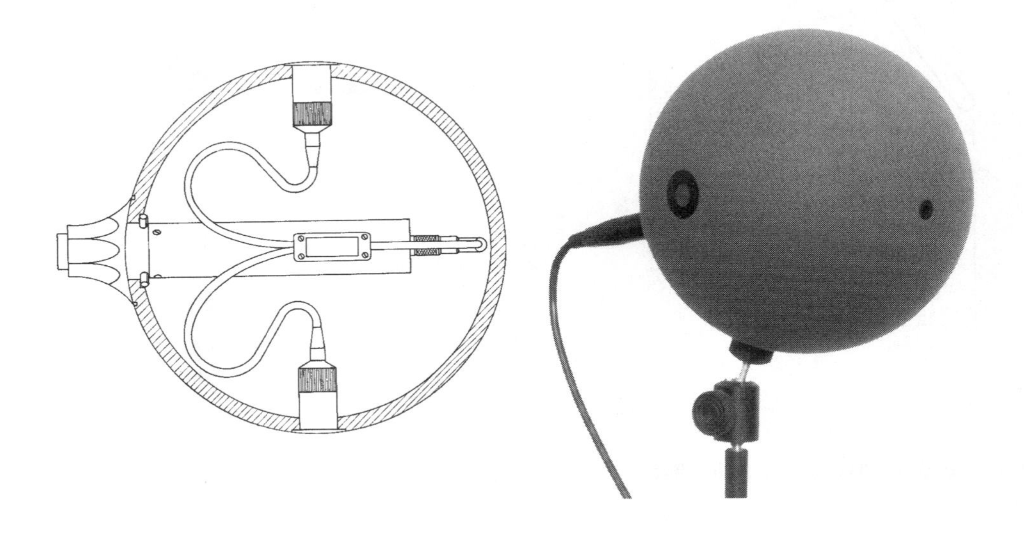

Figure 37: Cross-section of a spherical surface mic and one example, the KFM 360 from Schoeps

Since the sideways orientation of the microphone capsules inevitably means that a higher proportion of diffuse sound is picked up than normal, it's advisable to choose a room with good acoustics to do the recording and place the microphone carefully. Like those made via the ORTF system, recordings made using spherical surface microphones are mostly mono compatible due to the 180° angular offset of the two capsules.[144]

The second tried-and-tested form of acoustic-partition stereophony is the (OSS) Optimal Stereo Signal technique, which was invented by Jürg Jecklin. The configuration is essentially as follows: two omnidirectional microphones are placed 17.5cm apart (that being approximately the distance between most people's ears) and angled slightly outwards (around 20°). The two microphones are separated by a disc around 30cm in diameter and covered with foam plastic, as shown in Figure 38, allowing direct sound coming from the front and diffuse sound coming from the back to be recorded without any colouration at all, and direct sound from the side (which is reflected by the disc despite the foam plastic) to be relatively free from colouration.

The real advantages of the Jecklin disc, as it's popularly known, are most apparent when the microphone is comparatively far from the sound source. Provided that the microphone position is chosen carefully in order to ensure that a balanced blend of direct and indirect sound is picked up, recordings made using the Jecklin disc are characterised by a very well-balanced sonic image and a powerful sound, thanks largely to the use of omnidirectional microphones.

Although the angular offset of the two microphones (the stereo angle) is very small, the disc largely eliminates correlation problems, so OSS recordings are in most cases also mono compatible.[145]

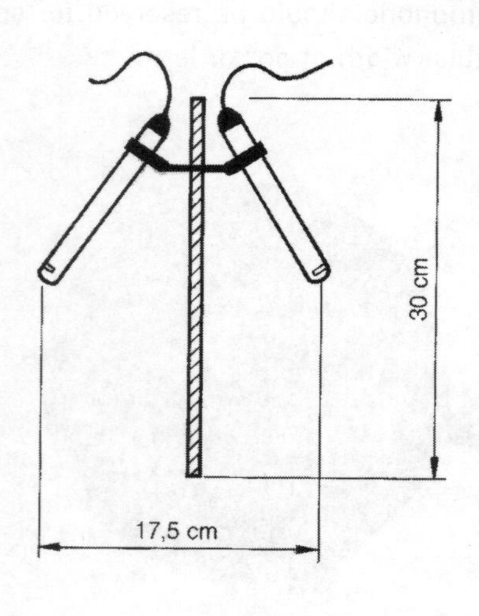

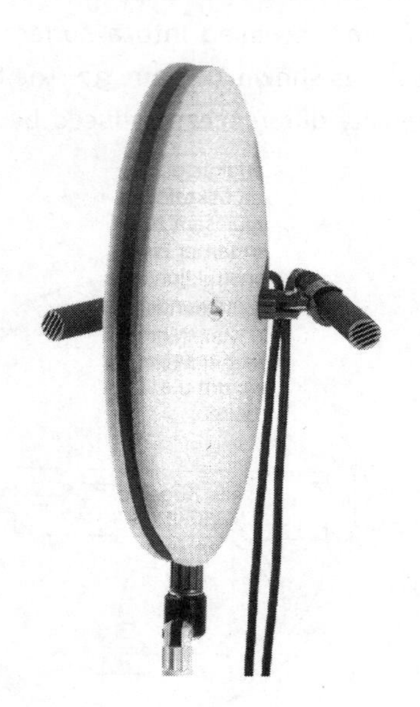

Figure 38: OSS recording using a Jecklin disc

Although strictly speaking binaural stereo recording can also be considered an instance of acoustic partition stereophony, the two systems should not be confused. Binaural stereo recordings – that is, recordings made using the dummy-head microphone – can only be played back through headphones, while recordings made using either the spherical microphone or the Jecklin disc can be played back using loudspeakers.

OVERVIEW OF DUAL-CHANNEL MIC TECHNIQUES

In his highly recommended book *Mikrofonaufsätze*, Jörg Wuttke offers a very helpful overview of the microphone techniques employed for dual channel stereophony, which are included in Table 5 to sum up the various techniques available.[146]

Multichannel Techniques

ICA 3 AND ICA 5

ICA (Ideal Cardioid Arrangement) 3 and ICA 5 are the product of research by Ulf Herrmann and Volker Henkels of the Fachhochschule Düsseldorf.[147] The ICA 3 technique involves recording one or more sound sources using three microphones in such a way as to divide the entire recording area into two segments, L-C and C-R, the former covering everything from the dead centre to the extreme left of the recording area and the latter everything from the dead centre to the extreme right. It's essential that the two areas do not overlap, and yet they do share a common border: the line that bisects the total recording area (in other words, 0°). The recording angle of the base L-R must be almost zero so that no L-R stereo base appears.

Type of stereo	Intensity stereophony		Small delay + intensity stereophony	Acoustic-partition stereophony	Delay-time stereophony
Name	XY	MS	eg ORTF	eg OSS	AB
	β d=0	90° M S d=0	β d	β d	β d
Distance between capsules	0cm, usually superimposed		5–30cm angle dependent	depends upon partition	40–80cm or more
Angular offset of microphones	45°–180°	90°	0°–180°	typically 20°	0°–90°
Receiver principle	pressure-gradient receivers (eg cardioids)			mainly pressure receivers (omnis)	
Sonic image	clean, often bright and brilliant			voluminous, especially good LF reproduction from omnis	
Spatial impression	slight		balanced	good	very good →
Localisation	← very good		good	satisfactory	indistinct

Table 5: Overview of the various microphone techniques for dual-channel stereophony

When played back on an ITU 775-compliant system, phantom sound sources are formed that are amenable to precise localisation. Research done by Hermann and Henkels suggests that the optimum mic arrangement is that illustrated in Figure 39, while the stereo angles for cardioid-mic use are indicated in the table.

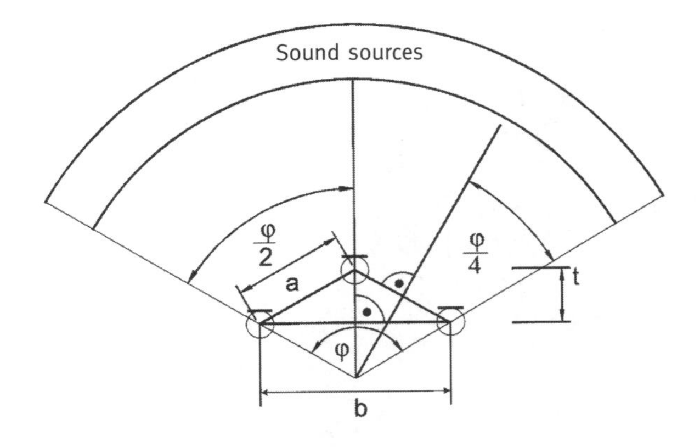

Figure 39: Microphone geometry and distance between microphones for various source widths

Sound sources	Angular width of source	Microphone distance a (in cm)	Microphone distance b (in cm)
100°	69	126	29
120°	53	92	27
140°	41	68	24
160°	32	49	21

The desire to introduce surround channels into the equation led to the creation of the ICA 5 technique, in which two rear facing cardioid microphones are added to the ICA 3 configuration. Through the comparison of two variants (ICA 3 + large-AB and ICA 5), you arrive at the relationships for a 3/2 main microphone (Ambience Cross ICA 5) as illustrated below in Figure 40. The ASM microphone serves to represent a practical implementation of the ICA 5 technique.

ICA 5 recordings are invariably compatible with the ITU 775 recommendation. In order to avoid rear localisation in applications, or with recording areas, that would make this undesirable, attenuation of the direction-determining frequencies 1.2kHz to 12kHz[148] is recommended in the surround channels.[149]

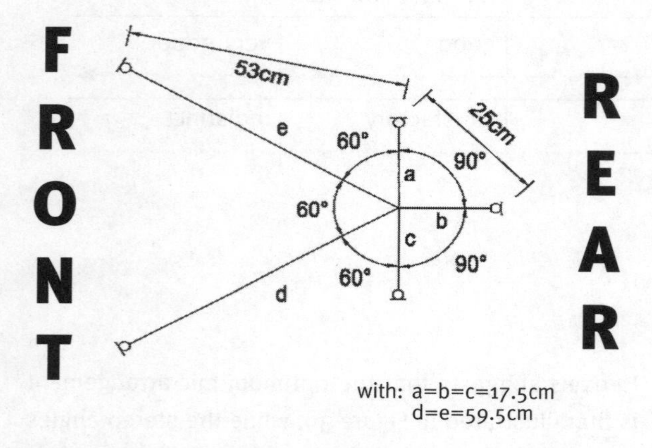

Figure 40: Microphone geometry for the Theile-Kreuz (Surround Ambience Microphone) ICA 5

DOUBLE MS STEREOPHONY

This coincident four-channel technique extends MS through the addition of a rear recording area. For this purpose, a second M microphone is placed above the figure-of-eight and aimed to the rear (180°), as shown in Figure 41. Depending upon the polar pattern employed for the two M microphones, a recording area of up to 360° can be produced (which should not be confused with that of the MS technique proper when an omni is used for the M signal).[150] The figure-of-eight microphone now serves to provide the S signal for both the front and the rear microphones, though the matrixing ratios have to be modified for the rear system. The double-MS system offers the same adjustment and post production processing flexibility as the MS system used for dual-channel stereophony, as well as its advantages and disadvantages.[151]

By using the front M signal separately, the four-channel system can be converted to 3/2, while separate use of the rear M signal opens up even more possibilities by introducing a centre surround channel for formats which support one, such as DTS ES and DD EX. However, outside the sweet spot, comb-filter-like effects are likely to be encountered.

Because of the great compactness of the main microphone and the associated advantages (the lightness of the arrangement, the fact that only one stand is needed and only a single windscreen), the double-MS technique is especially useful for ambience recordings for the film industry. Through the use of

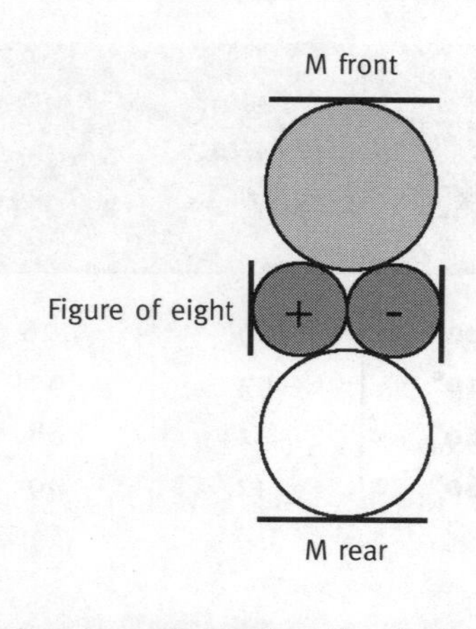

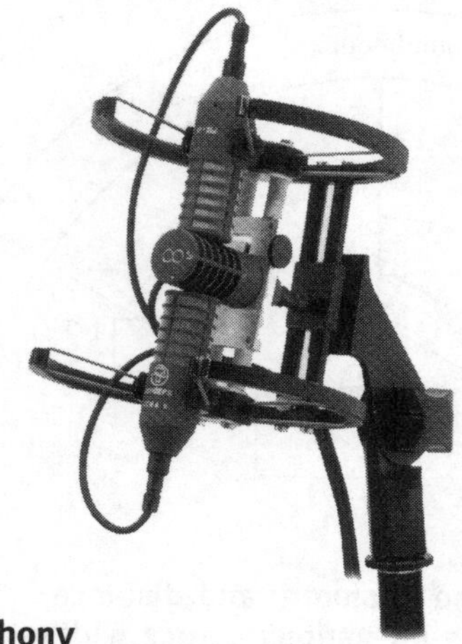

Figure 41: Microphone configuration for double-MS stereophony

different microphones for the front and rear M signals, the sound can be further adjusted in response to the demands of differing ambiences.[152]

ADJUSTABLE SURROUND MICROPHONE (ASM 5)

The Adjustable Surround Microphone (ASM 5) is based on the research of Hermann and Henkels. In the interests of flexibility, not only are the angle and distance between the microphones adjustable but their polar patterns, too, can be varied to adjust to different recording situations. The ability to switch between different polar patterns and therefore change the sound characteristics of the microphone provides a simple way, for example, to counteract the bass-heavy sound of PA reinforced concerts. In practice, this system's principal strengths are its ease of use and its simplicity of placement, along with its particular suitability for ambience recordings.[153] As with the ICA 5 concept, ASM 5 recordings are 3/2 compatible.

The best-known microphone of this type is the Brauner ASM 5 (shown in Figure 42), a high-quality main microphone employing five Brauner VM–1 large-diaphragm capacitor capsules. In addition to the mic's aforementioned adjustability, each of these capsules is capable of being rotated through 180°. To make the most of the ASM 5, you really need SPL's Atmos 5.1 controller, which allows continuous adjustment of the polar patterns, from omnidirectional to figure of eight.[154]

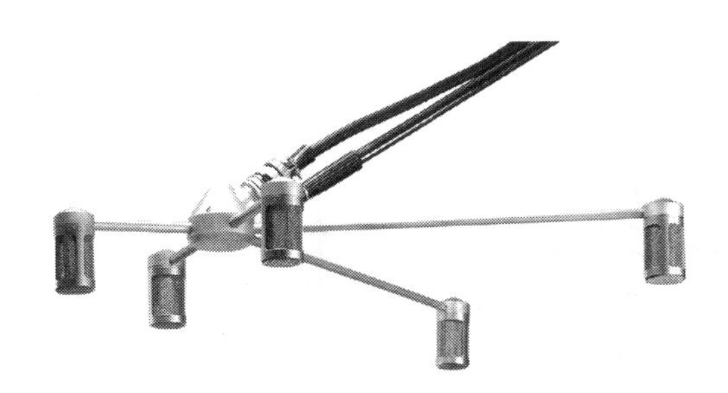

Figure 42: Brauner ASM 5

IRT CROSS

The Surround Ambience Microphone is a four-channel recording system that originated in the IRT (Institut für Rundfunktechnik) and is, again, the brainchild of Günther Theile, to a large extent. For this reason – and also because of its shape – it's generally known as the IRT (or Theile) Cross. It consists of four microphones arranged at the four corners of a square with sides measuring 20–25cm and aimed diagonally outwards, and a special X-shaped structure is used to hold the microphones in place, as shown in Figure 43. All four mics are cardioids, making the arrangement perfectly symmetrical. When played back through four loudspeakers positioned in the corners of a square room, 360° localisation is possible, as is the tracking of moving sound sources. As the name suggests, the system was designed for ambience recording in concert halls (where it picks up the indirect sound) and outdoors.

The Theile Cross can be regarded as two ORTF stereo systems, one facing forwards and the other facing to the rear, with the two front microphones mixed to the front L and R channels and the two rear microphones directly supplying the LS and RS channels.[155]

Theile actually recommends using the system as a way of extending the OCT technique through the addition of surround channels. The distance between the main and ambience microphones should not be greater than a few metres, in order to avoid excessive arrival-time differences. If, however, this is impossible, the main microphone signals should be delayed to create the desired spatial impression.

The Theile Cross is well respected in the profession for its ambient-recording qualities and is also very simple to use. For particularly rounded and powerful ambience recordings, omnis can be used in place of cardioids, which – besides improving low-frequency reproduction – reduces sensitivity to handling and wind noise.[156] The use of double-diaphragm capsules with switchable polar patterns can lead to gains in versatility.

Recordings made using the Surround Ambience Microphone are not automatically 3/2 compatible. To arrive at 3/2, their signals must be combined with those of a configuration comprising a main microphone with three front channels (OCT, ICA 3, Decca Tree).

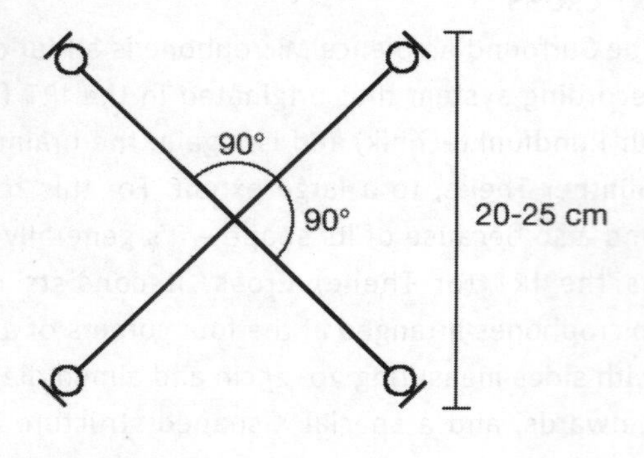

Figure 43: IRT Cross with four cardioids

SURROUND SPHERE

The Surround Sphere microphone sets out to do for surround recordings what the spherical-surface microphone did for dual-channel recordings. It's based on the Schoeps KFM 360, but two figure-of-eights mounted on the surface of the sphere just beneath the pressure transducers and aiming directly forwards (and therefore also directly backwards) are added to the two omnis recessed within it to yield two MS systems separated by the sphere, as describe in Figure 44.

Due to the comparatively wide coverage of the surround sphere (120°), the system can be placed far closer to the source than most other systems. Through the established matrixing procedure (L and LS = left omni ± left figure-of-eight; R and RS = right omni ± right figure-of-eight), virtual microphones for the front and surround channels are obtained, and the directional characteristic is continuously variable from omni to cardioid to figure-of-eight. This constitutes a far better way of adjusting to the recording situation than using EQ.[157]

It's possible to make a four-channel recording in 2/2 format with the microphone alone, but will be without a centre channel. In addition to matrixing the front and surround channels, this processor supplies the missing centre channel through the use of a Gerzon matrix.[158] It's also possible to derive a separate LFE channel (<70Hz) in the same way, and therefore a complete 5.1 format.[159]

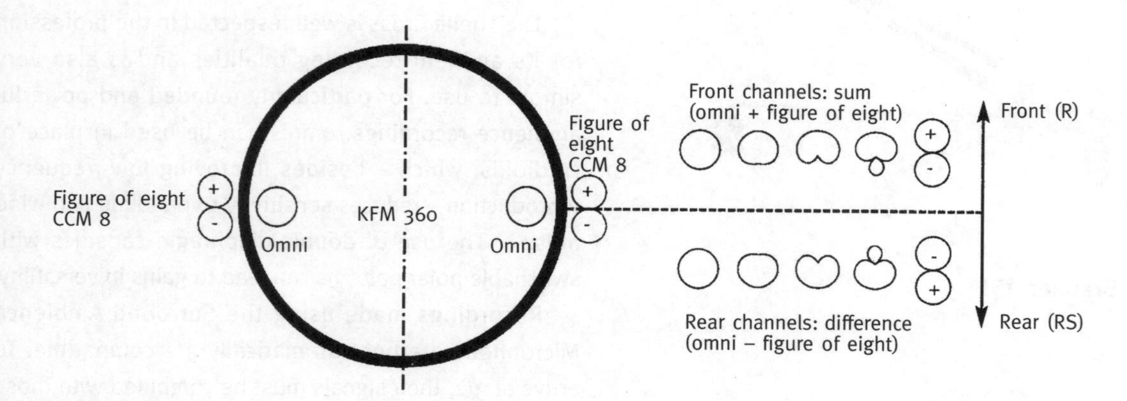

Figure 44a: Surround-sphere microphone (KFM 360) – schematic of signal derivation

Figure 44b: Surround Sphere microphone

Due to the processing and correction possibilities of the system, the recording quality is very good. This, coupled with the relative compactness of the structure and the good localisation of the sound source, make the Surround Sphere microphone especially effective for directional and effects-laden ambience recordings.[160] However, the system is also used for music recording, where the centre-channel matrixing has won praise for being so highly practical.[161]

SOUNDFIELD

The Soundfield system of multichannel recording is based upon the use of a single, specially designed microphone. The Soundfield microphone consists of four (near) cardioid capsules arranged in the form of a tetrahedron standing on end, as shown in Figure 45. The primary signals (known as the *A format*) of these four capsules are matrixed by a special processor into four new signals – W, X, Y and Z, which together constitute the *B format*. Of the B-format signals, the W signal has an omnidirectional characteristic and the other three are equivalent to figure-of-eight mic's signals, the X signal containing the left/right information, the Y signal containing the front/back (also called 'front/surround') information and the Z signal containing the vertical (up/down) information. The W signal is equivalent to that of an omnidirectional microphone placed in the centre of the configuration.

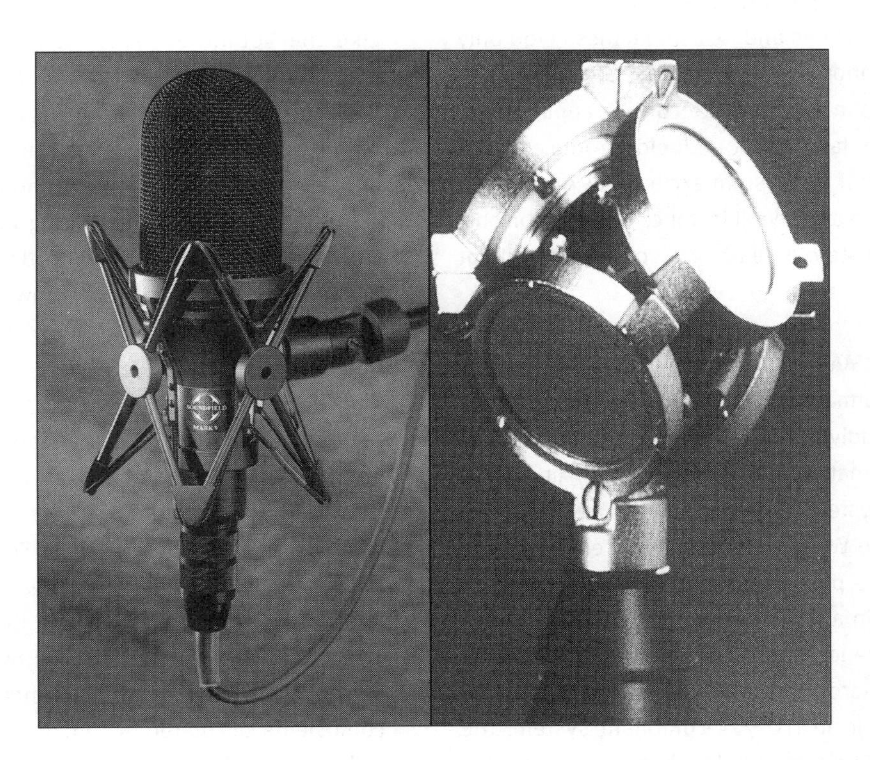

Figure 45: Soundfield microphone (left) with capsules arranged in the form of a tetrahedron (right)

Using a special decoder, the B-format signals can be converted into signals suitable for any one of a theoretically infinite number of loudspeaker layouts, from simple mono to dual-channel stereo to any of a multitude of surround formats, including 10.1. Since this process of conversion can be performed either during or after the recording, it's advisable to record not the primary (A-format) signals but the W, X, Y and Z (B-format) signals.[162]

The decoding of the B-format signals to signals in 5.1 format (as per the ITU 775 recommendation) is performed by the Soundfield SP-451 Surround Sound Processor,[163] and the speaker feeds are known as *G-format signals*. Since the ITU 775 format doesn't support periphony, the up/down information is ignored and the recording of the Z signal is therefore optional. The entire process of adapting the recording signals to the playback format (including modifying the orientation of the virtual microphones, recording area and apparent source width among other things) is performed by the processor.

The practical merits of the Soundfield system lie in its compatibility with virtually all playback configurations, the comprehensive post-production processing possibilities and its compactness (you only need one microphone). The system is said to produce very good results in all ambient recording applications.

Just one manufacturer, Soundfield, produces all of the components of the system exclusively. At present, demonstrating the archetypal instance of the ambisonic approach, the system is leading a somewhat twilight existence.[164]

DISCRETE B-FORMAT

The Discrete B-Format Microphone system represents an attempt to use individual mics in order to get the W, X, Y and Z signals that were obtained by matrixing using the Soundfield system. With this end in view, four mics – an omni for the W signal and figure of eights for the other three – are placed as close to one another as possible to obtain a coincident configuration.

Since coincidence is of critical importance, it's best to use small microphones. If the aim is simply to produce feeds for an ITU 775-compliant system, the up/down information can obviously be discarded. For the B format, much that was said both for and against the Soundfield system could be said again here, except that a wider choice of microphones is possible; you aren't limited to a single manufacturer, as most Soundfield processors have discrete inputs for normal mics as well as the special connector provided for their own, allowing you to obtain feeds for the same variety of loudspeaker configurations from Discrete B-Format signals as from decoded A-format signals obtained using the Soundfield microphone.

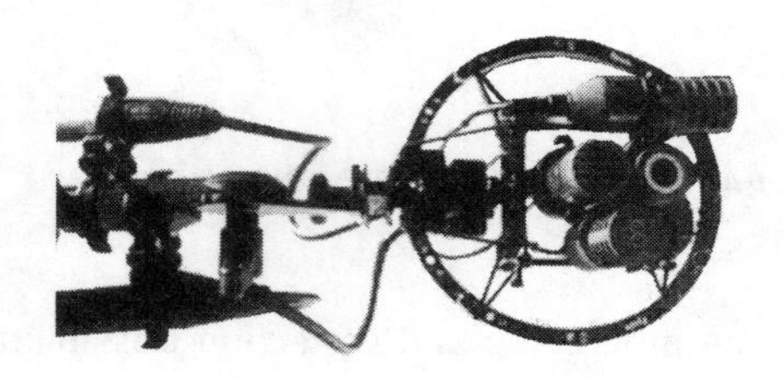

Figure 46: Discrete B-Format Microphone (Schoepsfield)

Like the Soundfield system, the Discrete B-Format microphone is suitable for all areas of recording and is especially recommended for ambience recording. Although the structure is compact, because it's possible to use so many different microphones, mounting them can often pose problems during mobile applications. One possible solution is afforded by the so-called Schoepsfield microphone,[165] shown above.

MID-SIDE DEPTH (MSD)

The Mid-Side-Depth system is another recording technique based on the principles of ambisonics. It comprises one omnidirectional microphone facing forwards and two figure-of-eights facing front/back and up/down, as demonstrated in Figure 47. Since the addition of two figure-of-eight mics arranged crosswise invariably produces a virtual figure of eight, the direction of which is determined by the ratio and sign of the two actual figure-of-eights, if the Ambisonic coefficients calculated by Gerzon[166] are used, matrixing will yield five different cardioid patterns, each of which can be added to the Mid signal (produced by the omni) to yield the L, C, R, SR and LR feeds needed for a 3/2 loudspeaker arrangement.

In practice, however, this system is almost never used as the results are not convincing and the matrixing is complex.[167]

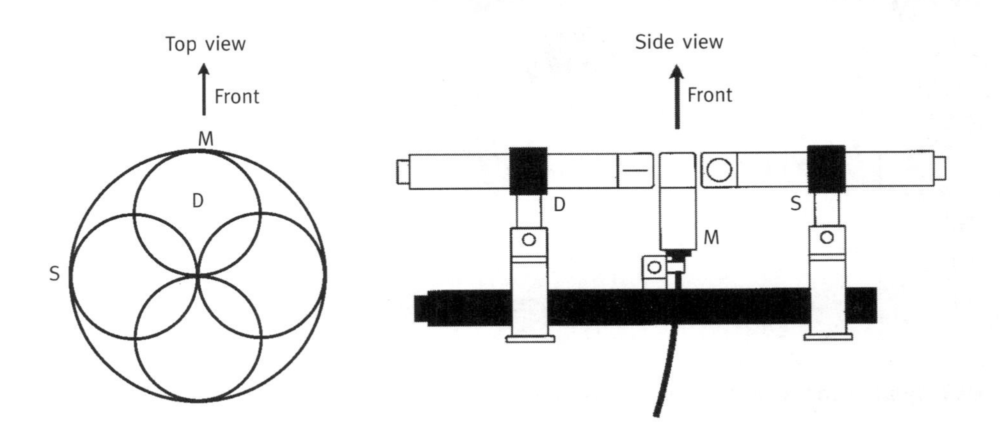

Figure 47: Mid-Side-Depth microphone configuration

OCT

The OCT[168] (Optimised Cardioid Triangle) is another brainchild of Günther Theile. In its basic version, it's a three-channel system for the discrete recording of the three front channels of the 3/2 format. The fundamental principle here, as with ICA 3, is that the L-C and C-R sectors are regarded as separate recording areas. To avoid overlapping, OCT employs five microphones arranged in the following manner:

The closest microphone to the stage (8cm closer than the Left and Right systems) is a cardioid pointing directly forwards (0°), which forms the tip of an isosceles triangle. In the two other corners are supercardioid microphones pointing to the sides (± 90°); these can be anywhere from 40cm to 80cm apart, the exact distance depending upon the recording angle, but 70cm (which corresponds to a recording angle of 120°, as recommended by the standard) is the distance most commonly encountered, in which case the format is described as 'OCT 70'.

To counteract the attenuation of the bass that's an inevitable consequence of the use of supercardioid microphones for the L and R signals, two additional mics – both omnis – are placed alongside them to capture more of the bass. To avoid AB stereophony and a lack of sharpness in the focus in terms of localisation, the signal of the omnidirectional microphones is sent to a low-pass filter with a roll-off frequency of 100Hz.

Sound arriving directly from the front (0°) is captured with maximum sensitivity by the cardioid at the 'prow' of the configuration and by the two side supercardioids (at the base of the triangle) attenuated by 9dB (–9dB), so the centre channel reproduction in this case will preponderate. If the sound arrives from the side, the nearest supercardioid will capture it with full sensitivity, the centre cardioid at –6dB and the more distant supercardioid (which is facing in the opposite direction) at –11dB (with the phase inverted), so there's excellent separation between the L-C and R-C sectors. However, the unsymmetrical combination of level and arrival-time differences necessarily leads to a lack of sharpness in the arc between ± 20–35°.[169]

The wisdom of using two omnidirectional microphones to compensate in the low-frequency range is open to question since most people are incapable of discerning the direction from which sounds with a frequency of less than 80Hz are emanating – besides

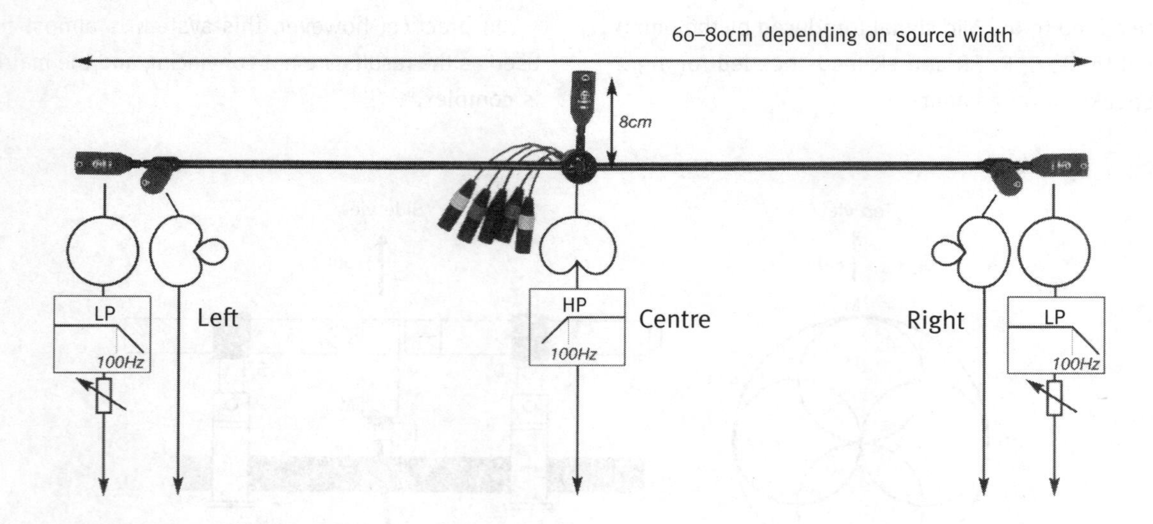

Figure 48: OCT system for recording in 3/0 format

which, in a large number of the playback systems on the market, all frequencies below 120Hz are sent to the lone subwoofer.

If you want to record in 3/2 or 5.1 format using the Optimised Cardioid Triangle, Theile recommends that you combine it with an IRT Cross, with the front two signals of the Cross mixed with the main L and R channels and the rear signals forming the LS and RS channels.[170]

Naturally, the quality of OCT recordings depends primarily upon the quality of the mics used. Small-diaphragm capsules are preferred – especially with supercardioids – since their frequency response is less influenced by the sound's angle of incidence. Due to the multitude of possible microphone combinations, no simple assessment of the sound quality of OCT recordings can be offered here, but it's worth noting that the large number of mics involved makes setting up a particularly laborious task, so the system isn't really suitable for mobile applications.

DECCA TREE AND FUKUDA TREE

The Decca Tree is a triangular microphone arrangement for recording in 3/0 format. It consists of three omnidirectional microphones arranged in a triangle, with the L and R microphones forming the base of the triangle 2m apart, and the C microphone – which forms the tip – 1.5m further forward, as shown in Figure 49. All three microphones are pointed forwards (0°). Because of the great distance between the front (C) microphone and the L and R microphones behind it – as well as the even greater distance between the L and R mics themselves, which is equivalent to a large AB configuration – the sonic image has great depth with an especially heavily emphasised centre channel.

If you are aiming for precise localisation of the sound sources in the frontal sonic image, the Decca Tree is

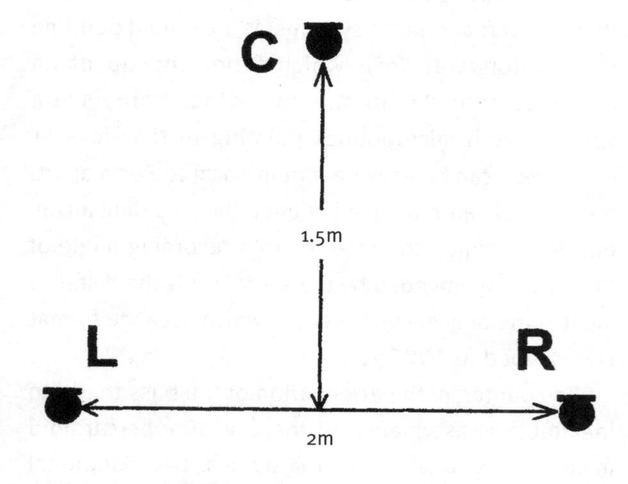

Figure 49: The Decca Tree

unsuitable. Of course, it's possible to substitute cardioid microphones (still facing forwards) for omnis to reduce the proportion of indirect to direct sound by some 6dB and in this way improve the localisation of the direct sound, or to even move the entire system further away from the sound sources in order to increase the recording area, but this will inevitably result in the sonic image being brighter and lacking in power in the bass register as a result of the poorer overall bass response of cardioid microphones. However, the extent to which the recording will suffer does of course depend on the quality of the mics used.[171]

In order to obtain 3/2 or 5.1 format recordings from the Decca Tree, you need to use a configuration known as the Fukuda Tree, which is reminiscent of ICA 5. The Fukuda Tree comprises seven microphones arranged as illustrated below in Figure 50. The L, C, R, LS and RS microphones are all cardioids while the flanking microphones – LL and RR – are omnidirectional. The L, R, LS and RS mics, which form a square, are aiming diagonally outwards, their axes being a continuation of the diagonals on which they are found (L, R ± 45°; LS, RS ± 135°), while the LL, C and RR mics face the front (0°). Provided that the proportions are maintained, the entire structure can be increased or reduced in size to match the acoustics of the room.

Due to the IRT-Cross-like arrangement of the L, R, LS and RS mics, it's possible to achieve 360° localisation, while the centre channel completes the sonic image. The omnidirectional 'outriggers', LL and RR, fulfil three tasks: they make it possible to use a LFE channel, they broaden the frontal sonic image and they ease the transition between the front and rear sonic images, making the entire sonic image more powerful and well rounded.[172]

With the Fukuda Tree, as with previous systems, the overall quality of the sound is heavily dependent upon the quality of the microphones used. Because of the complexity of the structure, neither it nor the Decca Tree are well-suited to mobile applications.

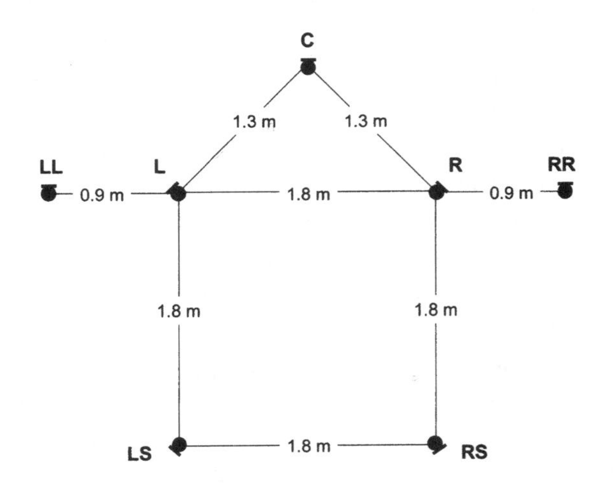

Figure 50: The Fukuda Tree

COMPACT SURROUND SYSTEM

The Compact Surround System (CSS) is a particularly rare configuration in which five cardioid microphones are mounted on a single microphone bar, with three of the mics facing forwards and two facing backwards. The sequence of the mics is as follows: L, LS, C, RS, R, the total distance between L and R being 60cm.

The orientation of the microphones depends on the recording situation, with the Williams curves being used to calculate the approximate recording area. When the CSS technique is used, the signals are usually recorded directly and only later processed to take into account level, relative timing and any discolouration that may be apparent.[173] Here, once again, the overall quality of the recording is heavily dependent on that of the microphones used.

MULTI-MICROPHONE ARRAY

The Multi-Microphone Array is to be regarded as more of a starting point for multichannel recording than a main miking technique *per se*. It's often mentioned in connection with Michael Williams, whose eponymous curves provided a very useful orientation for dual-channel stereophonic recording. In 1991, in a lecture delivered jointly with Guillaume Le Duc to the AES in 1999[174], Williams outlined his ideas on recording with microphone arrays.

With the Multi-Microphone Array for multichannel recording (in this case in 3/2 format), the room is divided into five equally large sections with a separate microphone configuration (using one of the established stereo microphone techniques) for each.[175]

FREE MIKING

As well as the techniques discussed here, people naturally come up with many other suggestions. Since the established techniques leave a great deal of room for experimentation and combination, over time many sound engineers have developed their own variations. Many then refer to this as *free miking*, although for the most part these innovations have their roots in one or other of the established techniques.

In 2000, Gerhard Betz conducted a survey into surround-recording practice, presenting the results at the 21st Sound Engineers Conference in Hanover. Of those who took part in the survey, a majority described themselves as devotees of free miking for multichannel recording. When Betz pressed them to say in a little more detail what this practice involved, the following points emerged.

1 Omnidirectional mics were used more often than cardioids (usually three to five of them, but sometimes as many as seven or nine).

2 For the frontal area, two to five microphones are normally used. When three front mics are used, the centre one is usually positioned slightly closer to the stage than the side ones (cp Decca Tree). With five mics, there are various systems in use to extend the frontal recording area and smooth the transition to the surround area.

3 In the interests of adequate decorrelation, a distance of two to three metres between the surround microphones is usually recommended, although this can be extended or reduced. The distance between the front and surround microphones can be anywhere from 1–20m (but beware of arrival-time differences).

4 Because of their more powerful sound, omnidirectional mics are recommended for the surround channels. They should, however, be turned away from the sound sources in order to avoided picking up direct sound (except for ambience recordings). Cardioids are simple to handle and can be placed closer to the source, although here some discolouration of the sound is to be expected.

5 When processing the signals, over-emphasis of the centre channel is to be avoided, since it can't always be assumed that this channel will be available. Most engineers felt, therefore, that it was sensible to provide an additional phantom sound source between L and R.

6 It's best to use parallel dual-channel/surround recording.

Certainly such pointers are likely to prove useful for those experimenting for the first time with microphone variations. The development of an individual style is undoubtedly highly prized. Betz therefore concluded his lecture by saying, 'There's no reason to approach the challenges of five-channel surround format – with all its possibilities and limitations – in a pragmatic manner.'[176]

Recording Criteria, Problems And Solutions

Delay Or Intensity Stereophony?

As you will doubtless have gathered by now, all microphone techniques are based on one, the other or a combination of both of these recording principles. Time-of-arrival (ie delay) stereophony delivers great spatial depth that can be appreciated even beyond the sweet spot, but when it comes to localisation of the individual sound sources, it's not that good. With intensity stereophony, which involves the use of coincident microphone techniques, it's the other way around: the spatial depth is unimpressive but localisation of the individual sound sources – for listeners near the sweet spot, at least – is very good.

In the case of dual-channel stereophony, the logical next step (typified by the ORTF technique) of combining the two principles pays dividends, but is the same true when you're operating under the more complex circumstances of multichannel recording?

By aiming to achieve a spatial impression that's as natural as possible, it's possible to latch immediately onto arrival-time stereophony to the neglect of all else. Here, the natural decorrelation of the signals results in an agreeably large sweet spot, which can be increased still further in the surround area through subsequent decorrelation. Since this is always achieved at the expense of localisation (which in the surround area is, in any case, unwanted), the question arises, does it make sense to adopt a miking technique for multichannel stereophony simply on the grounds that it delivers the most precise localisation?

When you actually look at the multichannel miking techniques in use, most undoubtedly have arrival-time stereophony as their underlying principle. Furthermore, many of the coincident techniques based on intensity stereophony (such as Soundfield, Discrete B-Format, MST) can be traced back to the ambisonic approach, which plays only a subordinate role in multichannel audio. This conclusion is supported by Betz's research amongst sound engineers,[177] who, he found, were using arrival-time stereophony almost exclusively. It's therefore clear that – at least as multichannel recording is concerned – spatial imaging is generally regarded as more important than precise localisation.

But does this mean we should abandon localisation altogether as an objective? When you consider some of the new formats employing up to 12 discrete channels and think about the number of microphones needed to implement them, the answer would appear to be yes. But on the other hand, there has to be localisation; even in multichannel audio, it must be possible to localise individual sound sources, at least to a certain degree. After all, in the absence of localisation, no listening impression could be described as realistic. The only way to resolve this dilemma, then, is to adopt the same approach as for dual-channel stereophony, combining the two techniques using something akin to the ORTF technique. And if the main mic doesn't provide enough localisation, it's always possible to use additional mics and combine their signals with those of the main mic later on.[178] The merits of this approach are hotly debated – indeed, hotly enough to merit a separate section...

Main Or Multi-Miking?

Even with dual-channel stereophony, this question is one of those that polarises opinion. While a great many practitioners have made the practice of recording with nothing more than a single, centrally placed stereo mic or two mono mics functioning as a stereo pair (which amounts to the same thing) into an art form, in either case this technique is designated the 'main microphone technique'.

There are others who avoid using a main mic altogether and instead prefer to use a separate mic for each individual sound source (within reason), reducing the spillage of sound from nearby instruments to a minimum. Nearly all studio productions, in fact, are based on this principle; as dry a recording as possible is made of each individual sound source (usually in mono), and only later is it panned into position in the stereo image. When we speak of a 'dry' recording, we mean one with as little reverberation as possible (reverberation is added artificially later), but initially the aim is to capture only the direct sound.

In the case of film soundtracks, panning method by which a sound source could be assigned a position in the stereo image; in science-fiction films, for instance, location recording is only very seldom possible![179]

Of course, there are many sound engineers who have sought to compromise, adopting first one and then the other of the two techniques, or even combining them in an attempt to get the best of both worlds. The quality of a main-mic recording is not, for example, unduly compromised if you place one or two spot mics close to the quietest sound sources in order to enhance their presence. Conversely, even if you've chosen to mic up each sound source separately and use panning to assign a place in the stereo image to each one, mixing in the signals of a main microphone can enhance envelopment and contribute a natural quality to the sonic image that it would otherwise lack. In other words, the evidence suggests that a blinkered, dogmatic approach seldom yields the best results. Of course, it's fine to have a basic strategy, but be open-minded enough to adapt it to the circumstances of each individual case.

Decorrelation To Augment The Sweet Spot

When multichannel audio is being discussed, one term that constantly crops up is *sweet spot*, referring to the ideal listening position. However, although the sweet spot is very important, any system that requires the listener to remain in a very limited area or else sacrifice the spatial effect altogether is plainly unsatisfactory, and for this reason more and more sound engineers are refusing to think in these terms. Of course, the only way of overcoming the need for listeners to occupy some very limited point in space is the adequate decorrelation of the channels, and as we saw in our brief look at the pros and cons of arrival-time and intensity stereo, only arrival-time stereo with mics positioned sufficiently far apart can deliver naturally decorrelated signals. We also saw, however, that this prejudged the listener's ability to localise individual sound sources, and concluded therefore that there had to be a better alternative. Nonetheless, natural decorrelation should certainly be seen as an important factor in any strategy to expand the sweet spot.

We know, too, from our comparison of sound reproduction in the cinema and in the home, that increasing the size of the sweet spot is an absolute necessity in the cinema. While in the front area several discrete channels are in operation, in the surround area artificial decorrelation comes into play to allow each of the surround channels to operate as a feed for several loudspeakers. In such cases, each loudspeaker delivers an individually modified signal in order to increase the listening area.

The same principle underpins home reproduction solutions that convert a 3/2 format to a pseudo 3/4 format. Here delay is often applied selectively, causing some loudspeakers to deliver the same signal later than others. However, arrival-time stereophony doesn't consist solely of differences in timing but is also the result of phase differences between coherent signals. Unfortunately, the simulation of natural arrival-time differences through the use of delay units or phase modification for recordings that already have a spatial element usually yields highly unsatisfactory results, so artificial decorrelation isn't really an acceptable solution, even though there are many areas of recording where it's the only practical one.

Since artificial decorrelation has a particularly adverse effect upon localisation, it can only be recommended – if at all – for the surround area, since (aside from ambience recordings) direct sound is generally unwelcome in surround channels. In practice, therefore, engineers seek to provide for an adequate degree of natural decorrelation, especially in the frontal area, resorting to artificial decorrelation only when absolutely necessary for the surround area. Using coincident miking techniques, however, this is virtually impossible, so in such cases the use of artificial decorrelation is the only remedy.

Large Arrival-Time Differences

Although the arrival-time differences that form the basis of delay stereophony represent an important foundation for the creation of phantom sound sources, they cease to contribute to the spatial imaging when they become too great. Open-air PA systems with several loudspeakers positioned a long way apart (which were once very common) provide a salutary example of the way in which delay can severely prejudice listening enjoyment. The kind of doubling and echo effects that appear as soon as delays of around 30–50ms are encountered spoil the overall sonic image and can ruin an otherwise good recording.

However, by looking again at Betz's research[180], it's possible to find instances of sound engineers placing the surround microphones as far as 20m from the main microphone. A distance of that magnitude will yield arrival-time differences way in excess of 50ms, so such recordings almost by definition can't sound good.

Or can they? In fact, the circle is easily squared by means of a neat trick. Given that the spatial impression captured a considerable distance from the sound source is often well worth reproducing, there's certainly a case for using widely spaced microphones. The detrimental effect of the delays can easily be removed at the post-production stage simply by delaying the front channels by the same amount. Obviously, when you do this, you have to be sure to delay all the front channels by the same amount or localisation will suffer. This technique in effect moves the sound sources closer to an ideal balance of direct and indirect.

The most common technique for eliminating unwanted arrival-time differences is to compare the signal of one of the spot mics (ideally a drum mic) with the centre signal of the room mic. The signals are sent to the left and right headphones and delay is then added until a clear phantom sound source appears in the centre of the sonic image. Bringing the two signals into sync in this way works particularly well if the recording is adapted in advance to the playback format. For example, if the playback is going to be in 3/2 format, a main mic designed for 3/2 use should also be used. In this case, a discrete centre signal from the room mic will be available for synchronisation, which can be carried out either at the recording stage (with a multichannel live mix) or later in the studio.

Since this is a very common technique in the post-production of multichannel audio, surround mixing consoles such as Euphonix's System 5 offer the requisite 'pre-delays' in every channel.

Location And Portability Of Multichannel Solutions

The uses of multichannel audio can be divided into two main categories: the reproduction of music and the addition of a soundtrack to film, video and other moving images. However, it's also possible to subdivide these groups further; in the music category, for example, there's a difference between multichannel production and multichannel live recording. The demands on the multichannel system you're using will vary depending upon the precise area of application.

Taking music first, for multichannel production in the recording studio, it's best to get dry mono recordings of the sound sources and then assign their positions in the multichannel image by way of surround panning, with the result that sound sources are reproduced with different intensities in different channels – and with intensity stereo, as we know, it's possible to obtain good localisation of phantom sound sources, and the amount of diffuse sound in the signals can be varied. If this manner of working is adopted, multichannel miking is actually superfluous, since it's only at the post-production stage that sources are placed in the surround image. Essentially, then, you need only a sound studio equipped with high-quality multichannel panning and surround-reverb processors[181]. Then, of course, you have to know what you're doing...

If you're engaged in multichannel music recording, the whole procedure is obviously different. As well as having a basic understanding of dual-channel and multichannel miking techniques, you also need to find a satisfactory solution for recording the diffuse sound and localisation of the sound sources – if necessary through the use of additional microphones. But whichever of the three approaches – main microphones only, main microphones plus spots or multi-miking – you adopt, you'll still need to play back the recording in the sound studio, if only to check it over. Regardless of whether they're recorded in the studio or live, music productions should be geared primarily towards ITU 775 reproduction – in other words, recordings should be made in the 3/2 or 5.1 formats.

In film recording, meanwhile, it's important to distinguish between post-production and location recording. The subject of film music has already been dealt with – monophonic sound sources are assigned with varying intensities to the available channels, as described earlier – but the dialogue, foley (footsteps, etc) and special effects pose quite different problems, and it's these we're concerned with here. The most obvious of these problems is that such sound sources are frequently in motion, and good all-round localisation is necessary if the listener is to perceive this.

In the case of location recording (the result of which is known as the *production audio*), the microphone has to be very near the camera (although out of shot!) or the entire illusion is shattered. Therefore, a reasonably compact solution is required, and since the camera position is constantly changing, it needs to be reasonably light. Bottom line: it has to be stand-mounted and the whole caboodle – stand and microphone(s) – must be capable of being carried, and in some cases held, by a single person (either the sound engineer or his/her assistant). It's also important to choose a mic that's pretty robust and won't pick up too much noise.

You also need to think about how many tracks you want to record. Bear in mind that, if you're over-ambitious here, you might not be able to use a portable recording device.

Ambience Recordings

With film sound, the more realistic the sonic image, the more realistic the entire scene. The use of multichannel techniques for the recording of ambient sound should not therefore be the exclusive preserve of Hollywood blockbusters. Multichannel recording systems exist that satisfy all the demands mentioned earlier without threatening the budgets of small productions.

At a recent Sound Engineers Congress in Germany, Florian Camerer of ORF presented research into the suitability of various multichannel microphone systems for outdoor recording, prefacing his assessment of the practical merits and failings of the various available solutions with a breakdown of the types of ambient recording commonly practiced, which have been summarise here.

- **Background And Foundation Ambience** – These establish the atmosphere and draw the audience into the scene. On a technical level, they also reduce dependence on the sweet spot. They can be thought of as the basic colours on the surround palette – wind, rain, snow, forest, traffic, crowd noise, etc

- **Directional Ambient Sounds** – These are sounds with a slight acoustic accent and a directional perspective, in the sense that they have a noticeable point or direction of origin. Under certain circumstances they may require the front/back and left/right dimensions to be treated separately. Typical directional ambient sounds are waves breaking on a beach, an open window in a room, the edge of a forest.

- **Ambient Effects** – These are ambient sounds with a clear focus of emphasis – singular audio events that form part of, but stand out from, the foundation ambience. Examples include distant birdsong in a forest, a car horn sounding in nearby traffic, a helicopter flying overhead in a street scene, a plane in the distance.

- **Effects** – Effects (as opposed to ambient effects) comprise foreground sounds (other than point sources), moving sound sources and point-of-view sounds. Examples include industrial machines, vehicles and airplanes outdoors and indoors, 'drive-bys' and 'fly-bys', avalanches, ice calving from a glacier, explosions, etc.[182]

Parallel Two-Channel Stereo And Surround Recording

As I said earlier, despite the advent of multichannel stereo, the traditional dual-channel variety continues to play an important role. Even aside from the fact that, in the home, surround-playback configurations complying with the standard are still vastly outnumbered by compromises and dual-channel stereo solutions, there are further reasons to pay close attention to the stereo mix, by no means the least of which is the fact that the DVD standard prescribes downward compatibility to dual-channel reproduction. Furthermore, since the overwhelming majority of recordings are released in dual-channel stereo (in the music sector, especially), the quality of these recordings will for the foreseeable future continue to be evaluated on how they sound in dual-channel stereo – especially since multichannel stereo requires new standards of evaluation.[183]

Nearly all sound engineers agree that you can't obtain a convincing dual-channel recording from a multichannel recording using a downmix matrix. The ambitious engineer therefore has no choice but to mix the entire recording twice, producing both a multichannel mix and a dual-channel one.

It can also be very useful – particularly during a live recording – to make a separate dual-channel recording. If the number of extra mics or tracks needed isn't a problem, you're best off using separate microphones, although good dual-channel recordings can also be made using certain multichannel miking techniques, such as the Decca Tree, in which case you don't need to use separate mics for the stereo recording. Techniques involving no centre microphone are particularly suitable for this purpose, although you might need to experiment a little with positioning the configuration. The ideal mic positions for surround and dual-channel recordings aren't necessarily the same.

Betz's research suggests a final observation on the differences between dual-channel and multichannel stereo. Betz asked his colleagues whether they had a tendency to evaluate multichannel recordings of music differently (more subjectively? more laid back? less critically?) from dual-channel stereo recordings. The overwhelming majority replied in the affirmative, and it emerged that, in the case of multichannel recordings, they were more ready to forgive small blemishes or intonation problems than with comparable dual-channel recordings.[184]

As long as both mixes are available (as is invariably the case with DVD releases), the quality of a recording is most often judged – certainly by consumers – on the basis of the dual-channel mix. One consolation is that, once you've produced an excellent dual-channel mix of your material, you can approach the multichannel mix in a more ambitious, objective and artistic manner, since the critics are liable to be more forgiving.

In conclusion, I would emphasise once again dual-channel stereo recording is still vitally important – more so, perhaps, than those working with multichannel audio are currently willing to admit.

Processing

Processing Requirements

When recording multichannel audio, it's very important to be able to monitor each recording channel very closely; you can't rely on the readouts of level meters and surround VDUs when attempting to find the optimal position for a microphone. Many miking solutions – such as the Double MS technique, the Surround Sphere and the Soundfield process – require the signals to be matrixed before the individual channels can be monitored, and even when you can monitor the individual channels it takes a great deal of experience and imagination to visualise the multichannel sonic image. If you don't have the luxury of an outside-broadcast van or a mobile recording unit and the right monitoring equipment, you have no choice but to rely on hope and to check the recording later in the studio.

It would nice, therefore, to find solutions that were capable of assigning mic signals to their correct positions in the multichannel spectrum during the actual recording. For live recording, this is at the moment impossible, which is why the (perhaps indefinitely) postponed launch of Studer's BRS system is particularly exasperating.

There are, however, solutions for studio and live use that are going in the right direction. Most of these, however, tie you to the use of one particular microphone or type of microphone, so we're still waiting for a universal solution. Processing without a suitable monitoring environment continues to represent a major problem, and for the foreseeable future there will be no other solution but to have faith in your own miking.

With that in mind, we can now take a look at how some of the problems associated with the live processing of multichannel recordings can be solved via techniques involving hardware, some of which are indispensable and others simply very useful. Their versatility (or lack thereof) won't be discussed further, since almost all of the available processors are tailored to one particular system.

Hardware Solutions

SPL ATMOS 5.1

SPL's Atmos 5.1 is a miking, mixing and monitoring solution for multichannel recording in 5.1 format. The input section boasts five strictly homogenous preamps that differ in gain by less than 0.1dB. Each of these channels can be positioned freely in the surround panorama using a mixing matrix, while the virtual distance between the front and back microphones can also be varied. As well as having the facility of allowing you to select the sources for the LFE channel, each channel is equipped with a switchable high-pass filter. The channels can be monitored individually using standard headphones, but to monitor the entire surround panorama you need a special set of headphones from Sennheiser.[185]

To make the best use of the Atmos 5.1 processor, you need to use the Brauner ASM 5 microphone, which offers continuous control of the directional characteristic of every capsule, from omni to cardioid to figure of eight and all points between. The result is a complete recording system of a very high quality, not simply because the components are ideally matched but also because they're high-quality components to begin with. If you can live with the limited flexibility of the ASM 5 miking technique, the Atmos 5.1 represents an ideal (if not exactly cheap) solution. The system has certainly impressed a number of well-known studios, who are already using it in mobile surround recording applications.[186] Naturally,

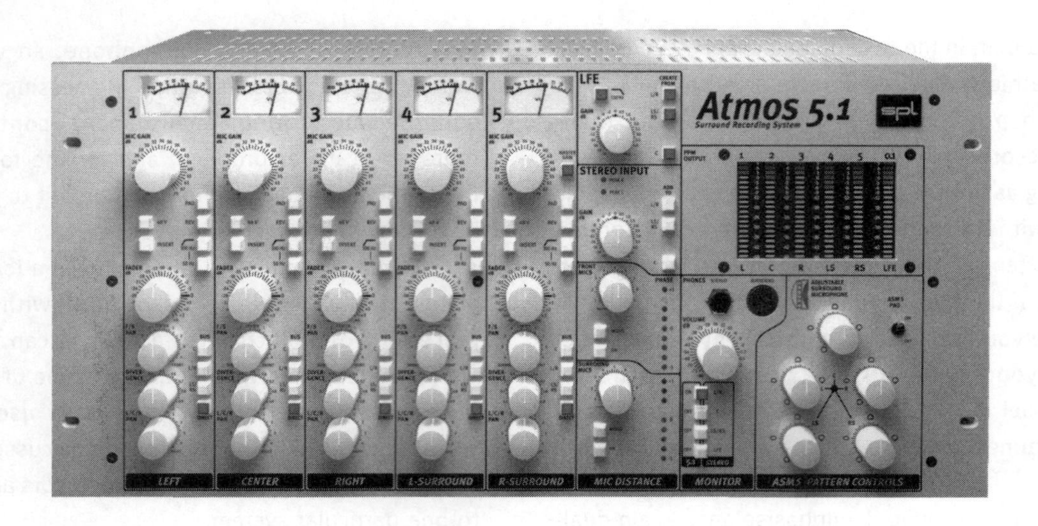

Figure 51: Atmos 5.1

it's also possible to use the processor with any five mono mics, but if you want continuous control of the polar patterns from within the processor, that function is limited to the Brauner model.

SPL AREA 5.1

The Area 5.1 system could to a certain extent be regarded as the Atmos 5.1's little brother, as it's very similar in structure, but is limited to basic multichannel recording in 5.1 format.

In the input section, there are once again five performance-matched mic preamps, whose signals can be solo-monitored using a normal set of headphones, and a Sub/LFE stage to determine the composition of the LFE signal.

The Area 5.1 dispenses with the panning matrix, the special headphones for monitoring and the polar-pattern matrix for the Brauner microphone offered by the Atmos 5.1. Instead, the entire system is designed for use with any five (matched) microphones, and there's also a special microphone holder available in the ICA 5 configuration.

One special feature of the Area 5.1 is the integration of a dual-channel downmix matrix that allows you to assign a level and a position in the dual channel panorama to each of the five channels, therefore allowing you to record in 5.1 and stereo simultaneously.[187] The entire system represents a useful alternative to the Atmos 5.1, if you don't mind dispensing with the Brauner ASM 5 and have access to a multichannel matrix for positioning the signals during post-production.

Figure 52: SPL Area 5.1

SCHOEPS DSP-4

The Schoeps DSP-4 processor is a matrix processor designed for use with the KFM 360 Surround Sphere Microphone. In addition to the signal processing available for the front and surround channels, the DSP-4 is capable of deriving a centre channel signal from the two front signals using a Gerzon matrix as well as offering a low-pass filter for the LFE. The polar patterns of the virtual mics for the front and rear channels are continuously variable, from omni to cardioid to figure of eight, while high- and low-frequency boost is provided to counteract any discolouration from the omnis and laterally positioned figure-of-eight mics. The inputs and the outputs of the processor are both analogue and digital (AES/EBU) to remove need for subsequent conversion.[188]

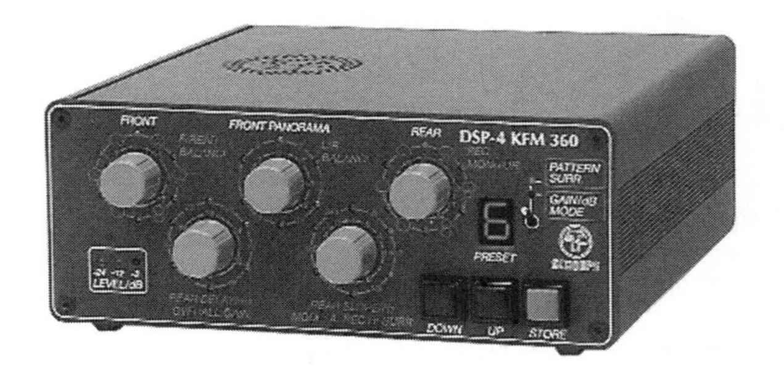

Figure 53: Schoeps DSP-4

If you're using the Surround Sphere Microphone, you'll find the DSP-4 indispensable for direct signal control, while the additional two channels permit recording in 5.1 format. Thanks to its integrated converters, the DSP-4 can even fill in for a mixer, if need be, so the entire system is portable.

SOUNDFIELD SP-451

The SP-451 processor is designed to generate a 5.1 signal from the B-format outputs of Soundfield microphones. Be warned, though, that the processor can't be connected directly to the microphone; first the signals must be converted from A format to B format, after which the SP-451 decodes six discrete channels, each with an individually adjustable level. It's also possible to widen the front or rear microphone base, while the virtual microphone arrangement and the individual polar patterns are determined by internally installed MAP (Microphone Array Pattern) cards. One such card, a cardioid L/C/R/SL/SR, is included in the package, but optional second and third cards can be added in almost any five-microphone-array configuration. The basic configuration positions are with the virtual channels on L,R = ± 45°, C=0° and LS, RS = ± 135°, but the front L/R and rear L/R mic positions can be changed by up to ±45° from these standard positions. Two additional outputs make the SP-451 compatible with both the 6.1 and 7.1 formats, provided that the requisite MAPs are installed.[189]

If you're using a Soundfield mic for multichannel recording, you have no choice but to use the SP-451, as Soundfield is the only manufacturer currently offering solutions for the processing of signals produced by Soundfield mics. To be able to monitor the multichannel signal during recording, you'll also need a mixing console, as the SP-451 has no monitoring capability.

Figure 54: Soundfield SP 451

STUDER BRS

Today, Studer's BRS processor is no longer part of the competition, as it still has to make it beyond the prototype stage.

The merits of binaural room scanning have already been discussed (see Chapter 2, 'Surround-Sound Fundamentals'). Assuming a room well insulated from environmental noise and a mobile solution to the head-tracker – neither of which poses an intractable problem given the current state of technology – the BRS processor would permit the monitoring of multichannel audio in 5.1 format in any desired situation. It would even allow you to monitor live recordings under studio conditions. The end result, however, is a discrete 5.1 signal, so the processor complements rather than rivals the other systems covered here.

Studer is currently stonewalling all enquiries as to whether or not they intend to manufacture the system. Hopefully, the concept of BRS won't fall prey to internal power struggles, as the technology would fill an existing gap in the market for multichannel recording equipment. Currently there is no alternative in sight.

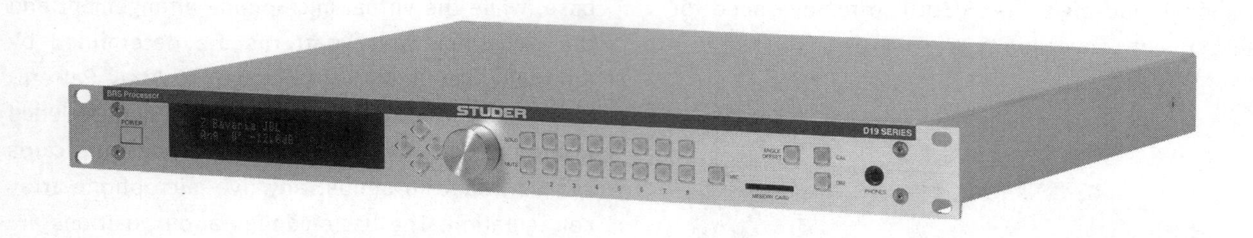

Figure 55: Studer BRS Processor

Data Formats And Intermediate Storage

Since the processing, editing and decoding of multichannel audio are digital processes, the analogue recording of multichannel audio makes little sense. There are many purist sound engineers and advocates of analogue technology who have some quite enlightening arguments concerning the respective merits and shortcomings of analogue and digital recording, but while for dual-channel stereophony a case can be made for analogue recording, multichannel audio is clearly a creature of the digital domain. Theoretically, apart from the encoding, there's no intrinsic reason why analogue processing might not be possible, but none of the existing multichannel systems support it.

Once high-quality analogue-to-digital converters have done their work, the microphone signals should remain on the digital level without further conversion until finally the decoder converts them back into analogue signals, and here the AES/EBU and ADAT formats are best. Depending upon the reproduction being aimed for, the audio resolution could be as high as 24 bits and 192kHz, although 16 bits and 44.1 (48) kHz or 24 bits and 96kHz are more common, since they generate far less data and are still of very high quality.

The number of recording tracks you'll need will depend on which recording technique you're using. If you're using eight mics or fewer, it makes sense to use an eight-track recorder (certainly that's what ITU 775 recommends), and in 5.1 format the recommended track assignments should also be adhered to. If you need more than eight tracks, use a second eight-track recorder rather than ending up with a recording split between two different recording media and data formats. For location recording, you're going to want a portable recorder, which effectively limits you to four tracks most of the time.

Whatever system of intermediate storage you choose, it should be one that supports audio resolutions from 16 bits and 44.1kHz to 24 bits and 96kHz. For post-production work, the recording system needs to be present in the studio, so a portable studio/live combination makes sense. Given the speed of developments in this sector of the market, it would be unwise to recommend any one system.

Summary

Any survey of multichannel audio will quickly establish that it's a subject in which there are very few universally valid rules. Current practice runs the gamut, from creative experimentation with the enlarged number of channels to the automated upmixing of old dual-channel recordings with a view to re-releasing them, and within this spectrum many different approaches are possible.

Also, just as we saw that, with microphone techniques, there can be no simplistic division of systems into 'good' and 'bad', but rather – at the very most – into those that are 'more' or 'less' suitable for a particular application, the same type of subjectivity pervades the entire field of multichannel recording. There's very little agreement among sound engineers over the wisdom (or otherwise) of certain practices, and even those who find themselves in accord often turn out, upon closer examination, to understand them differently.

The upshot is that no two multichannel recordings of the same source material ever sound alike. Of course, in view of the generally more lenient attitude of critics to multichannel recordings, there is obviously greater scope for creativity in this field. This doesn't mean you can do whatever you like and get away with it, but only that, if you think the results are better when you adopt a particular approach – even though you can't explain why – you should trust your ears.

The mere substitution of one type of mic for another within the ASM configuration drastically changes the quality of the sound, and sound engineers often conclude that the appropriateness of a particular type of mic is solely dependent upon the style of music being recorded.[190] Even though a *de facto* standard does exist in ITU 775, this recommendation is concerned only with playback.

Also, the flexibility available at both ends of the multichannel production chain is typical of the possibilities available. While this means that those new to the world of multichannel sound will take far longer to find their feet than perhaps they expect, it at least affords them gratifying scope to exercise their creativity and to develop their own working practices and, ultimately, their own sound.

4 SURROUND PROCESSING

Fundamentals Of Processing

Once the source material has been recorded, the many-faceted task of processing begins. This is generally done in a recording studio and includes the entire process of positioning each of the signals in the sound spectrum, adding reverb (if needed), mastering and finally encoding.

As well as a technical understanding of this production process, a great deal of experience is required. A detailed theoretical examination of the production process would require a separate book four times the size of this one,[191] so I'll restrict myself here with providing an outline of a multichannel recording studio's basic structure and explaining how to use the fundamental components.

The Layout Of A Surround Studio

At first glance, a surround studio looks little different from a normal studio for dual-channel stereo. There will normally be a recording room and an acoustically optimised control room. Even the control room looks much the same as that in a conventional studio, with the obligatory mixing console, multitrack recorders and a variety of peripheral devices housed in 19" racks.

The first difference is the number and placement of the monitor loudspeakers: in a dual-channel control room there should generally be five, plus perhaps a subwoofer,[192] arranged as per the ITU 775 recommendation.

The speaker configuration around the sweet spot is one of the most important features of the studio layout. The speakers are one of the few obligatory analogue components of a surround studio, and before they can produce any sound, the multichannel mix must undergo conversion from digital to analogue – ideally the first such conversion since the signals were converted to digital at the start of the recording process. Certain surround speaker systems, such as Dynaudio's Air system, can be driven with AES/EBU signals and the D/A conversion does not occur until just before the power amplifier stage. These systems have the additional advantage of having integrated processors capable of correcting any audio discolouration caused by poor speaker positioning, so optimal monitoring is possible even under less than ideal circumstances.

If you're fitting out a surround studio from scratch, you should take account of the extension of the frequency range brought about by sampling at 96kHz or 192kHz and using DSD-coded audio material. You can now buy monitoring loudspeakers that are capable of reproducing frequencies as high as 100kHz – the signal components that give the overall sound a more transparent and realistic sound than normal sampling rates are capable of reproducing – although this still isn't a good enough reason to throw out good monitors that are perhaps capable of reproducing frequencies only up to 22kHz. If the overall sound of the monitor is good, it will remain a valuable component of the studio. And besides, the upward extent of a monitor's frequency range is *a* factor, but it's far from being the most important one in determining its quality.

The next most important component of a recording studio is the mixing console. Even though a surround console might not look much different from a conventional dual-channel mixer, it differs in being able to place signals in the multichannel spectrum, mostly through the use of busses which route the signals to their desired destinations.

Instead of just using the a pan pot, the business of assigning signals in varying amounts to the available loudspeakers of a multichannel system (which is known as *surround panning*) is performed with the help of a graphical display of the loudspeaker configuration displaying the phantom sound sources. Given timecode support and a suitably equipped desk, it's even possible to place a moving source in the surround panorama and determine its path. Since with multichannel productions it's highly advantageous to keep the entire production process on the digital level, surround mixing consoles are generally digital. As well as allowing you to control the movement of phantom images, timecode synchronisation brings with it the possibility of automation.

To permit any assessment of the multichannel mix, a surround monitoring matrix is needed to control the total volume of all channels, the monitoring or muting of individual channels, a change of monitoring system and ideally the solo logic of the desk. This matrix can be regarded as the heart of the entire monitoring system and can either be integrated into the mixing console or be a stand-alone model.

In many cases, further processing of the source material is necessary prior to mastering. This could take the form of dynamic processing, sound correction or the addition of synthetic reverb. Since these tasks need to be performed for all channels at the same time, you can't use dual-channel processors; instead, you need a special multichannel processor like the TC System 6000[193]. Such devices usually have an open architecture that allows different multichannel algorithms to be combined with one another. Given a good multichannel recording that requires no further signals to be added to it, the entire business of processing can be left

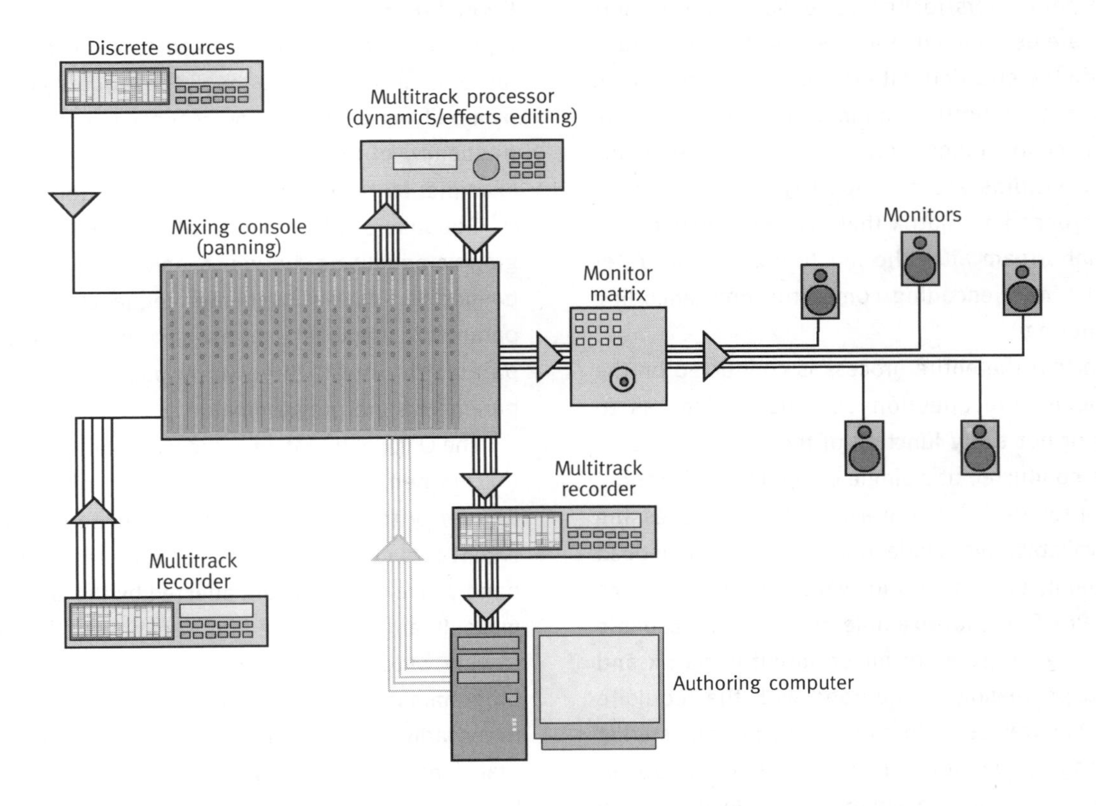

Figure 56: Schematic structure of a surround studio

to the processor, thus removing altogether the need for a mixing console.

When the multichannel mix is ready, the maximum level and the dynamic range have to be tailored to the application and the final mix once again recorded onto discrete tracks. This is generally done on a separate hard-disk recorder, which can then be used to encode the data directly, but it could be done just as well by some other recording device, provided that it offers the right number of tracks and supports the same audio resolution. (The ITU 775 recommendations regarding track assignment should be complied with here, too.)

The final step is the encoding of the discrete channels into a data stream. This encoding is not, strictly speaking, part of the audio processing, and is not even performed in the recording studio in most cases, but is instead carried out by a special authoring workstation which processes the DVD, SACD or sound film. Nonetheless, this encoding is an important element of the entire process, since it's at this stage that the parameters for the corresponding downmix matrices are determined. And besides, it's a good idea to decode the encoded data stream one more time in order to determine the minimum data transfer rate and to check for coding errors. For this purpose, many surround studios are equipped with a switchable encoding/decoding matrix that can be switched into the signal stream after the mastering section. After this preliminary encoding comes the final encoding and authoring.

Given that the entire process is conducted on the digital level, the question obviously arises as to whether or not every function of the surround studio could be conducted at a single computer workstation. Indeed, provided that there's sufficient processing power available, this is indeed a possibility, and indeed many (mainly project) studios work this way. Systems such as Pro Tools, for example, are perfectly capable of assuming the roles of mixer, monitor matrix and surround processor (if equipped with the requisite plugins[194]) as well as performing the tasks of mastering and encoding. As long as there's enough power available, it's possible to achieve highly flexible studio configurations this way.

Important Studio Components And Their Uses

FILTERS

Filters allow part of the frequency range to pass unhindered and attenuate the other part or parts, and come in three flavours: high-pass, low-pass and band-pass. These terms are pretty much self-explanatory: a band-pass filter attenuates frequencies both above and below a specific band, for instance. In the case of variable filters, the frequency at which the attenuation begins to take effect – strictly speaking, at which the signal is attenuated by 3dB – is known as the *corner cut-off-frequency* or the *roll-off-frequency*, or else as the *3dB down point*, and the rate of attenuation (measured in decibels per octave) is known as the *filter slope* or *roll-off rate*. Microphones are often equipped with switchable high-pass filters (also called 'low-cut filters') to eliminate footfall, handling noise and other types of solid-borne sound; the 3dB down point and roll-off rate in such cases is not normally adjustable.[195]

EQUALISERS

Equalisers[196] are primarily used to correct any tonal discolouration (to make the output *equal* to the input) by modifying the frequency response (amplitude versus frequency) of the signals passing through them – for example, by boosting the bass or the treble.

Equalisers fall into one of two distinct groups: graphic equalisers, on which only the amplitude can be modified but not the corner frequencies and Q; and parametric equalisers, with which the first two (semi-parametric) or all three (fully parametric) of these parameters are programmable.

The Q (Quality) rating is the width of the filter 'skirt' (in mathematical terms, the ratio of the centre frequency to the bandwidth) and it determines the extent to which the frequencies on either side of the band you're modifying are affected by the changes you make. It range can range from very narrow (1/20 octave) to very wide (three octaves or more). If the Q is not programmable, however (which is not to say that it's necessarily constant), an intermediate value is chosen that depends to a certain extent upon the number of bands provided by the equaliser.

Equalisers are mostly applied to mono signals and

can be used to raise the profile of quiet sound sources within the overall sonic image in a more subtle fashion than the crude application of gain. In a live mix, of course, you might want to put an equaliser in the sum – for example, to attenuate booming frequencies or feedback – but in the studio this should never be necessary.

COMPRESSORS, EXPANDERS AND LIMITERS

These three device control in various ways the level of the signal and are known collectively as *dynamic processors*.

Compressors reduce the dynamic range of a signal passing through it. This can be useful on occasions when you want to improve the compatibility of instruments with widely different dynamic ranges, such as the grand piano and guitar. Originally, compressors were designed to make loud sounds quieter and quiet sounds louder (applied to vocals, this could result in the singers' breathing becoming almost as loud as their voices, and is indeed an effect still often heard in recordings), but more often a threshold is set beneath which no changes occur, in which case the only effect is that the loudest signals are turned down (ie their dynamic range is reduced.)

Compression is frequently applied to the sum (the main L/R output), particularly in pop music.[197] In this case, the quiet passages *are* made louder, so that they can be heard above the noise of a car engine, for example, and also to increase the subjective impression of loudness. There are pop recordings being released nowadays that have a dynamic range of only 1dB over the entire track, and further compression is often added by radio stations anxious to (appear to) be the loudest without exceeding the legal limits. The effect, of course, is to eliminate dynamic expression altogether from the performer's bag of tricks, but there you go.

Compressors offer two basic parameters: threshold and ratio. As soon as the level goes over the threshold, it's compressed by an amount determined by the ratio; if the ratio is 4:1, for example, then once the threshold has been exceeded, a further increase of 4dB in the input will result in an increase of only 1dB in the output. Suppose, for example, the maximum level of an uncompressed recording is 0dB (as shown in Figure 57, the straight line beginning at –50dB in the bottom-left-hand corner and extending to 0dB near the top-right-hand corner) and we set the threshold to –20dB and the ratio to 2:1. After compression (marked out by the bold line following the same course as before but deviating at the threshold), the maximum level would be only –10dB.[198] This makes it possible now to raise the overall level by 10dB without the original maximum level (0dB) being overstepped (illustrated by the thin line running parallel to the bold line and deviating at –10dB). Compressors usually provide two additional parameters – attack and release – that control the speed at which the compressor reacts when the level exceeds and drops back below the threshold, respectively.

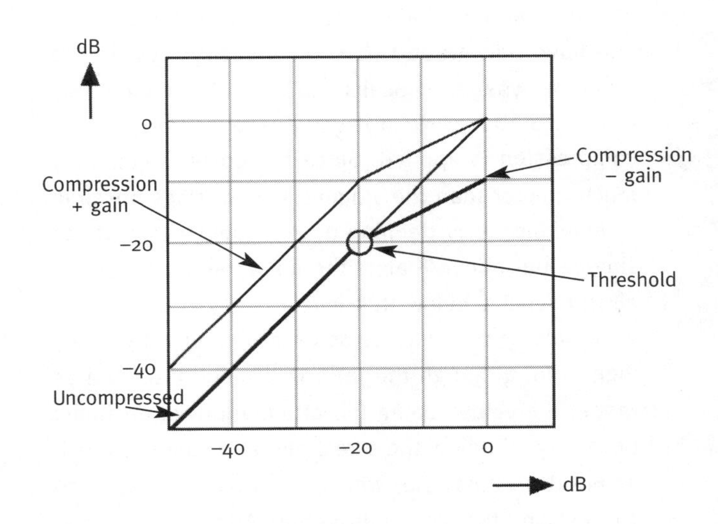

Figure 57: Amplitude before and after compression

Multiband compressors represent a further refinement of the theme of compression. These are generally used in the sum and they divide the signal into various frequency bands, applying variable amounts of compression to each, so that, for example, the bass is more strongly compressed than the treble and midrange. After compression, 10dB of gain can be added to the signal without exceeding the original maximum level.

An expander is the opposite of a compressor: it increases the dynamic range of a recording. Ideally the compressor and limiter should operate as a pair, offering the same parameters and levels.[199]

A limiter is designed to prevent the signal from going over the maximum permitted level at all. Essentially it's just a compressor with the ratio set to 20:1 and a with very fast response (ie attack and release rates). For instance, you might want to set the threshold to a level slightly below the legally permitted limit to eliminate the risk of contravening regulations to control noise levels.

Limiters are almost always used in the sum and should affect only peaks, as constant limiting noticeably reduces the quality of a recording.[200]

NOISE GATES AND DENOISERS

A noise gate is a processor that lets only those signals above a certain minimum level pass. If, for example you have background noise in a vocal track, in the moments when the vocalist isn't actually singing, this noise can be quite obtrusive – even more so if compression is applied. Since the noise is generally much quieter than the singing, however, it's possible to eliminate it by defining a level (below that of the singing but above that of the noise) and attenuating all frequencies below that level.

A noise gate operates as an expander with a very high ratio, although the ratio is usually described as *range*, the values being the attenuation (in decibels) of the signal below the threshold, and values as high as 80dB are possible, which is almost equivalent to suppressing the signal altogether. Attack and release parameters can also be set.

Noise gates are especially valuable when recording drums as, without them, noise from the snare drum (for example) can easily spill into the hi-hat mic and vice versa, making it impossible to process the signals of the two instruments separately. Finding the right threshold values in this case, however, is an art, as the difference in volume between the instrument you want (played quietly) and the one you don't (played loudly) might not be very great.[201]

Denoisers are frequency-dependent level amplifiers that attenuate the high-frequency signal elements of the sum when the output level is low. Normally, at low levels, no high-frequency signal elements are required, so attenuating them has little effect upon the overall sound. High-frequency hiss, on the other hand, can be very distracting during quiet passages, and since it's this that the denoisers eliminates, the result is a far more pleasant sonic image. At loud volume levels, the natural high-frequency content of the program material is very loud and drowns out the noise.

Most denoisers are also programmable, with variable parameters governing threshold and degree of attenuation, as well as attack and release times.[202]

EFFECTS

It would be hard to imagine popular music – still less cinema sound – without the extensive use of effects of all kinds. By *effects* I mean artificial reverb, as well as delay, phasing, flanging, chorus and harmonising, either singly or in combination. Many modern multi-effects units offer several and sometimes all of the above. Other devices specialise in a single effect and these are generally regarded as *reference effects units*, examples being the Lexicon Reverb or Eventide Harmonizer. In the case of workstations and hard-disk recording systems, effects devices usually come in the form of plugins.[203]

Reverb effects are designed to give recordings a more natural spatial impression (for example, by simulating the effect of sound reflecting from walls and ceilings). For post-production work on films, in particular, there are a series of high-quality reverb units on the market capable of simulating the acoustics of various surroundings – a car interior, for example, or a bathroom – for dialogue. It has to be said, however, that reverb effects can't compete with natural reverberation; artificial reverb sounds a little unnatural, and since one of the prime objectives of multichannel recording is a more natural sound, wherever possible the diffuse sound should be captured with a microphone rather than simulated using reverb. All the same, reverb units are the most important of all effects devices in the studio.

Delay and echo effects, meanwhile, store the signal for short periods and then release it. Much use is made of the latter in music production, especially for vocals and instrument solos.

Another frequently used effect, the phaser, operates

by way of a narrow notch filter sweeping up and down through a given frequency range, with the output then summed with the original input to create the effect of a sweeping comb filter.

With a flanger, the effect is much the same, only more pronounced. Here, though, signal delay is used to simulate the effect of two identical signals running in parallel, with each in turn slowing slightly.

Chorus, meanwhile, imitates the small blemishes that result from the imperfect doubling of instrumental or vocal parts. Like phasing and flanging effects, chorus can be used to give a mono source a two-channel stereo feel.

Harmonisers or pitch-shifters alter the pitch of signals without influencing their duration. Similar devices are often referred to as *octavers*. The altered signals can either replace the original or be added to it. There's a difference between static harmonisers (which invariably raise the pitch of a signal by a set amount) and intelligent harmonisers (which recognise the pitch of the input signal and refer to a predetermined scale to determine whether a minor sixth or a major sixth, for example, is called for, providing a simple, if somewhat crude, method of part-writing).

Processing Tasks

This section takes a closer look at the separate steps involved in the post-production process. Since no two sound engineers work exactly the same way, and since the process in any case is heavily dependent on the nature of the source material, the purpose of the recording and the genre, we're not dealing with a fixed set of tasks that must invariably be performed in a set order. Nonetheless, it may prove instructive to describe a few such tasks.

Surround Panning

Panning is the process of assigning to each mono source a position in the stereo image. In the case of multichannel stereo, the process is known as *surround panning*.

Whilst the circuitry required to implement this process for dual channel stereo is relatively simple, when more than two channels are involved, a considerable amount of processing is required to calculate how much of the signal of each source needs to be sent to each channel in order for the phantom image of that source to appear at the desired location. For this reason, you need a digital matrix equipped with digital signal processors, the exact power and number of which depends on the number of channels involved. The configuration of the matrix is tailored to the current playback format and speaker configuration.

Once the surround panning has been performed, there's usually no going back in terms of choice of playback format. Even so, it makes sense to perform the panning fairly early in the post-production stage, as a number of other tasks can't really be performed until the process of panning is complete. Normally, the graphic interface displays the speaker configuration as well as indicating the position of the phantom image of each sound source within it. Figure 58 illustrates two possible formats for the user interface.

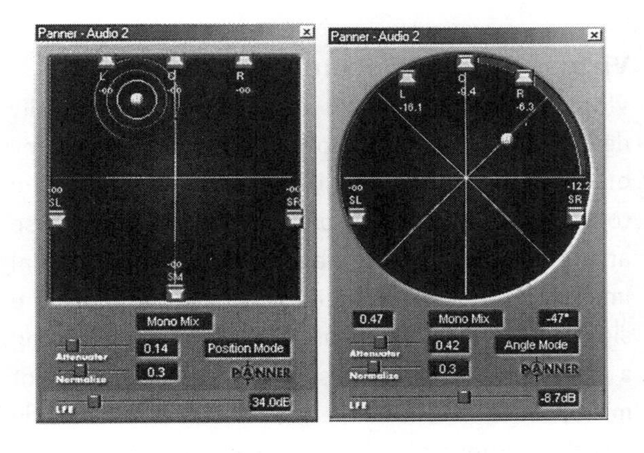

Figure 58: Surround panning interfaces for 6.1 cinema and 5.1 home formats

Surround panning is generally a standard feature of multichannel mixing consoles and hard-disk recording systems. Timecode automation also permits the simulated movement of sound sources, whereby the path and duration of each movement is specified so that, during playback, the position of the source within the matrix is moved in real time. This is especially important for film post-production, where sound sources are constantly moving and this movement can't always be recorded as production audio. Figure 59 illustrates the panning of a moving sound source using the channel matrix of a Sony DMX R–100 console.

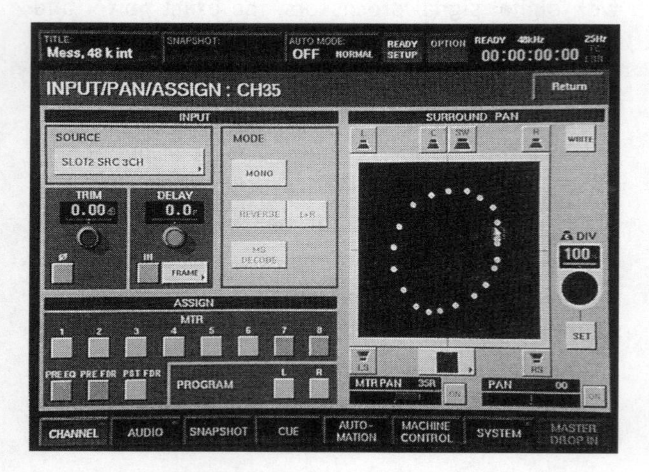

Figure 59: Panning a moving sound source

Virtual Surround Panning

Virtual Surround Panning is a special process originally developed by Studer but now also available from many other manufacturers. VSP is predicated on the desire to free sound engineers from the need to compromise at the post-production stage between good spatial imaging and acoustic balance when combining the signals of main and spot mics. The problem with using a main microphone for its spatial impression and spot microphones to capture the sound sources individually (for the purpose of balance correction) is that, when you come to mix them all together, no matter how careful you might be to assign the mono signals (from the spot microphones) to their correct positions in the sonic image, it doesn't alter the fact that the more mono signal you add to the mix, the greater the tendency for the diffuse sound to be drowned out, so that the spatial image gradually fades.

Studer's solution is to simulate (for the mono sound sources only) both the early reflections and the late reflections (reverberation) that would be generated in a simulated room, the acoustic properties of which have been tuned as closely as possible to match that of the actual room (the Albert Hall was used in one test).

Unlike conventional processors that create artificial reverberation, VST enhances rather than replaces the natural reverberation of the room; the recorded reverberation captured by the main and ambience microphones is still present in the recording. VST ensures that, as the mono signals of the spot mics are added to the mix, their (simulated) reflections are added in the same measure, so that the balance between direct and indirect sound is preserved.

Besides calculating the early reflections (based on the virtual positions within the room that have been assigned to each mono sound source), VSP panning employs the complete toolbox of intensity, time-of-arrival and frequency-response cues to assist localisation, revealing not only the direction but also the distance (depth) of each sound source. The primary benefit of VSP is a heightening of the sense of 'being there' (which is known as *envelopment*), although the improved sharpness of both the directional and the depth imaging is also a valuable spin-off.

Surround-Sound Processing

Processing is one of the most time-consuming tasks in a recording studio. There are a great many tasks involved, including level adjustment, frequency-response correction (using filters and EQ), dynamic processing (using compressors, expanders and limiters), noise reduction (using noise gates and denoisers) and the addition of sound effects (using a variety of effects units or a multi-effects unit).

The processing of multichannel recordings imposes a far heavier burden upon processors than that of dual-channel recordings. The problem is that the various channels are interdependent, so that if there's a change in one channel, the repercussions on each of the other channels has to be calculated – for instance, when an alteration in the tone of a source in one or more of the front channels is matched by a corresponding change in the tone of the diffuse sound in the rear channels. Conventional two-channel processors therefore can't be used for surround applications, as they are incapable of calculating the interaction between more that two channels at a time. Doubtless because of this complexity, there are very few dedicated surround processors on the market, which is why the few that really can cut the mustard – the Lexicon 960L, TC System 6000 and Yamaha's SREV 1 – can be found in virtually all surround studios.

The SREV1 occupies a special position since it's a convolution-sampling-based reverb with only four channels, and therefore supports neither the 3/2 nor the 5.1 format, so I'll omit it from the discussion that follows. The same goes for the numerous plugins that are now available for computer-supported production systems since, even though they may offer extensive processing possibilities, their exact specifications are constantly changing, as with most software in general.

The other two best-known multichannel processors – the Lexicon 960L and the TC System 6000 – represent the state of the art in surround-sound processing. Here's a short introduction to each, along with a brief synopsis of a relatively new dynamic processor, the Orion, made by the Berlin firm Jünger Audio. (No inferences should be drawn from the order in which they are presented.)

LEXICON 960L

The Lexicon 960L[204] is the successor to the well-known Lexicon 480L studio reverb. Strictly speaking, it's a stand-alone computer with a powerful DSP card as well as eight digital inputs and outputs. A second DSP card can be added, thereby doubling the processing power, and additional inputs and outputs can be incorporated.

Figure 60: Lexicon 960L mainframe and LARC2 remote control

The 960L operates throughout in 24-bit resolution at sampling rates up to 96kHz. Configuration and editing are performed using a remote control. In large studio complexes with several control rooms, several remote controls can access the same mainframe. A CD-ROM drive is integrated, allowing the user to update the operating system.

The configuration of the 960L is variable – ie the inputs and outputs can be mapped individually to the DSPs that perform the necessary calculations. For multichannel audio, two DSPs are provided for each channel, so the 960L is capable of producing two[205] multichannel effects simultaneously.[206] Surround panning is used to position the discrete source signals in the acoustic environment generated. The 960L is equipped with special algorithms that can place dual-channel recordings in a multichannel spectrum. The additional phantom channels are obtained through matrixing, to create a pseudo-multichannel format.

The Lexicon 960L is a true multichannel effects and reverb device that enjoys reference status due to the quality of the acoustic environments it produces. It's generally considered to be the best reverb processor on the market.

TC SYSTEM 6000

The TC System 6000[207] is similar in structure to the Lexicon 960L, as it too has a stand-alone mainframe accommodating the entire processing unit with four DSPs. The inputs and outputs can be expanded in a modular fashion either with eight-channel AES/EBU or four dual-channel analogue I/O cards, with the upper limit being 16 digital or analogue inputs and outputs. The system comes with a separate communication interface, the CPU6000, which allows multiple remote controls to access multiple frames via standard Ethernet connections, while USB ports allow a range of standard USB controllers to access the functions of the connected System 6000 mainframes. The Icon desktop control unit (shown in Figure 62 over the page). offers a colour touch-sensitive screen and six touch-sensitive motorised faders.

The System 6000 operates in 24-bit resolution at sampling rates up to 96kHz, although all the basic

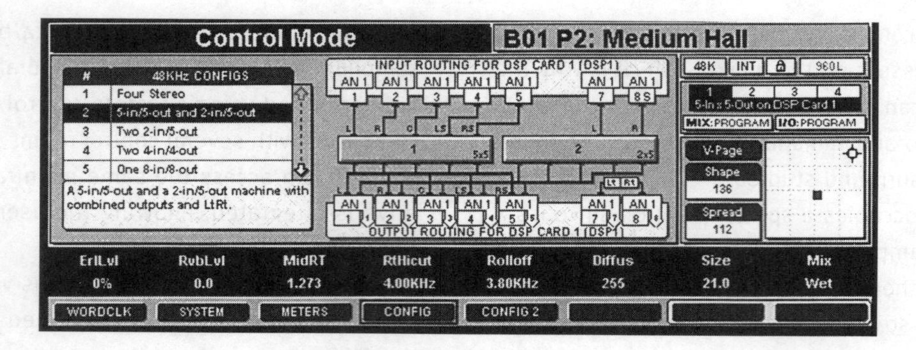

Figure 61: Configuration and sound panning using the Lexicon 960L

configurations relate to 44.1kHz or 48kHz. Therefore, if the 96kHz format is selected, only two DSPs are effectively available.

The operating system of the System 6000 can also be updated, and a free slot for an additional DSP card means that you can ensure that it has sufficient processing power for the future.

Figure 62: TC Icon – the remote control for the System 6000

Like the 960L, the System 6000 is freely configurable, and all the inputs and outputs can be connected to the four processing engines or each other, as shown in Figure 63. Unlike other effects units, the various programs don't all come as standard but can be purchased when required, allowing the device to be adapted to the current application. The algorithms are purchased as bundles and can also be retrofitted.

In addition to the reverb and modulation effects that come as standard, there's a special audio restoration package and a 5.1 package for multichannel audio. Along with numerous multichannel reverb and ambience effects, this contains a multiband dynamic processor (shown in Figure 63), equaliser and pitch-shifter for multichannel audio as well as a 5.1 toolbox that fulfils a wide range of monitor matrix functions. Naturally up to eight sources can be placed in the virtual acoustic spaces and even moved around by using the touch sensitive display or optional joystick.

For dual-channel stereo editing, the System 6000 offers not only dual-channel versions of the aforementioned functions but also a series of additional effects, such as a phaser, chorus, delay and binaural mapping.

These optional algorithms make the TC System 6000 the most flexible stand-alone multichannel effects device currently on the market, and the only one that covers not only effects but also the entire area of post-production for multichannel audio. The System 6000's multichannel compressor/limiter algorithms make it the ideal solution for the mastering of multichannel recordings in 5.1 format, and the quality of the signal processing is also very high.

For all these reasons, the TC System 6000 is to be found in virtually every multichannel studio and is regarded as an unparalleled piece of equipment by most users.

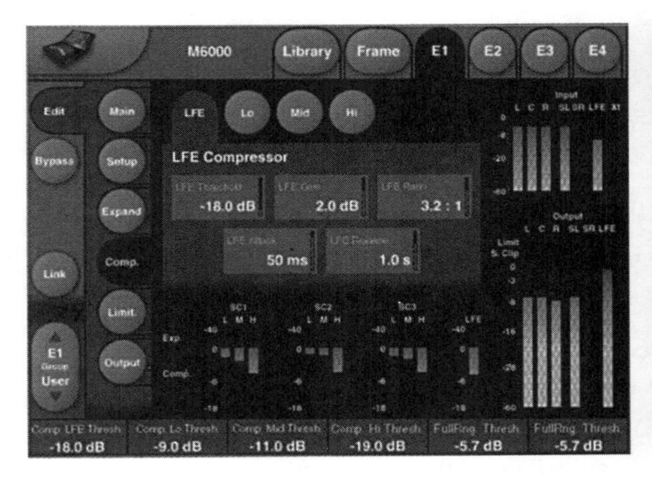

Figure 63: The multichannel multiband compressor and monitor matrix of the TC System 6000

JÜNGER AUDIO ORION

Unlike the last two systems, Jünger's Audio Orion is not a multi-effects unit; its capabilities are limited to dynamic processing, but it's specially tailored to the special demands of multichannel audio and offers a number of highly innovative and interesting possibilities.

Like the Lexicon and TC Electronics devices, the Orion is based around a modular 19" mainframe equipped with two DSP cards, eight AES/EBU inputs and outputs, and countless synchronisation possibilities. The basic system can also be equipped with analogue inputs and outputs as an option as well as MADI/SPI or AES/EBU interfaces with sample-rate conversion. The system can be controlled by any PC running Windows NT4.

What is especially interesting about the Orion is the fact that it allows the integration of an 'embedded PC' in the mainframe, thus transforming it into an independent system. The system comes as standard with the Orion Control remote-control unit, which provides direct access to parameters via four faders and three rotary controls.

Figure 64: Jünger Audio Orion with Orion Control

The Jünger Audio Orion is based on the compression algorithms Jünger developed for their Access series and are notable for their wide-ranging automation capability, whereby, unlike conventional compressors, loud levels are not attenuated but quiet ones are adaptively amplified, depending upon the input level. Therefore, the quieter the input signal is, the higher the boost in level. In order to prevent noise from being amplified unnecessarily, the maximum level boost can be set in advance, with 10dB being a sensible figure. The great advantage of this system is that dynamic differences may be reduced but their structure is preserved, with the result that the material sounds more natural. In times of multiple sum compression – with broadcasters the principal culprits – this is a commendable new approach.

What's special about Orion is the use of these algorithms for surround processing, especially with the advent of Dynalink technology, which makes it possible to link up dynamically the gain controls of correlated audio channels, as well as allowing flexible, user-defined adjustment of dynamic links. For example, the amount by which the levels of the surround channels is raised can be linked to the levels of the LCR channels, thus preserving envelopment during quiet passages, or the centre-channel compression during film production can be linked to the level of the L/R channels to ensure that intelligibility is maintained even during loud scenes, especially around the edges of the sweet spot. All these processes take effect rapidly and without disturbing artefacts such as pumping or the amplification of the noise floor, thanks to the Orion's largely automatic and adaptive algorithms.

With the Orion Control, the most important parameters are always under your control, and the PC-supported user interface can be used for a multitude of other tasks, such as controlling the link and gang functions, link editing, preset and project administration, track assignment, memory and input switching and so on. With all this in place, the Orion is capable of adapting swiftly to any conceivable variety of multichannel processing, performing outstanding service, but doing it unobtrusively, which is the hallmark of a good dynamic processor.[208]

Mixing

If the task of mixing traditional dual-channel stereo is mainly limited to assigning each sound source a place in the spectrum and then adding sound processing, the additional channels involved in surround processing offer a great deal of scope for creativity. Depending on your aims, you can use the centre and surround channels to improve the spatial impression or to position sound sources with maximum precision.

Despite the relative freedom of the user when mixing multichannel audio, there are certain guidelines[209] that are worth following. These are designed primarily to improve spatial imaging.

FRONT CHANNELS[210]

When mixing the front (or 'screen') channels, you now have three channels instead of just two at your disposal. Whereas before, if you wanted to place a sound source in the centre of the stereo image, the only way of doing so was to assign the signal in equal amounts to the right and left channels (which was fine for listeners who were ideally placed), the new centre channel offers you a more satisfactory option. By assigning the signal to the centre channel, you can ensure that the signal can be correctly localised by listeners anywhere in the room. This is one reason why, in cinema systems, there are sometimes as many as three centre channels: LC, C and RC.

However, assigning a sound source exclusively to the centre channel can result in a very cramped or fragmented sonic image. It's therefore usually a better idea to assign parts of the signal to the sides, in effect creating a phantom image of the same source in the same place. That said, creating a fully-fledged phantom source in the dead centre of the sonic image is an extreme measure that's best avoided, since it increases the likelihood of introducing noticeable comb-filter effects, most likely to be heard by those at the sides of the listening area. True, such effects can be eliminated to a large extent by modifying the pitch or presence of the side channels relative to the main centre signal, but often just the level of the centre channel is reduced (usually by –3dB, especially with centre matrixing) to give the side channels more presence.

The existence to two additional triangles – listener, left speaker, centre speaker, and listener, centre speaker, right speaker – extends the possibilities for frontal signal assignment. Since the speakers are closer together, phantom sound sources can be localised more precisely and the front sonic image is consequently more stable. When a main microphone technique (such as ICA 3) is employed, the positioning of mics should take this into account.

When it comes to the triangle formed by the listener and the left and right speakers, the spatial impression can be improved by adding to each channel phase-inverted portions of the other's signal, as this results in a broadening of the sonic image. When combined with the rear channels, this helps to envelop the listener, and any tendency for a hole to appear in the centre of the sonic image can be counteracted through the use of the centre channel. Care must be taken, however, that the gains in spatial impression and envelopment aren't at the expense of an excessive blurring of the phantom images.

SURROUND CHANNELS[211]

If the addition of the centre channel represents an extension of the possibilities of dual-channel stereo, the surround channels introduce a whole new dimension, and while their use in films has been relatively clearly defined, in music production there's still plenty of room for experimentation.

In the case of classical recordings, the surround channels are normally used to reproduce reflections from the rear of the concert hall, the idea being to recreate the aural impressions obtained from occupying the best seat in the house, and the surround speakers should therefore carry no direct sound; they're there to support, not divert attention from, the front channels. As with the front corner channels, here, too, it's possible to supply a little of the (out-of-phase) surround-left signal to the surround-right channel in order to increase the breadth of the image and thus improve envelopment. The fact that a hole may appear in the sonic image midway between the rear speakers isn't too much of a problem, given the limited ability of humans to localise sounds coming from directly behind them. Of course, if a 6.1 speaker configuration is used, with a central channel supplied by a Gerzon matrix, this isn't a problem.

Multichannel audio is not tied to this concept, however. For example, it's perfectly possible to give the listener the impression of sitting in the middle of a circle of musicians, in which case the surround channels would be reproducing discrete sources; the frontal sources would still tend to predominate, simply because of the way in which we hear sounds, but the aim of not distracting the listener unduly from the front sonic image is perfectly consistent with the type of arrangement described here.

LFE[212]

The most common misconception regarding the LFE channel is to equate it with a subwoofer; while a subwoofer reproduces the low frequency range of all the channels – or, at least, of the left and right channels – the LFE is a discrete (albeit frequency-limited) reproduction channel. The fact that both tasks are capable of being performed by the same device (the subwoofer) is no reason to confuse them.

An important point to bear in mind when dealing with the LFE channel is that no source should ever be assigned to it exclusively, for two reasons: firstly, because it's impractical, due to the limited bandwidth; and secondly, because the LFE channel is optional, which means that it has to be possible to reproduce all sources and signals on a system that doesn't have it. Therefore, only the very lowest frequency components of bass-laden effects should be assigned to the LFE channel; the rest should be directed elsewhere, usually to the main L and R channels. To ensure the lowest frequencies have sufficient penetration, the LFE channel is usually 10dB louder than the other channels, although obviously the maximum permitted level must not be exceeded.

Many loudspeaker configurations take advantage of the presence of a subwoofer to employ smaller loudspeakers for the front and surround channels, in which case all frequencies below a certain level (usually 120Hz) are assigned to the subwoofer. In order to compensate for the fact that in such systems the subwoofer often is performing two tasks, it's a good idea to check how the mix would sound on such a system using bass management. This involves putting an electronic bass-frequency crossover (in this case, at 120Hz) on all the channels and redirecting the bass frequencies below 120Hz from each of the channels to a common subwoofer. This has absolutely no effect on the actual mix, and indeed many multichannel processors support such bass management.

DOWNMIX AND UPMIX[213]

Downmixing a multichannel mix for a playback format with fewer channels is an essential and frequently performed task, involving an intelligent reassignment of all relevant sources to the channels actually available. There are three basic ways of doing this: you can either create a separate mix in the relevant format, you can set the individual parameters for the downmix matrix or you can let the decoder perform the entire task automatically.

This last option doesn't really merit serious consideration, since it involves abdicating all control over the sonic image; the decoder will consult the existing channel ratios for orientation, and while acceptable results may be achieved occasionally, the results generally tend to be unsatisfactory.

One example of the second option occurs during the authoring of an audio-format DVD, when it's possible to define an individual downmix, thereby retaining a certain degree of influence over the new mix. This involves defining the mixing ratios of the individual channels. For downmixing from 3/2 to 2/0, for example, Theile recommends a ratio of Lo = L + 0,7C + k LS and Ro = R + 0,7C + k RS, whereby the factor *k* determines the proportion of diffuse sound, which can be anything from 0 to 1, although the recommended ITU 775 value is 0.7. (Incidentally, if you're trying to create a multichannel mix from a dual-channel mix – ie upmixing – *k* should always equal 0.[214])

Meanwhile, the first option – creating a separate mix in the desired format – obviously provides the highest level of control over the quality of reproduction and should certainly be regarded as the best solution. In the case of DVD playback, there are eight tracks available, which leaves room for both the six tracks of a 5.1 mix and a separate dual-channel mix.

As well as compatibility with dual-channel reproduction, traditionally the DVD should also be capable of playing back in Dolby Surround format. The Dolby Surround downmix is easier to control than the stereo downmix, so a separate mix is normally not necessary. Downmixing to Dolby Surround generally involves summing the surround channels and lowering their levels accordingly. The signal of the centre channel (insofar as it's not already present in them) is divided equally between the L and R channels to create a phantom source in the centre of the sonic image. Theoretically, Dolby Surround can be encoded in two channels, but this is inadvisable; a Dolby Surround mix produced from a 5.1 mix should sound better, if only because of the presence of a fully-fledged surround channel.

A little earlier, I referred briefly to upmixing. This process usually involves the creation of a surround mix from a dual-channel or mono mix. The actual number of channels, however, isn't of essential importance, but the process is known as *upmixing* only as long as the output contains more channels than the source. Many DVD reissues of old films contain upmix formats, although really you have to wonder why the manufacturers bother; rather than experiencing an increase in quality, a good dual-channel mix often loses quality as a result of upmixing. If discrete source material is available, it would be better to create a new multichannel mix from scratch. In many cases, anyway, an upmix is totally superfluous; an old black-and-white film, for example, lacks authenticity in 5.1 format, and in many cases the original mix is far more appropriate. It's a mistake to assume that you'll automatically make something better by converting it from its original format into a newer one.

If you do have to perform an upmix, you might as well resign yourself to the fact that localisation of the individual sound sources is going to suffer. In most cases, upmixing will involve generating a 3/2 signal from 2/0. A Gerzon matrix is the most practical solution for the centre channel, while for the surround channels the L/R signals are generally used, out of phase and attenuated to make them seem like reflections. However, you should take special care with the downmix parameters of multichannel recordings that were created through the use of an upmix.

Mastering

Mastering represents the final point of the sound-processing stage of production. Here, the dynamics of the final mix will be checked one last time before the mix is stored in the designated playback format.

In the case of multichannel recordings, the reference quality is also defined at the mastering stage. If a lossless system has been used for the storage, no loss will occur at the encoding stage, but if lossy compression has been used, the reproduction quality of the mix will deteriorate further after mastering.

Mastering multichannel stereo is essentially little different to mastering dual-channel stereo. Usually compression is applied to the sum until the desired dynamic range has been achieved, after which limiting is applied in order to ensure that the maximum permissible level is not exceeded. If, for example, a multichannel recording is going to be stored on DVD, the maximum level is odB. If the same material is destined for broadcast, however, the maximum level is only –9dB.[215] It's advisable to check how the mix sounds over various monitor configurations as well as under living-room conditions.

When the mix is finished and all the levels have been set, the complete recording is transferred to as many tracks as the selected format requires. This final recording will form the basis of all subsequent formats, since access to the source material will be impossible after this. Since in most cases the next stage is the encoding of the multichannel recording, it's therefore advisable to record to a hard disk, from which it's then possible to record the encoded data stream to the authoring workstation's hard disk.

In order to avoid incurring encoding errors and be able to listen to the recording in its final quality, after the mastering stage many sound engineers encode the material in the desired transmission format and then decode it again.

Encoding

Since the capacity of all data-storage media is limited, the problem often arises concerning how best to reduce the data to manageable proportions. In the past, the few storage media capable of storing the vast amounts of data required by multichannel audio – whether or not it was combined with video – were prohibitively expensive. With the advent of DVD, however, there is now an affordable storage medium capable of satisfying the demands of modern video and multichannel sound reproduction.

However, there is a limit to the amount of data that even DVD is capable of storing, and also a limit to how much data can be read from it. With DVD-Audio, where it's almost exclusively audio data that's being played back, there's enough bandwidth for uncompressed (and therefore error-free) multichannel sound, while with films, the fact that both images and sound have to be played back at the same time means that the use of lossy compression of the video and sound material is unavoidable.

There are great differences between the various encoding formats and not all are equally suitable for every medium. Some are defined in standards while others are merely optional formats permitted in combination with standard ones. The quality of the compression also varies from format to format, and the choice of encoding format can therefore have a decisive effect upon the quality of the final recording. So it would be useful perhaps to look now at the most important encoding formats for multichannel audio and their primary areas of application. (No value judgement should be inferred from the order in which each format is presented here.)

Lossy Encoding And Delivery Formats

DOLBY SURROUND AND SURROUND PRO LOGIC[216]

Dolby Surround is an analogue matrix transmission format in which a centre channel and a frequency-limited[217] mono rear channel are encoded into a dual-channel stereo signal. The level of the centre channel is reduced by 3dB and the signal is then assigned in equal amounts to the main L and R channels. During playback, either a phantom centre channel is formed or the centre channel is separated using a matrix and played back through a separate loudspeaker.

The level of the surround channel is also reduced by 3dB during encoding, and an additional band-pass filter and a noise-reduction system are applied to the channel. Then the surround channel is added in equal proportions but with a ±90° phase reversal to the L

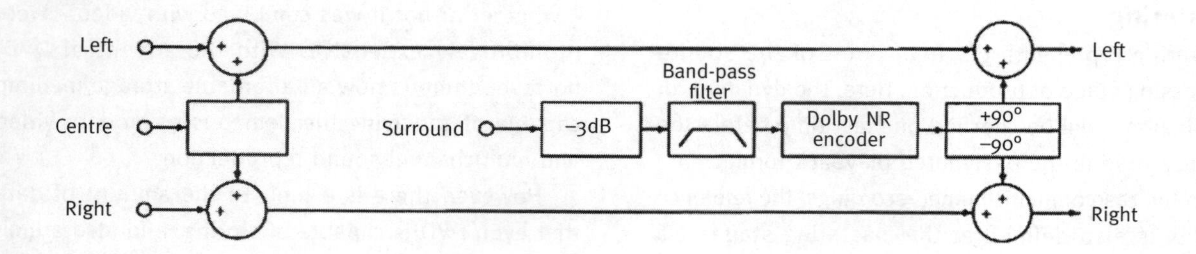

Figure 65: Dolby Surround Pro Logic signal encoding

and R channels, as shown in Figure 65. During playback, the decoder recognises this difference in the channels and assigns the signal to the surround channel. The surround channel then cancels itself in the main channels as a result of the phase reversal.

Since four channels are matrixed into two transmission channels – which, after decoding are then played back as four channels – Dolby Surround is described as a 4:2:4 encoding format for a (pseudo) 3/1 reproduction.

Dolby Surround is only important for dual-channel analogue media such as VHS cassettes and is almost exclusively confined to the reproduction of film sound. Standards such as the DVD standard stipulate for downward compatibility with Dolby Surround.

Dolby Surround Pro Logic, Pro Logic II and Pro Logic IIx are further developments of Dolby Surround. With Pro Logic, the sound reproduction was improved through a superior (synthetic) channel separation.

Then, at the beginning of 2001, Dolby Pro Logic II was released, the chief improvement here being the additional surround channel, so that Pro Logic II now represented a 'genuine' 3/2 format. The frequency range of the centre and surround channels had also been improved to 20Hz–30kHz. Dolby Pro Logic II is most often encountered in games consoles and car hi-fi systems.

The latest Dolby matrix system, Pro Logic IIx, was introduced in August 2003. Here, two additional surround channels and the so-called Movie, Game and Music modes are the chief difference between this system and its immediate predecessor. While the Movie mode assumes that material has already been mixed in surround, the Music mode – which is based on two-channel stereo material – is said to improve surround reproduction and eliminate the surround artefacts that, in the past, have been the cause of much criticism.[218]

MPEG-2 AUDIO/MPEG 2 AAC[219]

MPEG-2 is the standard video format[220] for DVD. The audio encoding format that goes with it is MPEG-2 Audio, which is essentially based upon MPEG-1.

MPEG-2 is a digital lossy encoding format for multichannel audio with up to eight channels. The channels are transmitted discretely, but with data reduction, to produce anything from 2:2:2 to 8:8:8 format results, depending on the output material.

Like MPEG-1, MPEG-2 is divided into various layers. The maximum compression for audio data in MPEG 2 format is around 12:1 and the data-transfer rate for six channels averages at 400kbps. MPEG-2 Audio is also backwards-compatible, so MPEG-2 recordings can be played back under MPEG-1 (the only limitation being that they are then limited to two channels).

MPEG-2 AAC (Advanced Audio Coding) is an improved version of MPEG-2 Audio for bit-rate-reduced multichannel transmission that has been specially designed to anticipate future developments. Technically, AAC can be regarded as a further development of MPEG-1 Layer 3 (better known as MP3), allowing up to 48 channels to be encoded in 24-bit resolution with sampling rates up to 96kHz. The average data-transfer rate for MPEG-2 AAC is around 50% less, even though there is no audible difference between the two formats.[221]

MPEG-2 Audio and MPEG-2 AAC are the ISO standard for multichannel audio encoding. In countries using the PAL norm, MPEG-2 is a key component of the DVD video standard and can be used in place of PCM Audio or AC-3.

AC-3 (DOLBY DIGITAL)

Audio Coding 3 (AC-3)[222] is the encoding standard for the Dolby Digital format, constituting a further multichannel development of the AC-2 algorithm. It was introduced in 1991 by Dolby Laboratories, initially intended for the reproduction of film sound.

AC-3 is designed as a 6:6:6 format for multichannel recordings with up to six channels and a sampling rate of up to 48kHz in 20-bit resolution. PCM material is compressed using a perceptual coding algorithm, the ratio of compression being around 10:1 at an average data rate of 384–448kbps for 5.1 audio and 192kbps for dual-channel stereo, in each case in 48kHz and 16-bit audio resolution. Admittedly, sample rates of 32 and 44.1kHz are possible using AC-3, but they are almost never used because the DVD standard stipulates for 48kHz. Using AC-3, it's possible to encode one to five channels with a frequency range of 3Hz–20kHz, in each case with an optional LFE channel limited to 120Hz.

When encoding dual-channel recordings, you can also choose between a stereo or a dual mono version with separate channel information. AC-3 can also be used for the encoding of Dolby Digital EX, with the out-of-phase analogue signal of the rear centre channel matrixed into the LS and RS channels. Since an analogous system is used to encode the surround channel with Dolby Surround, Dolby Digital EX's out-of-phase signal components make it downwards-compatible with Dolby Digital, although the rear centre channel requires a special decoder and its frequency range is limited.

AC-3 is one of the most widely used encoding formats in current use, since it forms part of the DVD video standard for multichannel audio worldwide. Every DVD video player must be capable of decoding AC-3 and deliver at least one discrete dual-channel stereo signal. In return, each DVD video must include one encoded format as an alternative to PCM, and AC-3 is usually chosen since DVD players all over the world are capable of decoding it. It's true that, in countries that use the PAL video standard, MPEG-2 Audio or MPEG-2 AAC can be used as an alternative, but they're seldom encountered; most DVD video titles use AC-3.

AC-3 is also the only encoding algorithm that's available for consumer use, so authoring programs such as Apple's DVD Studio Pro are capable of encoding multichannel recordings in AC-3. The other encoding formats are generally reserved for professional use.

DTS

DTS[223] (Digital Theatre System) is another encoding format developed for films. It was introduced in 1993 in the formats DTS Stereo, DTS 6 and DTS ES and is capable of handling up to seven channels in 24-bit resolution at sampling rates up to 96kHz (7:7:7). The codec (compression/decompression) employed by DTS is called Coherent Acoustics and is capable of encoding audio at a wide range of bit rates, although only two of these – 1509.25kbps (1509 for short), which is recommended, and 754.5kbps (754) – are compatible with the DVD standard.

The choice of bit rate is governed by the overall capacity of the disc and the maximum data transfer rate. In each case, the sample rate is 48kHz and the resolution 16 bits.

The DVD video norm also allows the decoding of DTS data in 96kHz and 24 bits, whereby the data is divided into a core stream and an extension stream, the ratio between which is selectable (eg 1.5Mbps + 380kbps). To ensure downwards compatibility, the core stream contains the normal 48kHz information and the extension stream the data added as a result of the 96kHz sampling.

Since this DTS extension is new, the first DVD players and discs capable of decoding 96kHz/24-bit material became available only as recently as 2002.

DTS can be used to encode recordings in 1/0, 2/0, 2/1, 2/2, 3/2 and 3/3 formats, in each case with the optional LFE channel. With the 3/3/1 format, it's possible to include a downwards-compatible matrix version (DTS ES Matrix 6.1), analogous to Dolby Digital EX, as well as a discrete seven-channel version (DTS Discrete 6.1).

DTS data-transfer rates are much higher than those of AC-3 or MPEG-2 Audio, but since the process involves less compression, the quality of the sound is considerably higher, which is why many sound engineers prefer it. Despite this, DTS can be played back only on video DVDs in combination with a standard format (PCM, MPEG-2, AC-3). Multichannel recordings in DTS are therefore relatively rare, even though they're preferable to AC-3. You sometimes see special-edition DVDs that offer both formats.

SDDS

SDDS[224] (Sony Dynamic Digital System) is an 8:8:8 format using Sony's own ATRAC codec that achieves a compression rate of around 5:1. Although SDDS, like DTS, can be used as a supplementary multichannel format on video DVDs, it's seldom encountered because few domestic players support it and because it uses a 5/2/1 configuration. In the cinema, however, SDDS is one of the most important formats due to its high playback quality.

DOLBY E

Dolby E[225] is a relatively new encoding format aimed particularly at the broadcasting industry. The basic idea behind it is to make it possible to transmit multichannel audio over two digital transmission channels. Dolby E encodes up to eight channels (20 bits, 48kHz) on two transmission channels and is therefore an 8:2:8 format with a bit rate of 1.9Mbps. Using Dolby E, eight discrete channels – for example, a complete 5.1 mix and a separate stereo or Dolby Surround mix – can be transmitted on one AES/EBU channel. In addition to the discrete channels, metadata can be transmitted, thus making it possible to achieve the optimal adaptation of playback in the home. In the future, Dolby E should be able to support 24-bit audio resolution.

Dolby E is especially important for post-production work, where the material can be encoded and decoded up to ten times without noticeable loss of sound quality. The sizes of the audio blocks also match those of the video blocks, thereby facilitating synchronisation. The comparatively high data-transfer rate provides an open processing base for encoded material and therefore helps to establish a standard for the digital transmission of multichannel audio. Dolby E is not yet a standard but is already regarded as such by many broadcasters.

Compensating For Lossy Compression

Unfortunately, some deterioration of the sonic image is inevitable whenever lossy compression is used. However, it's generally not noticeable, except in direct comparisons, and the popularity of systems such as MP3 would even suggest that a large number of listeners aren't too bothered whether the sound quality is compromised or not. On the other hand, it's reasonable to assume that those who invest in multichannel sound systems do so in the expectation that the sound quality is going to be better than that, say, of a mobile phone or a Discman.

The prevalence and need for encoding and compression systems, and the inevitable deterioration of the quality of the sonic image they bring with them, must be taken into account at the processing stage, prior to encoding. The extent of the deterioration varies from algorithm to algorithm, and also depends largely on the input. The quality of the spatial impression (one of the main objectives of multichannel recording) is generally the first thing to suffer, but peaks and sibilants also harden and acquire undue prominence within the overall sonic image. As a rule a thumb, the slower the bit rate, the greater the degree of deterioration.

With each production, it's therefore important that you keep comparing the sound after compression with the original to see what changes have taken place before going back to the uncompressed mix, applying processing and then encoding the material again – an expensive and tedious process. Other than a general warning to eliminate excessive peaks prior to encoding, there are no objective rules as to how best to avoid compression artefacts. A great deal of experience and practical knowhow is called for – especially at high compression rates – to ensure that the final product sounds as close as possible to the original. Beginners are advised to favour formats like DTS that apply less compression, even though they may be less widely used than AC-3 and the codecs in question more difficult to obtain.

Most of the research into the effects of lossy compression and the best ways to counteract them has been done on AC-3, since that's the system favoured by the DVD standard, but DTS (which is generally considered less culpable in this respect) has also come under the microscope, without yielding any kind of concrete results – other than the fact that each production presents a new set of problems and that combating them takes practice. The golden rule, it appears, is that there are no golden rules!

Lossless Encoding And Delivery Formats

PCM

PCM[226] (Pulse Code Modulation) isn't actually an encoding process but simply the most common system for the uncompressed sampling of analogue audio data. Nonetheless, it should be mentioned here since, with all digital media (CD, DVD, etc), you have the option of recording the uncompressed PCM data. The DVD-Video standard lists PCM alongside MPEG-2 and AC-3 as one of the three main audio standards and provides for up to eight channels in 24-bit resolution and sample rates as high as 96kHz. The DVD-Audio standard even provides for sampling at 192kHz, although in this case you're limited to dual-channel stereo. If you record the audio in PCM format, there's no deterioration in signal from the master, so PCM is one of the highest-quality recording formats out there.

MLP

MLP[227] (Meridian Lossless Packing) is the main encoding process for DVD-Audio. With MLP, it's possible to encode up to eight channels in either 16-bit or 24-bit resolution, and with sample rates as high as 192kHz, with no data loss. The compression rate is around 2:1, and the bit rate (depending upon the application) is somewhere between 1.4 and 9.4Mbps.

As with AC-3 and video players, every audio DVD player must support MLP. However, since the algorithm is relatively simple and is also licensed by Dolby, both formats can be decoded by the same chipset, hence the existence of dual-format DVD-Video/DVD-Audio players. For high-quality music productions on DVD audio, MLP and PCM are the two best formats, and here the fact that MLP doubles the capacity of the disc without any loss of quality obviously gives it the edge. With MLP, a single-layer DVD can store around 74 minutes of music in 5.1 format in 24-bit resolution with a sampling rate of 96kHz or 86 minutes of dual channel stereo in 24-bit resolution at 192kHz.

DSD

DSD[228] (Direct Stream Digital) is the encoding format for Sony's Super Audio CDs (SACDs). Unlike the systems discussed so far, all of which base their coding on a PCM data stream, DSD represents an alternative to PCM.

With DSD, the analogue signal is sampled at the extremely high sampling rate of 2.8MHz, which is 64 times faster than that used for standard CDs, using a single-bit converter. The sampling frequency produces a great deal of quantising noise which DSD's Noise Shaping facility transfers to an inaudible high-frequency band. In this way, SACD achieves a dynamic range of 120dB. The revised version of the SACD standard, 1.1, is designed for multichannel audio use in 5.1 format.

Despite its interesting values, DSD is the subject of no little controversy, since the sampling technique it employs is radically different to that used by most digital studio devices, such as PCM.

To get the best out of DSD, the entire production prior to encoding would need to take place on the analogue level. This is feasible, of course, and would delight the purists, but the majority of modern studios are no longer capable of producing music this way. What's more, the DSD algorithm is highly complex, so even simple operations like crossfades require a great deal more processing power to implement than they would if PCM were used. As things stand, therefore, and in the absence of a further technological breakthrough, those studio devices that *do* currently employ DSD sampling are far less powerful than comparable devices with PCM converters, and so very few studios are equipped to produce exclusively in DSD. The best that most studios and DSD-capable devices can do is employ high-resolution PCM data (24-bit/96kHz or better) and then convert the signal at the end of the production process or, at the output stage, to DSD, respectively. However, research has shown that listeners can discern virtually no difference between the quality of material produced using this hybrid technique and that produced using PCM alone.

Research has also shown that unlike their PCM counterparts, DSD converters are incapable of functioning without producing distortion – although here we are talking about artefacts so subtle that no one is capable of evaluating them objectively. Nonetheless, given the already high quality of PCM data sampled at 192kHz, such flaws can't be dismissed out of hand.

When it comes to archiving, too, most studios prefer PCM, since even though the Noise Shaping algorithm might have banishing the sampling artefacts to a frequency range beyond human detection, they still take up space on the archiving medium.[229]

Despite these problems, it should be re-emphasised that the audio quality of DSD-encoded recordings is very high – clearly superior to CD. Besides which, if you're producing for SACD, the final encoding must employ DSD, regardless of whether or not you've used PCM at some prior stage in the production.

Data-Carrying Media

At the end of the production process, the material has to be transferred to a carrying medium. Of course, the exact format of this will have been chosen earlier in the production, since it will have a bearing on how the material is prepared.

In the case of multichannel recordings, the choice of available media isn't that great. For cinema productions, the sound will be transferred either to the film (as is the case with Dolby Digital) or to a sound-storage medium, such as a CD or DVD (in the case of DTS). Since this choice is not generally within the sound engineer's remit, and since the work is generally done by a duplication facility, little more needs to be said here regarding the choice and preparation of storage media for cinema production.

This leaves productions designed for playback in the home, presentations and internal studio reproductions (eg for research purposes). In the latter case, you don't need a permanent storage medium; a multitrack backup of the master will suffice, or you might want to use the master itself.

For all other applications, the recording will leave the studio on a multichannel medium that must be portable (obviously), capable of being played back in any studio or the home and conforms to the relevant norms. Currently, this narrows the choice to five media: DVD (Audio/Video), SACD, CD, hard disk and the relatively new Blu-Ray Disc or similar blue-laser formats. Of the five, DVD is currently the one most often chosen for multichannel reproduction, so we'll take a look at it here in some detail before discussing the advantages and disadvantages of it in comparison with the other four other media.

DVD

Digital Versatile Discs (DVD) resembles CDs but have a considerably greater storage capacity and data-transfer rate. These advantages are achieved through the use of smaller pits, narrower tracks, two layers (in place of one) and the ability to use of both sides of the disc. Table 6 shows a direct comparison of the CD and DVD formats.

DVDs with different formats can be physically identical. Whilst the CD is primarily used for musical and computing applications, DVDs can be used for the storage of moving images and sound at the same time. The DVD can therefore be considered a successor to the music CD, the computer CD and the video cassette, and represents a considerable improvement on all three.

	DVD	CD
Diameter	120mm	120mm
Thickness	1.2mm (2 x 0.6mm substrata layers)	1.2mm
Track width	0.74µm	1.6µm
Minimum pit size	0.4µm	0.83µm
Capacity	DVD-5 (single-sided/single layer) 4.7GB	650MB (700MB)
	DVD-9 (single-sided/dual layer) 8.5GB	
	DVD-10 (double-sided/single layer) 9.4GB	
	DVD-18 (double-sided/dual layer) 17GB	
Maximum data-transfer rate	9.8Mbps	1,4112Mbps

Table 6: Comparison of DVD and CD specifications

For the computer, a distinction has to be made between DVD-ROM, DVD-RAM, DVD-R (DVD-RW) and DVD+R (DVD+RW). DVD-ROM (Read Only Memory) is designed as a pre-recorded data-carrying medium capable of storing either computer data, films or audio, depending upon the format selected.

DVD-RAM (Random Access Memory), on the other hand, is a rewritable data-carrying medium designed for the temporary storage of large amounts of data. Here, though, the figures do not quite match those quoted for the DVD-ROM above; DVD-RAM discs are capable of storing between 2.6 and 9.4GB of data (depending on whether one or both sides of the disc are used) and can't be used as a DVD-Video or DVD-Audio disc; they can only be written to and read by special DVD-RAM drives, as they need to be kept in a special closed caddy to protect their sensitive write layers. DVD-RAM drives are, however, usually capable of reading DVD-ROM discs; the Fostex DV40, for instance, is one device that uses DVD-RAM as a four-channel mastering medium.

DVD-R and DVD-RW are the equivalent of CD-R and CD-RW discs in that computer or video data can be written to them. (Here, the suffix *-R* stands for 'recordable' and *-RW* for 'rewritable', meaning that you can record onto the disc, erase what you've recorded and then record something else.) DVD-R and DVD-RW – the 'minus' format, developed by the DVD Forum – now has a rival, the 'plus' format (DVD+R and DVD+RW), which was developed by the DVD+RW Alliance, a group of well-known firms including Sony, Philips, Hewlett-Packard and Yamaha, in response to the fact that the recording of films in real time was problematic using the established DVD-RW format. One advantage enjoyed by members of the Alliance is that they don't have to pay fees to the Forum, which controls the licensing rights to the DVD-R format. From a technical standpoint, the DVD-R and DVD+R formats are almost identical, apart from certain mechanisms on older recorders that prevent those designed for each from writing on the media of the other.

The real differences, however, are encountered in the rewritable formats. Oriented towards the CD-RW, the DVD-RW can experience problems in the writing of video data. Because the writing process takes place at a constant bit rate, the writing process constantly needs to be suspended and resumed, which results in a linking loss, making the disc incompatible with read-only devices like DVD video players and DVD-ROM drives.

With DVD+RW, it's possible to perform lossless linking – ie to suspend and continue the writing process without linking loss. For lossless linking, it's necessary to write any data block in the correct position with high accuracy (within 1 micron). For this purpose, the groove is mastered with a high wobble frequency (817kHz at n = l), which ensures that the writing can be started and stopped at an accurately defined position. This feature makes the format very efficient and suitable for random writing in data as well as video applications. Additionally, lossless linking makes it possible to replace any individual 32KB block (recording unit) with a new one without losing compatibility.

In the computer area, the trend is towards multiformat recorders that support both formats, so the choice of recording media will in the future be determined by the available playback devices.

In the near future, it should also be possible to create dual-layered DVD+RW discs. The first prototypes, demonstrated in August 2003, were capable of storing 9.4GB of data per disc, instead of the 4.7GB that is the current limit of the DVD-RW and DVD+RW formats.[230]

With the requisite formatting, either format can be used to create an audio or video DVD, so DVD±R – like DLT tape – represents an ideal proofing and transfer medium for DVD authoring. Video and audio DVDs created in this manner can now be played by virtually all video and audio DVD players,[231] as thankfully the days are gone when players were deliberately designed so that they couldn't play back non-pressed discs.[232]

In the video and audio sector, there are special requirements for DVD designed to ensure international standardisation. The guidelines and possibilities relating to video and audio DVDs will be explained in greater detail in the following sections.

DVD-VIDEO

The video DVD can be regarded as the digital successor to the video cassette. It scores over conventional VHS tape in that it offers superior image resolution and rapid access to different parts of the disc, doesn't wear out and is generally less fragile.

The video material is usually divided into chapters or scenes that you can select individually like the tracks on a CD. It's possible to interact with the disc in various ways, such as by bookmarking favourite scenes or looping sequences. Since the data is divided into several smaller data streams, films usually offer the sound in a number of different languages with subtitles in up to 32 languages. Parallel video streams are also supported, allowing you to watch the same scene from different camera angles. There is also usually space for supplementary material such as outtakes, interviews, filmographies of cast members, commentary from the director, 'making of' clips and so on. In other words, a DVD is superior to a video cassette in virtually every respect.

The main image standard for DVD-Video is MPEG-2 MP@ML, although MPEG-2 SP@ML (a lower resolution format) and MPEG-1 can be used for applications where the quality of the picture is less important. Most DVD players support not only PAL but also NTSC playback, as well as two different aspect ratios: 4:3 (the aspect ratio of a standard TV screen) and 16:9 (that of widescreen TV).

However, deliberate measures have been taken to hamper international compatibility (each disc carries a regional code designed to prevent it from being played back in a zone other than that for which it was intended) in order either to protect copyright or else because films are released at different times in different parts of the world and the film companies want to stagger their DVD releases accordingly. There are also fears of an international black market in pirated DVDs. To what extent such measures are necessary or, indeed, justified is open to question, especially since – like the refusal of older players to accept DVD±R discs – they deliberately complicate DVD production. Furthermore, consumers with a little technical knowhow can easily circumvent the restrictions. More drastic action is needed to fight copyright piracy; the solutions being adopted at present are a nuisance and objectionable.

As well as being able to store video data, a video DVD offers a wide range of possibilities for the storage of multichannel audio. The main formats that every DVD video player must support are PCM audio (eight channels at sampling rates as high as 96kHz), AC-3 (six channels) and MPEG-2 Audio[233] (eight channels). In addition to these formats, multichannel recordings can also be stored in DTS[ES] (six [seven] channels) and SDDS (eight channels). A video DVD can therefore also be used as a carrier medium for high-quality multichannel recordings, although the audio stream must also be integrated into a video stream, so it's therefore impossible to create a video DVD that contains only audio. The video could, however, be something as simple as a still picture or even a black screen. Video DVDs are generally navigated using menus.

DVD-AUDIO

DVD-Audio is a newer standard than DVD-Video. The difference between the two is essentially one of priorities. DVD-Audio was designed to be the successor to the CD, which, in comparison, has extremely limited multichannel capabilities. Because of its large storage capacity, an audio DVD is capable of accommodating uncompressed multichannel recordings as well as offering various multimedia functions – text, accompanying slideshows and a limited amount of video. Physically, an audio DVD is no different from a video DVD, and apart from a few minor differences they share the same format.

The encoding formats stipulated by the DVD-Audio standard are PCM and MLP, with up to six channels in each case. PCM audio can even be recorded at a sampling rate of 192kHz, although in this case only two channels are supported. Since MLP is a lossless compression method, both formats deliver exceptionally high-quality reproduction.

The audio format is also scalable, which means, for example, that it's possible to employ a sample rate of 96kHz for the front channels and only 48kHz for the surrounds. In practice, however, the use of two different sample rates considerably complicates the task of processing; if disc space is limited, the use of MLP is a far more satisfactory solution.[234]

An audio DVD can be navigated in a similar fashion to a CD using a TOC[235] (in which case it's described as a black disc) or through the use of screen menus. It's also possible to output a certain amount of image and text material at the same time as the audio. This takes the form of stationary images that have previously been loaded into the memory of the DVD player. By this means, slide shows and the like can be implemented. The text information can be directed either to the DVD player's own display or to a video output. Besides containing information about which track is playing, this could include a song's lyrics, allowing the disc to be used in a karaoke situation.

Audio DVDs can also contain moving pictures conforming to the DVD-Video specifications and stored on a separate area of the disc. They also supports web links, allowing users to download bonus tracks over the internet, for example, and manufacturers are especially interested in this ability to establish contact with the customer.

Audio DVDs don't have regional codes, which makes them considerably more flexible than video DVDs. An algorithm called CSS-2 (Copy Scrambling System) is used to combat piracy, and it's also possible to watermark the discs so that the origins of copies can be proved.

Audio DVDs can't be played back on simple video DVD players, but since most DVD players purchased nowadays combine the two functions (the playback of video and audio DVDs), it's possible to combine the advantages of both formats on a single disc – for example, by providing a high-resolution audio recording of a concert on a black disc on one side and a video version of the same concert (but with inferior sound quality) on the other. The possibilities for such combinations are far-reaching and also include the ability to integrate DVD-ROM material for computer access.

AUTHORING[236]

The creation of a DVD is seldom a simple matter of copying the audio data to the disc the way you would with a music CD; instead, the process is more like the creation of a multimedia CD, using an application like Director, and it takes careful planning. You need to link all the various audio and video elements with the menus as well as with each other – an exception being a black-disc audio DVD, where it really is a simple case of copying the encoded audio material to a DVD-R or DLT tape with the correct formatting, as the TOC handles the entire business of navigation.

The layout, menu creation and content linking is performed at the computer using a dedicated authoring workstation, such as that produced by Sonic Solutions. Such applications are designed to manage the processing, encoding and space constraints of DVD production.

You begin any such production by defining your objectives and planning carefully how best to meet them. A crucial factor in DVD production is what's known as *bit budgeting*, which involves calculating the data-transfer rate and apportioning it to the various data streams. Once this has been done, it's possible to choose the most appropriate encoding format.

It's probably helpful here to give an example of bit budgeting. Suppose you need to create a DVD containing 120 minutes of video material and three soundtracks: an English-language soundtrack in 5.1 format and two stereo (2/0) soundtracks, one in French and the other in German. You're also planning to provide subtitles (around 1,500 per language) in a number of other languages. The entire production has to fit on a DVD-5.

First of all, you have to calculate how many bits are at your disposal: 4.7GB x 1000^3 [bytes to GBs] x 8 [bits to bytes] / 1,000,000 [bits to megabits] = 37,600Mbits. Of this, you need to set aside around four per cent for the menu graphics and navigation information and to provide a safety margin: 37,600Mbits x 0.96 = 36,096Mbits.

The remaining space is now divided by the duration of the production: 36,096Mbits / (120 min x 60 s/min) = 5.01Mbits/s. This, then, is the total data-transfer rate, and you need to subtract from it the data-transfer requirements of the encoded audio tracks and subtitles: 0.385Mbps (English 5.1) + 0.192Mbps (French 2/0) + 0.192Mbps (German 2/0) + 0.16Mbps (subtitles) = 0.928Mbps, leaving 4.08Mbps (because 5.01 – 0.928 = 4.08), which is the average data-transfer rate that the video compression needs to achieve.

Such bit budgeting is very important, since DVD authoring is not simply a question of fitting all of the data onto the disc; it's just as important to ensure that DVD players are capable of reading it fast enough. Therefore, simply adding up the storage requirements of the various data components and ensuring that they don't overflow the disc capacity is a necessary first step, but it's by no means the whole story.

Once you've divided up the storage space on the DVD, you can produce and encode the contents accordingly. In the case of the audio material, you may also need to specify the parameters for the downmix matrix. Once these are ready, the data needs to be assembled by the authoring workstation and linked using menus and navigation commands.

At this point, it's a good idea to test the compilation using a DVD simulator or a virtual remote control to make sure all the links work. If it's a commercial production, you also need to add copy protection.

The final task is to create an image file of the entire contents of the DVD, which (depending on what further processing needs to be done) you can then write to a DVD-R or a DLT tape to take to the duplication service.

Other Media

HARD DISK

For many applications, it's often a good idea to store multitrack recordings or video-and-sound content on a hard disk. This means that they can be made available more quickly for presentation purposes, they can be played back directly from the computer and they can be edited at any time. Hard disks also have a higher capacity than other media, and their prices in recent years have fallen to such an extent that hard-disk storage is scarcely more expensive than any other storage media.

The data-transfer rate of a hard disk is also considerably faster than that of a DVD – how much faster, of course, depends upon the computer configuration – so even high-resolution image and sound data can be played back with no difficulty.

Faster access times, however, are another factor. Since the data format on a hard disk isn't standardised, you can also play back any format combination you like, such as HDTV image and eight-channel audio in 96kHz resolution – provided, of course, that you have the requisite hardware and software. The only limitations, therefore, are those imposed by the computer itself, and as we know the pace of development in this area is very rapid. Hard disk is therefore the most powerful and versatile medium for the storage of multichannel audio and image-and-sound content. Having said that, of course, the data thus stored is heavily dependent upon the operating system as well as on the hardware and software configuration of the individual computer, so a hard disk obviously doesn't offer the broad compatibility of a standard DVD.

CD

Since a CD is essentially a very small DVD, multichannel recordings could naturally be stored on a CD. Obviously, when it comes to moving images and sound, the limited capacity and lower data-transfer rate of the CD is obviously a problem, but multichannel audio reproduction is still possible, although the maximum playing time is far less than that of a DVD. Theoretically, given suitable compression, the data-transfer rate of 1.4Mbps offers almost an hour of playing time, but CDs are nonetheless almost never used for the storage of multichannel audio since the reproduction is not standardised. If they're used at all in multichannel productions, it's simply for the transfer of data from one computer to another, or else for archiving. For dual-channel stereo in 16-bit resolution at 44.1kHz, the CD will remain the most important medium for some time yet, since CDs are relatively cheap to produce and there almost every home has a CD player.

XRCD

The Extended Resolution CD (XRCD), developed by JVC, is based on a normal CD format upon which audio data is recorded using a special mastering process (K2 Super Coding), reducing the data resolution from 24 bits to 16 bits.

JVC distinguishes between two formats: XRCD 24-bit Refined Digital and XRCD 24-bit Super Analogue. The combination of K2 Super Coding with various JVC converters and the low-jitter K2 algorithm is said to lead to a considerable improvement in the sonic image. Since the Red Book standard is adhered to, XRCDs are compatible with all popular CD players and can therefore be played back without difficulty on any system. Since JCV hasn't licensed the manufacturing process, in an effort to protect the system, there's only one mastering studio capable of processing audio material for XRCDs and manufacturing the necessary glass masters. This means that, if you want to produce an XRCD, you have to send the finished production to Japan! A further problem is that each glass master is capable of producing only a limited number of copies before pressing errors start to crop up.[237]

Because of the inconvenience of this system, the XRCD has made little impact on the audio market, and since it's now possible to record data without compression in 24-bit resolution, with the standardisation of DVD-Audio, it's unlikely that many producers will be prepared to go through this whole rigmarole just to end up with a bit-reduced recording. In other respects, the XRCD has the same advantages and disadvantages as CD.

SACD

The SACD[238] (Super Audio Compact Disc), developed by Sony and Philips, can be regarded as a direct competitor of DVD-Audio. Technically, both are based on the same medium; the SACD is just a specially formatted DVD. The essential difference between the two media is the recording process. While DVD-Audio employs PCM-coded data, SACD uses the new DSD system.[239]

In addition to the aforementioned shortcomings of DSD, the SACD has been criticised on other grounds, one being the fact that it's purely a sound carrier and is generally incapable of image reproduction. Furthermore, only a few studios are capable of performing the mastering process, and the number of DSD-capable studio devices is limited. On the other hand, the number of duplication facilities has recently increased, so we can expect to see an increase in the number of SACD titles on the market. Already more titles are available in this format than in DVD-Audio, and certain audio productions are now set to appear exclusively on SACD.

However, despite reproducing outstanding sound quality SACD has obtained mixed reviews from users. The complicated copy-protection system and the absence of a digital output on first-generation devices (dictated by the same concern to hinder copying) are a thorn in many users' sides. Without such an output, it's impossible, for example, to upgrade to a better DSD decoder and use the digital signal of the player to control it. Even so, this is a common practice in the hi-fi sector, and – in view of the fact that the current generation of DSD converters is unlikely to be final word in the format's development – this would have been an option worth keeping open.

The lack a multimedia capability, meanwhile, is offset by the increasing number of multiformat players on the market capable of playing not only CDs and SACDs but also video and even audio DVDs. Such devices offer consumers the security of knowing that, whatever medium they've purchased, they'll always be able to play it back, which is likely to ease the transition to high-definition audio for many consumers.[240]

One argument often used in favour of SACDs is that they are *hybrid*, implying that they can also play back on normal CD players. While it's undoubtedly true that SACDs generally contain a second layer that can be played back by a normal CD player (naturally in 16-bit/44.1kHz audio resolution), thus making SACD downwards-compatible with CD, the same can also be said for DVD; a DVD can be designed to play back on a CD player in precisely the same way – which is hardly surprising, given the fact that SACDs and DVDs are based on the same medium. The record label Dabringhaus & Grimm has produced just such an 'all-in-one' DVD combining DVD-Audio, an AC-3 data stream for a DVD-Video player and a CD data track. The hybrid SACD is therefore a useful marketing ploy but hardly an exclusive technology.[241]

BLU-RAY DISC AND OTHER BLUE-RAY LASER FORMATS

While the DVD-Audio and SACD formats offer sufficient capacity for current requirements in terms of audio production, in the film and video sector – especially in Japan and the USA, where HDTV is in the process of establishing itself – there was disquiet at the formats' limitation of only 4.7GB per layer (a limitation that affects all of the current recordable media), and people were soon asking for a similarly convenient medium but with a higher storage capacity. It was quickly decided that any new format would need to be compatible with the CD and DVD, and therefore 12cm in diameter, so the only way of achieving an improvement in the storage capacity was to reduce the track width and make the pits and lands smaller.

While this was all very well in theory, it only became a serious commercial possibility with the mass-production of blue lasers, which can be focused and positioned more accurately than the current system.

Since the beginning of 2003, a number of potential successors to the DVD have emerged, most of which are based on blue-laser technology. Another thing almost all have in common is the use of new video codecs (primarily designed to support HDTV) and an increase in the maximum data-transfer rate. The following table provides a quick run-down of the possible formats:

	Depth of the data layer	Laser	Video codec	Capacity (single layer/dual layer)	Data-transfer rate
HD-DVD-9	0.6mm	Red (650nm)	new codec	–/8.5G (ROM)	11Mbps
Advanced Optical Disc (AOD)	0.6mm	Blue (405nm)	HD MPEG-2 and new codec	15GB/30GB (ROM), 20GB/40GB (–R)	36Mbps
Blue-HD-DVD-1	0.6mm	Blue (405nm)	Advanced Video Codec (AVC)	17GB/–	25.05Mbps
Blu-ray Disc (BD)	0.1mm	Blue (405nm)	HD MPEG-2	27GB/50GB	36Mbps
Blue-HD-DVD-2	0.1mm	Blue (405nm)	Advanced Video Codec (AVC)	17GB/–	31.59Mbps

Table 7: Hard-disk-capable successors to DVD

HD-DVD-9 doesn't represent any technical innovation not already present in the DVD format; it simply uses a new codec that permits HD material to be stored and read. While DVD drives in computers could read such material through the use of additional software, HD-DVD-9 is incompatible with conventional DVD players, and if the purchase of a new playback device is inevitable, it seems impractical to employ a technology for which clearly better alternatives exist. The blue-laser formats – including the Advance Optical Disc (Toshiba and NEC), officially introduced by the DVD Forum; the Blu-Ray Disc (Sony, Philips and Panasonic, among others); and the Blue-HD-DVD-1 and 2[242] (developed by the Advanced Optical Storage Research Alliance in Taiwan) – would all seem to have a better chance of succeeding the DVD.

The Blu-Ray Disc (BD) is now the first blue-laser format ready for mass production and has already been used (mainly by Sony) in professional photography. The pitches of the tracks on this format and the minimum pit length are considerably smaller than those of the DVD, giving the BD a storage capacity of up to 27GB. Here are some of the other technical specifications:[243]

Diameter 12cm
Thickness 1.2mm
Thickness of data layer 0.1mm
Track width (pitch) 0.32µm
Minimum pit size. 0.16–0.132µm
Storage capacity 23.3–27GB
Maximum data transfer rate 36Mbps

While the use of MPEG-2-HD clearly offers more potential for image transmission, the BD format changes little from an audio perspective when compared with DVD, although it does support PCM and the commonest codecs, such as AC-3, DTS and MPEG Layer 2. The most interesting feature is the possibility of higher data-transfer rates, since a maximum bit rate of 36Mbps offers scope not only for very high-quality encoded HD images but also for a great deal of audio data. BD would also allows the combination of HD video with MPEG-AAC sound – a good basis for the use of Wave Field Synthesis. We can therefore look forward to the release of high definition films on Blu-Ray Disc with considerably better sound quality than that offered by DVD, but not before 2005/2006, and in the meantime much could change.

In the absence of the necessary hardware, BD and related blue-laser formats are at the moment irrelevant as carrier media for multichannel audio. However, in view of the often criticised lossy compression techniques used in DVD-Video, the new technology – with its considerably faster data-transfer rates – has great promise as a medium for multichannel audio.

5 THE FUTURE

Surround sound isn't a new technology; multichannel audio has been used extensively in the cinema for many years and has been established for some time even in the home, in the form of analogue matrix systems. What makes surround sound so important today for the audio industry is the development of digital carrier media that make it possible to reproduce multichannel audio discretely and with a level of quality previously unattainable in the home.

While the industry may view DVD as being the long-awaited successor to the video cassette and CD, giving distributors an opportunity to re-release films and music recordings, for sound and recording engineers what is primarily of interest is the opportunity to achieve new levels of quality. On the one hand, surround sound – with its rear loudspeakers – makes it possible to scale new heights in terms of realism and spatial imaging, while on the other the larger number of channels offers greater scope for creativity, as well as a far greater potential for drawing the listener into the acoustic events, to engage, involve and envelop.

But first there needs to be far greater uniformity among the playback systems people use in their homes. While most consumers know (more or less) how the loudspeakers of a dual-channel stereo system are supposed to be positioned – even if, for one reason or another, they fail to act on this knowledge – the level of public awareness of the ITU 775 recommendations, which constitute the *de facto* standard for surround sound, is hopelessly inadequate. Most surround loudspeaker sets are designed primarily for the reproduction of film sound, and even these are very rarely positioned properly. Admittedly, the whole idea of 'multichannel audio for its own sake' is very new, and one can't expect people to go to the same lengths to establish optimal listening conditions in the home as recording engineers do in the studio, but nonetheless there's an urgent need to make the public better acquainted with the ITU 775 recommendation, especially since it deals specifically with the 5.1 format, which, of the many possible formats, is the only one established as a standard in the home.

When you look at multichannel recording, it's clear that it holds parallels with dual-channel stereophony and its recording principles. Nearly all the main miking techniques for surround recording have their roots in techniques such as AB, XY and MS, developed for dual-channel stereophony, so it goes without saying that a thorough grounding in dual-channel stereophony should be considered essential for anyone planning to embark on a career in the much more complex and demanding field of surround recording. Also, any serious examination of multichannel recording practice will quickly establish that there are no right and wrong ways of doing things, any more than there are good and bad main miking techniques; in each case, the best procedure depends on the objectives of the recording, and each recording engineer will develop his own way of doing things over time. And this is a good thing; after all, no one could seriously want all multichannel recordings to sound the same.

The same goes for multichannel processing in the recording studio. Here, too, a solid technical basis and a great deal of experience with dual-channel practice are essential, since multichannel equipment is often very similar to that used for dual-channel recordings, while sound engineers naturally need to understand the consequences of adopting a given course of action, and a thorough grounding in theory can be helpful in this respect. Trial and error is unlikely to achieve anything of value in the area of multichannel audio, due to the complex interaction of the channels.

It's also important that the equipment used to record and process multichannel sound is powerful and sophisticated enough to anticipate and control these complex relationships. Generally speaking, multichannel production should start and finish on the digital level.

Practice and experience are also vital when it comes to minimising the effects of lossy compression. This is actually one of the most important areas in multichannel audio production, since the data-transfer rates required by error-free compression can seldom be achieved. The object is not to produce as good a *master* as possible but rather as good a *product* as possible – in other words, it's the quality of the recording *after* the encoding and decoding has taken place that counts. However trite this sounds, it's nevertheless something that many studio engineers lose sight of. Lossy compression inevitably means compromised sound, but the exact nature of the compromise is unpredictable. It depends upon the codec used, the material itself and the production process. Compensating for (and thereby minimising the effects of) such deterioration is therefore an art which, if mastered, allows you to obtain impressive results with even low data-transfer rates.

Regardless of which carrier medium eventually prevails in the coming struggle to replace DVD, and regardless of whether technology such as Wave Field Synthesis or 3D audio ever become established in the home, it's clear that, one way or another, multichannel audio will soon be making a major contribution to our enjoyment of both films and music in the home. Already the gains are impressive: with a little imagination, the listener can really feel part of the acoustic events. Nonetheless, dual-channel stereophony remains the dominant format, and the majority of music productions will continue to be released on CDs in dual-channel stereophony for some time yet. We shouldn't become so dazzled by the possibilities of surround sound that we lose sight of commercial reality.

APPENDIX

Current Standards

Deutsches Institut für Normung: *DIN 1320 – Akustik-Begriffe*, Berlin, Ausgabe 61997

European Broadcasting Union: EBU Technical-Recommentation R 64: *Exchange Of Sound Programmes As Digital Tape Recordings*, 1993

European Broadcasting Union: EBU Technical Recommendation R 68: *Alignment Level In Digital Audio Production Equipment And In Digital Audio Recorders*, 1992

International Telecommunication Union: ITU-R BS 645-2: *Test Signals And Metering To Be Used On International Sound Programme Connections*, Geneva, 1986–1992

International Telecommunication Union: ITU-R BS 775–1: *Multichannel Stereophonic Sound System With And Without Accompanying Picture*, Geneva, 1991–1994

International Organisation For Standardisation: ISO 1996: *One-third Octave Band Background Noise Level Limits Noise Rating Curves (NR)*, Geneva, 1972

Society of Motion Picture and Television Engineers: SMPTE N 15.04/152–300B: *Loudspeaker Placement for Audio Monitoring in High Definition Electronic Production, SMPTE Recommended Practice*, 1991

Online Resources

5.1 Production Guidelines, Dolby Laboratories Inc, 2000, S. 5-2 (www.dolby.com)

A Chronology of Dolby Laboratories – 1990–1999 (www.dolby.com/company/chronology1990_1999.html)

A Chronology of Dolby Laboratories – 2000 to present (www.dolby.com/company/chronology2000_present.html)

Allan, John F: *The Eight Channel Advantage* (www.sdds.com)

Digital Audio Compression Standard (AC-3) (www.dolby.com)

Dressler, Roger: *Dolby Surround Pro Logic Decoder – Principles Of Operation* (www.dolby.com)

Elen, Richard: *5.1 Past And Present – Surround Sound: A Brief History and Introduction*, Ambisonic.net Articles, August 2000 (www.ambisonic.net/about5.1.html)

History Of Multichannel Cinema Sound, Sony Cinema Products Corporation (www.sdds.com)

Kramer, Lorr: *DTS – Brief History and Technical Overview* (www.dtsonline.com/technology/technical_literature.php)

Large-Capacity Optical Disc Video Recording Format, 'Blue-Ray Disc' established (www.matsushita.co.jp/corp/global/news_m.html)

Taylor, Jim: *DVD Frequently Asked Questions (And Answers)* (www.dvddemystified.com/dvdfaq.html)

The Selection Of Audio Coding Technologies For Digital Delivery Systems (www.dolby.com)

THX – History (www.thx.com)

XRCD – Learn About The Process (www.xrcd.net/Shopping/process.asp)

Sources Of Illustrations And Tables

1, 10: Surround Sound Forum: Hörbedingungen und Wiedergabeanordnungen für Mehrkanal-Stereofonie

2, 6, 14 (right), 20, 22, 23, 46, 49, 50, 55 – Verband Deutscher Tonmeister: 21. *Tonmeistertagung – Bericht*

3, 4, 11, 12, 13, 14 (above), 15 – Hull, Joseph: Surround-Wiedergabe Gestern, Heute und Morgen

5, 37 (right), 38 (right), 41, 42, 43, 44, 48: Wuttke, Jörg: *Mikrofonaufsätze*

7, 8, 16: Webers, Johannes: *Handbuch der Tonstudiotechnik*

9, 17, 18, 19, 25, 56, 57: Christian Birkner

21: product information, Studer

24: *Der Spiegel*, December 2001

26, 27, 28, 29, 30, 31, 32, 33, 34, 35, 36, 37 (left), 38 (left): Dickreiter, Michael: *Mikrofon-Aufnahmetechnik. Aufnahmeraum, Schall-quellen, Mikrofone, Räumliches Hören, Mikrofon-Aufnahme*, third edition, S Hirzel Verlag, Stuttgart 2002

39, 40, 47: *Studio Magazin*, September 1997

45, 54: product information, Soundfield

51, 52: product information, SPL

53: product information, Schoeps

58: product information, Nuendo

59: *Studio Magazin*, October 2000

60, 61: product information, Lexicon

62, 63: product information, TC Electronics

64: product information, Jünger

65: *Studio Magazin*, October 2003, and Jünger Audio

Table 1: Surround Sound Forum: Hörbedingungen und Wiedergabeanordnungen für Mehrkanal-Stereofonie, SSF 1

Tables 2, 3: Surround Sound Forum: Mehrkanalton-Aufzeichnung im 3/2-format, SSF 2

Table 4: Verband Deutscher Tonmeister: 21. *Tonmeistertagung – Bericht*

Table 5: Wuttke, Jörg: *Mikrofonaufsätze*

Table 6: Block, Dave/Ely, Mark: *Publishing in the Age of DVD*

Endnotes

1 Cf Ausstattung privater Haushalte mit Empfangs-, Aufnahme-, und Wiedergabegeräten (figures for 27/5/2003) (www.destatis.de/basis/d/evs/budtab4.htm). (Cf also 'Haushalte mit VCR- bzw. DVD-Playern in Deutschland 1999 bis 2002 and Umsatzentwicklung im Videomarkt 1998 bis 2002' in *Media Perspektiven*, September 2003, S 446, and *Business Report zum Videomarkt*, 2003, Published by the Bundesverband Audiovisuelle Medien)

2 International Telecommunication Union: Recommendation ITU-R BS 775–1 – *Multichannel Stereophonic Sound System With And Without Accompanying Picture*, Geneva 1991–1994

3 Hoeg, Wolfgang/Steinke, Gerhard: *Stereofonie-Grundlagen* (hereafter abbreviated to Hoeg/Steinke), Verlag Technik, Berlin, 2/1972, p 9

4 Ibid, p10

5 There is comparative unanimity, however, among sound engineers that the absence of a natural spatial impression cannot be made good by reverb processors. There are admittedly very good simulations available for multichannel audio, but even these are incapable of matching reality in various respects. Virtual Surround Panning pursues one possible line of compromise between a natural room element and artificial reverberation.

6 In some publications, LFE is expanded to 'low-frequency extension' or 'low-frequency enhancement'. Since there is no universally valid multichannel standard, all three terms are permissible. (Cf. Steinke, Gerhard: *Surround-Sound: Wie viele Kanäle/Signale braucht der Mensch? – Plädoyer für die Standard-3/2-Stereo-Hierarchie und ihre Optimierung im Heim* (hereafter abbreviated to Steinke-3/2), p 303. In *21 Tonmeistertagung 2000*, Hanover – Bericht (hereafter abbreviated to *TMT 21*), Verlag KG Saur, Munich, 2001, pp283–328

7 Cf Dickreiter, Michael: *Mikrofonaufnahmetechnik* (hereafter abbreviated to Dickreiter), Hirzel Verlag, Stuttgart/Leipzig, 2/1995, p110

8 Cf Ders, p122f

9 Cf Webers, Johannes: *Meilensteine der Audiotechnik* (hereafter abbreviated to Webers – *Meilensteine*), in *TMT 21*, CD-ROM collection

10 Reinecke, Hans-Peter: *Stereo-Akustik – Eine Einführung in die physikalischen, psychologischen und technischen Grundlagen des stereofonen Musikhörens* (hereafter abbreviated to Reinecke), Musikverlag Hans Gerig, Cologne, 1966, p20ff

11 Cf Große, Günther: *Von der Edisonwalze zur Stereoplatte – Die Geschichte der Schallplatte* (hereafter abbreviated to Große), Musikverlag, Berlin, 1981, p8. (Other sources give the date as 1857)

12 Große, p8

13 Webers – *Meilensteine*, p1
14 Große, p9
15 Ibid, p28. See also Webers – *Meilensteine*, p5
16 Webers – *Meilensteine*, p7
17 Ibid, p9
18 Ibid, p10
19 Ibid, p14
20 Reinecke, p112
21 Webers – *Meilensteine*, p16
22 Ibid, p25
23 Ibid, p25
24 Cf *Phonetische Sammlung des Institutes für Sprechwissenschaft und Phonetik Halle/S* (www.sprechwiss.uni-halle.de/sammlung)
25 Webers – *Meilensteine*, p32
26 Reinecke, p109. Webers gives the date as 1941
27 Initially the real values fell short of these theoretical ones (cf Webers – *Meilensteine*, p33)
28 Reinecke, p29
29 Große, p104
30 Ibid, p124ff
31 Ibid, p125
32 Disney employs a system known as Fantavision that, in fact, involves the use of three optical sound channels (cf Hoeg/Steinke, p15: *Verweise auf 'Fantasia'*, and Hull, Joseph: *Surround Sound – Past, Present And Future: A History Of Multichannel Audio From Mag Stripe To Dolby Digital* (hereafter abbreviated to Hull), Dolby Laboratories Inc, 2000, p30 (also available online at www.dolby.com)
33 Hoeg/Steinke, p11 (cf also Große, p140)
34 Große, p140
35 Ibid, p140
36 Hoeg/Steinke, p13 (cf also Große, p140)
37 Webers – *Meilensteine*, p33ff
38 Hoeg/Steinke, p13
39 Ibid
40 Cf Webers, Johannes: *Tonstudiotechnik – Analoges und Digitales Audio Recording bei Fernsehen, Film und Rundfunk* (hereafter abbreviated to Webers – *Tonstudiotechnik*), Franzis Verlag, Poing, 6/1994, p150
41 Webers – *Meilensteine*, p42
42 Consultative Committee for International Radio
43 Hoeg/Steinke, p14
44 Ibid, p14
45 Cf Webers – *Tonstudiotechnik*, p571
46 Ibid, p589ff
47 Ibid, p533ff
48 Ibid, p553ff
49 In autumn 2001, DAT recording in 24-bit resolution was possible on only one device, the TASCAM DA-45 HR, in which the tape runs at double speed to make it possible to record the greater quantity of data
50 Compact-Disc Recordable
51 Compact-Disc Rewritable
52 Two norms exist for DVD: DVD-Video and DVD-Audio (see 'DVD', p98)
53 At present, DVD audio and the SACD are engaged in a kind of format battle to succeed CD, with Sony being the only media company putting its weight behind SACD
54 Extended-Resolution Compact Disc, developed by JVC, the only company currently producing it
55 See 'XRCD', p102
56 See 'Data-Carrying Media', p98
57 Cf Hull, p2 (cf also Elen, Richard: *5.1 Past and Present – Surround Sound: A Brief History and Introduction*, Ambisonic.net Articles, August 2000 [www.ambisonic. net/about5.1.html])
58 Cf *History of Multi-Channel Cinema Sound*, Sony Cinema Products Corporation (www.sdds.com)
59 Ibid
60 Cf Hull, p1 (cf also *History of Multichannel Cinema Sound*)
61 *History of Multichannel Cinema Sound*
62 Hull, p1
63 Cf THX – History (www.thx.com) (cf also Webers – *Tonstudiotechnik*, p598ff)
64 Hull, p3 (cf also Webers – *Meilensteine*, p55)
65 Webers – *Meilensteine*, p56 (cf also Hull, p5)
66 Low-Frequency Effects or Low Frequency Extension
67 Hull, p6
68 Digital Theatre Sound
69 Kramer, Lorr: *DTS – Brief History and Technical Overview* (hereafter abbreviated to Kramer) (www.dtsonline.com)
70 Sony Dynamic Digital Sound
71 Cf *History Of Multichannel Cinema Sound*

72 Cf *A Chronology Of Dolby Laboratories – 1990 To 1999* (www.dolby.com/company/chronology 1990_1999.html)

73 Cf also Kuhn, Clemens: *Wellenfeldsynthese* – 'Wiedergabetechnik der Zukunft' (hereafter abbreviated to Kuhn – 'WFS') in *Production Partner*, 11/2003, pp32–40

74 Cf also Kuhn, Clemens: Wellenfeldsynthese – Wiedergabetechnik der Zukunft (hereafter abbreviated to Kuhn – 'WFS') in *Production Partner*, 11/2003, pp32–40

75 Reinecke, p58

76 For fundamental physical terms in general, cf Webers – *Tonstudiotechnik*, pp21–90

77 For the perception of sound in general, cf Blauert, Jens: 'Räumliches Hören' (hereafter abbreviated to Blauert), *Monografien der Nachrichtentechnik*, S Hirzel Verlag, Stuttgart, 1974 (cf also Webers – *Tonstudiotechnik*, pp91–137)

78 Webers – *Tonstudiotechnik*, p96

79 Ibid

80 $\Delta L = 20 \lg \frac{p_1}{p_0}$ [dB] ($p_0 = 2 \times 10^{-4}$ µbar) (cf Webers *Tonstudiotechnik*, p102)

81 Ibid, p105ff

82 Cf Webers – *Tonstudiotechnik*, p110ff

83 Cf Reinecke, p129

84 www.tonmeister.de

85 The title of this standard is often abbreviated to 'ITU 775'

86 Cf Surround Sound Forum: *Hörbedingungen und Wiedergabeanforderungen für Mehrkanal-Stereofonie* (hereafter abbreviated to SSF 1), Empfehlungen für die Praxis (SSF-01), 1998 (www.tonmeister.de)

87 'NR10' is short for 'Noise-Rating curve 10' (63Hz–40dB; 125Hz–30dB; 250Hz–20dB; >1kHz–10dB) (Cf ISO 1996 [1972]: 'One-third Octave-Band Background Noise Level Limits Noise-Rating Curves')

88 The format code is in each case based primarily upon the number of sound channels, not the number of loudspeakers attached, which may be different

89 In general, these configurations are based around two large loudspeakers (L and R) two smaller shelf loudspeakers for LS and RS and a centre loudspeaker optimised for dialogue

90 High Definition Television, a high-resolution TV format with quadruple (1,440 x 1,152 pixels) the resolution of the current European PAL standard (720 x 576 pixels), the values for NTSC (as used in the States) being comparable though not identical

91 See *Mehrkanalwiedergabe im Heim- und Kinobereich*, p45 (cf *SSF* 1, p15)

92 See Mehrkanalwiedergabe im Heim- und Kinobereich, p45

93 The 3/1 format was included in the recommendation at the request of Japan, due to the popularity of the MUSE system there

94 The term *tracks* is a holdover from the days of magnetic tape recorders, where a track was a real physical entity. With the digital hard-disk recordings of today, there are no real tracks, but the term is still useful

95 The relevant formula is L ref = 85 – 10 log(n) dB, where n is the number of playback channels. n=5 therefore yields 78dB. (Compare with *SSF* 1, p7)

96 ITU recommends ±0.25dB, but in practice up to ±1dB is tolerated (cf *SSF* 1, p7)

97 Reference tone 1.02Hz pink or white noise

98 EBU Technical Recommendation R.64: *Exchange Of Sound Programmes As Digital Tape Recordings*, 1993

99 EBU Technical Recommendation R.68: *Alignment Level In Digital Audio Production Equipment And In Digital Audio Recorders*, 1992

100 ITU-R BS 645-2: Test Signals And Metering To Be Used On International Sound Programme Connections, Geneva, 1986–1992

101 Surround Sound Forum: *Mehrkanalton-Aufzeichnung im 3/2- Format* (hereafter abbreviated to SSF 2), Empfehlungen für die Praxis SSF-02 (follow links from www.tonmeister.de)

102 Retranslated from Hoeg, Wolfgang: 'Multichannel Audio: Aktivitäten der EBU', p502 in *TMT* 21 (pp495–506)

103 Cf Rathbone, Birgit/Fruhmann, Markus/Spikofski, Gerhard/Mackensen, Philip/Theile, Günther: 'Untersuchungen zur Optimierung des BRS-Verfahrens (Binaural Room Scanning)', p94 In *TMT* 21 (pp92–106)

104 Cf Webers – *Tonstudiotechnik*, p209ff
105 Cf Herrmann, Ulf/Henkels, Volker: 'Mikrofonierungen für den 3/2-Stereo-Standard' (hereafter abbreviated to Herrmann/Henkels), p54f in *Studio Magazin*, 9/1997, pp51–63 (extracts online at http://members.surf.eu.de/ulf.herr-mann/ vortrag.html)
106 Webers – *Tonstudiotechnik*, p210ff
107 Ibid, p211
108 Hull, p4
109 Cf Dressler, Roger: *Dolby Surround Pro Logic Decoder – Principles Of Operation* (www.dolby.com) (cf also Küster, Jörg: 'Back To The Roots [hereafter abbreviated to Küster-Mastering] in *Production Partner*, 9/2001)
110 Ibid
111 See Gerzon-Matrix
112 Cf *Internet Presentaton* by Martin Gansel (http://home.ins.de/~martin.gansel/sen.htm)
113 Cf Steinke-3/2, p295ff
114 357 Society of Motion Picture and Television Engineers
115 SMPTE N 15.04/152–300B: 'Loudspeaker Placement For Audio Monitoring In High-Definition Electronic Production', *SMPTE Recommended Practice*, 1991
116 See *Codierung*, p140
117 In PAL countries, Dolby Digital, MPEG-2 Audio and PCM Audio must be supported by every DVD player. In NTSC countries, only Dolby Digital and PCM Audio must be supported
118 Cf Steinke-3/2, p311ff
119 Cf Blauert, p80ff
120 Cf Steinke-3/2, p324f
121 Cf Karamustafaoglu, Attila: 'BRS-Prozessor: Praxis und zukünftige Entwicklungstendenzen', p86 in *TMT* 21, pp85–91
122 Sometimes the term *wavefront synthesis* is preferred, although the terms are, in effect, synonymous
123 de Vries, Diemer/Hulsebos, Edo/Bourdillat, Emmanuelle: 'Auralisation durch Schallfeldsynthese', p121ff in *TMT* 21, pp121–128
124 Cf Paetsch, Martin: 'Wohlklang im Plattenbau', in *Der Spiegel*, 12/2001
125 Cf Kuhn – 'WFS', pp32/33
126 Cf Kuhn – 'WFS', pp37/38 (cf also Kaminski, Peter: 'Carrouso 3D-Audio-Zukunft' in *Production Partner*, 3/2002, pp68–71)
127 The exact height is given as half the base width. In the home, if the base width is 2m, the third channel pair should be 1m above the front loudspeakers. In the studio, if the base width is 3m, the appropriate distance would be 1.5m
128 Dabringhaus, Werner: '2+2+2 – Kompatible Nutzung des 5.1- Übertragungsweges für ein System dreidimensionaler Klangwiedergabe klassischer Musik mit drei stereophonen Kanälen', in *TMT* 21, pp265-272 (cf also Kaminski, Peter: 'Dabringhaus und Grimm Audiovision', in *Production Partner*, 7/2003, pp28–31)
129 Cf Wuttke, Jörg: 'Allgemeine Betrachtungen zur Audio-Mehrkanal-Stereofonie' in his *Mikrofonaufsätze* (hereafter abbreviated to Wuttke – *Mikrofonaufsätze*), Schoeps GmbH, Karlsruhe, 2/2000, pp=98–103 (cf also the same author's *Betrachtungen zur Audio-Mehrkanal-Stereofonie* [hereafter abbreviated to Wuttke – *Vortrag*], Vortragsmanuskript, 2001)
130 Such microphones are also called *moving-coil microphones*. Another type of dynamic mic is te ribbon microphones, in which two very thin aluminium ribbons suspended close to each other take over the function of the coil
131 Special miniature microphones exist with the electronics located externally
132 Pressure receivers retain their omnidirectional response in the low-frequency range for only as long as the microphone is smaller than the wavelength of the sound. This means that smaller microphones remain omnidirectional at lower frequencies than larger ones. In each case, the response becomes increasingly directional and eventually club-shaped (line cardioid) in the high-frequency range, which makes it advisable to point even omnidirectional microphones at the sound source
133 See 'MS Stereophony', p55
134 The figures given for sensitivity are theoretical values
135 See 'Processing Requirements', p75
136 The surround recordings discussed in this section are based on the idea of recording a sound source

located in front of the listener – for example, an orchestra – along with the corresponding diffuse sound in the room (eg a concert hall) with an ITU 775 playback configuration. The microphone systems, especially the surround systems, could be used in many other situations. If a given system is especially well suited to some other application, this will be pointed out when the system is discussed

137 Cf Dickreiter, p126

138 Cf Wuttke – *Mikrofonaufsätze*, p9ff

139 A decisive factor here is the echo effect of the room, which should always be imperceptible (cf Dickreiter, p129)

140 Cf ibid, p114

141 Cf ibid, p116f

142 ORTF stands for Office de Radiodiffusion-Télévision Française, which, until 1974, was France's publicly owned radio broadcasting corporation, where the idea originated (cf Dickreiter, p132f)

143 Cf Dickreiter, p116f; also Wuttke – *Mikrofonaufsätze*, p9ff

144 Cf Dickreiter, p134f; also Wuttke – *Mikrofonaufsätze*, p34ff

145 Cf Dickreiter, p136f; also Wuttke – *Mikrofonaufsätze*, p34ff

146 The use of such microphones was recommended by J Wuttke

147 Herrmann, Ulf/Henkels, Volker: 'Vergleich fünf verschiedener Surround-Hauptmikrofonverfahren. Abschlussarbeit an der FH Düsseldorf', 1997; also under the same title in *Tonmeistertagung*, Tagungsband, 1998, pp508–517

148 Cf Blauert, p89f

149 Herrmann/Henkels, p59

150 See 'MS Stereophony', p55

151 Cf Wuttke – *Mikrofonaufsätze*, p100

152 Cf Camerer, Florian: 'Mehrkanalton bei Außenaufnahmen – Eine Systematische Betrachtung (hereafter abbreviated to Camerer), p476 in *TMT* 21, pp473–484

153 Cf Betz, Gerhard: 'Surround-Aufnahmen – Praktische Erfahrungen' (hereafter abbreviated to Betz), p485f in *TMT* 21, pp485–494

154 Cf Wuttke – *Mikrofonaufsätze*, p100 (also 'Empfehlung Für Einen Neuen Standard – Atmos 5.1', SPL product information, p5

155 Cf Wuttke – *Mikrofonaufsätze*, p101

156 Cf Camerer, p479

157 Cf '5.1 – Surround – Mikrofonsystem nach Bruck', Schoeps product information

158 The Gerzon matrix generates an extra-wide dual-channel stereo image with a hole in the centre from an ordinary stereo signal through the addition of out-of-phase elements of, in each case, the other channel. A mono signal is then used to supply the centre channel (cf Gerzon, Michael, A: 'Three Channels – The Future of Stereo', *Studio Sound*, 1990)

159 See 'Schoeps DSP-4', p77

160 Cf Camerer, p478

161 Cf Betz, p486

162 Cf Camerer, p481f. Cf also '5.1 Surround From A Single Microphone'; Sowie: 'The Soundfield SPS 422 Studio Microphone System (Soundfield product information)

163 See SP-451, p77

164 Cf Camerer, p482

165 Ibid, p482

166 Gerzon, Michael/Barton, Geoffrey: *Ambisonic Decoders HDTV* (AES preprint 3345, 1992)

167 Cf Herrmann/Henkels, p54f

168 Optimised Cardioid Triangle

169 Cf Wittek, Helmut/Theile, Günther: 'Untersuchungen zur Richtungsabbildung mit L-C-R-Hauptmikrofonen', p443 in *TMT* 21, pp432–454

170 Cf. 'Surround-Aufnahmen mit OCT-Mikrofonanordnung nach Theile', Schoeps product information

171 Cf Theile, Günther: 'Mikrofon- und Mischkonzepte für 5.1- Mehrkanal-Musikaufnahmen' (hereafter abbreviated to Theile-5.1), p396 in *TMT* 21, pp384–431

172 Ibid, p416

173 Cf Camerer, p483

174 Cf Williams, Michael: *Microphone Arrays for Natural Multiphony* (AES preprint 3157, 1991) (cf also Williams, Michael/Le Duc, Guillaume: *Multi-Microphone-Analysis für Multichannel Sound Recording* [AES preprint 4997, 1999])

175 Cf Wuttke – *Vortrag*

176 Betz, p494
177 Cf ibid, pp485–494
178 See 'Virtual Surround Panning', p86
179 Cf Wuttke – *Vortrag*
180 Cf Betz, p488
181 See 'The Layout Of A Surround Studio', p80
182 Camerer, p474
183 See 'Surround-Sound Evaluation', p28
184 Cf Betz, p491f
185 Cf. 'Empfehlung Für Einen Neuen Standard – Atmos 5.1', SPL product information
186 Eurosound, or the Galaxy Studios, in Belgium are well-known studios (cf *Studio Magazin*, 3/2001, p16, and *Sticks – Magazin für Schlagzeug und Percussion*, 4/2001, pp36–42)
187 Cf 'Area 5.1', SPL product information,
188 Cf. '5.1-Surround-Mikrofonsystem nach Bruck', Schoeps product information
189 Cf '5.1 Surround From A Single Microphone', Soundfield product information
190 Cf Kaminski, Peter: 'Live-Aufnahme für DVD-Audio' in *Production Partner* 9/2001, pp20–27
191 For a basic introduction, the *Handbuch der Tonstudiotechnik* by Johannes Webers and *Das Tonstudio Handbuch* by Hubert Henle are recommended
192 Depending upon the desired mix format, also more (eg seven monitor loudspeakers with the 3/4 format, etc)
193 See 'TC System 6000', p87
194 Plugins are small progam modules offered (for the most part) by third-party developers which take advantage of the open interface offered by the host application, expanding a particular aspect of its functionality
195 Cf Henle, Hubert: *Das Tonstudio-Handbuch – Praktische Einführung in die Professionelle Aufnahmetechnik* (hereafter abbreviated to Henle), CG Carstensen Verlag, Munich, 3/1993, p212
196 The terms *equaliser* and *equalisation* are generally shortened to EQ
197 Independently of the distinction between classical music (in the broadest sense of the term) and rock, pop, jazz, etc
198 Cf Henle, p220
199 Cf ibid, p230
200 Cf ibid, p226
201 Cf ibid, p232
202 Cf ibid, p233
203 Cf ibid, pp237–249
204 All the data comes from the Lexicon 960L product information
205 At a sampling rate of 88.2/96kHz, however, only one multichannel effect can be processed
206 Since the device only has eight inputs, the first effect is derived from six and the second from two discrete input channels, so in effect it's possible to process only one discrete multichannel source (assuming 5.1 format)
207 All the data comes from the TC System 6000 product information
208 Cf (on the subject of the Jünger Orion) Kahlen, Dieter: 'Orion an Erde...' in *Studio Magazin* 10/2003, pp24–37
209 The suggestions are orientated towards a multichannel mix in 5.1 format
210 Cf '5.1 Production Guidelines', Dolby Laboratories Inc, 2000, p5 (2) (www.dolby.com)
211 Cf ibid, p5 (2f)
212 Cf ibid, p5 (3f)
213 Cf ibid, p5–(4ff)
214 Cf Theile: *5.1*, p427
215 Cf *SSF* 2, p3 (see also 'Production Parameters', p26
216 Cf Dressler, R: 'Dolby Surround Pro Logic Decoder' (www.dolby.com)
217 Frequency range limited to 100Hz–7kHz
218 Cf 'A Chronology of Dolby Laboratories – 2000 To Present (www.dolby.com/company/chronology 2000_present.html) (see also 'Introducing Dolby Pro Logic IIx', 'Dolby Pro Logic IIx Frequently Asked Questions' and 'Alles über Pro Logic II' – www.dolby.com)
219 Cf 'Dolby Laboratories: The Selection of Audio Coding Technologies for Digital Delivery Systems' (www.dolby.com, 20/8/2001); cf also 'DVD Video – Technik und Praxis' (background paper, Fast Multimedia AG product information)
220 The precise standard is MPEG-2 MP@ML (Main Level/Main Profile), which is equivalent to a

resolution of 720 x 576 pixels at a data rate of approximately 10Mbit/s

221 Cf 'MPEG-2 AAC, Fraunhofer Institut Integrierte Schaltungen' (www.iis.fhg.de/amm/techinf/aac/index.html)

222 Cf 'The Selection of Audio Coding Technologies for Digital Delivery Systems – Comments from Dolby Laboratories' and 'Digital Audio Compression Standard (AC3)' (both available online from www.dolby.com; cf also Küster – *Mastering*

223 Kramer. Cf also Küster – *Mastering*

224 Cf Allan, John F: 'The Eight-Channel Advantage' (www.sdds.com)

225 Cf 'Dolby-E-Mehrkanal-Codierung für die Tonproduktion und -verteilung im Digitalen Fernsehen', Dolby production information (www.dolby.com)

226 Cf 'DVD Video – Technik und Praxis' and also Hintz, Markus: 'Die DVD-Audio – Chancen und Problemlösungen' (hereafter abbreviated to Hintz) in *Studio Magazin*, 9/1999

227 Cf Hintz; cf also Elen, Richard: 'Audio Reality – Next-Generation Audio' in *Audio Media*, 4/1999, pp54–9

228 Cf Müller, Swen: 'DSD Statt PCM – Fort- oder Rückschritt?' (hereafter abbreviated to Müller) in *Production Partner* 3/2001, pp16–40

229 Ibid, p22. Cf also Kaminski, Peter: 'DSD-Praxis bei den Emil Berliner Studios' in *Production Partner* 9/2003, p22–5

230 Cf 'DVD+R And DVD+RW', also 'DVD+R/+RW: The World Standard That Puts The User First', and 'DVD+ReWritable: How It Works' – all at www.dvdrw.com

231 Cf 'DVD Video – Technik und Praxis'

232 In many first-generation DVD players, the hardware was deliberately designed to prevent the playback of CD-R, CD-RW, DVD-R and DVD-RW media. This practice was, however, quickly abandoned for two reasons: firstly, components quickly appeared on the market that circumvented the restriction; and secondly, rival manufacturers were quick to point out that their devices were not hamstrung in this way, which made them more attractive to consumers

233 Only in PAL countries

234 Cf Hintz

235 Table Of Contents, a digital list of the contents of a DVD or CD that appears at the beginning of the disc

236 Cf Kaminski, Peter: 'DVD-Audio Authoring Workshop' in *Production Partner* 5/2001, pp26–34; cf also Ely, Mark/Block, Dave: 'Publishing In The Age Of DVD – A Primer For Creating Content For DVD (Sonic Solutions product information)

237 Cf Garver, Andrew: 'XRCD – 24-bit Refined Digital' and 'XRCD – 24-bit Super Analog (both JVC product information, www.xrcd.com); cf also 'XRCD – Learn About The Process (www.xrcd.net/Shopping/process.asp)

238 Cf Müller; cf also Müller, Johannes: 'DVD-Audio Produktion' in *TMT* 21, pp888–905

239 See 'DSD', p97

240 Cf Müller; cf also Kaminski, Peter: 'DVD-Audio und Super Audio CD auf der Tonmeistertagung' in *Production Partner* 1/2003, pp35

241 Cf Müller; cf also Kaminski, Peter: 'Dabringhaus und Grimm Audiovision' in *Production Partner* 7/2003, pp28–31

242 See also Taylor, Jim: 'DVD Frequently Asked Questions (And Answers)' (www.dvddemmystified.com/dvdfaq.html)

243 Cf 'Large-Capacity Optical Disc Video Recording Format "Blu-Ray Disc" established' (www.matsushita.co.jp/corp/global/news_m.html)